T0248344

PRAISE FOR
BRAVE
TOGETHER
BY CHRIS DEAVER AND IAN CLAWSON

Brave Together is a groundbreaking book that challenges the status quo and offers a refreshing perspective on work, culture, and leadership. Chris Deaver and Ian Clawson invite readers on a transformative journey to break free from fear and embrace the power of co-creation. Through their innovative concepts like the Mirror Test and the Hero's Sacrifice, they provide a road map for unleashing our collective potential and building a better future. *Brave Together* is a beacon of hope that empowers us to reimagine our experiences and embrace a new way of life. Get ready to be inspired and join the co-creation movement with this remarkable book.

—Dr. Marshall Goldsmith, Thinkers50 #1 Executive Coach and *New York Times* bestselling author of *The Earned Life*, *Triggers*, and *What Got You Here Won't Get You There*

Brave Together is an exhilarating exploration of genuine collaboration, where every voice matters and every idea is a potential catalyst for transformation.

—Daniel H. Pink, #1 *New York Times* bestselling author of *Drive*, *To Sell Is Human*, and *The Power of Regret*

A vital, generous, and urgent book, it will transform the way you think about teams. And then it will help you become a better leader.

—Seth Godin, author of *The Song of Significance*

The leadership we need in the future is not about command and control or maximizing shareholder value. It's about inspiring hearts, unleashing human magic, and building purposeful organizations together. If, like I do, you believe this, you MUST read *Brave Together*, as you will find that it is such a helpful guide on this journey. Thank you, Chris and Ian, for giving us such a precious companion!

—Hubert Joly, former CEO of Best Buy and Harvard Business School faculty

The world has shifted. To solve our greatest problems, we don't need more fighting or ego. We need more connection, collaboration, and co-creation. *Brave Together* can power us all, especially leaders, to change our work and world for the better!

—KAREN DILLON, bestselling author of *The Microstress Effect* and *How Will You Measure Your Life?* (with Clayton Christensen) and former editor of the *Harvard Business Review*

Being brave is good but not enough. *Brave Together* helps us shrink down our egos and find ways to work as a team. It shows us how to harness the power of connection, co-creation, and most importantly, selfless love, as we work together in unity. Thank you, Chris and Ian!

—STEVE YOUNG, NFL Hall of Fame, Super Bowl MVP quarterback

Brave Together is the antidote to a disconnected world. For those of us feeling isolated and stuck, this book offers the path to becoming brave together: giving us the chance to move beyond selfish leadership, the possibility for deep empathy, and the magic of co-creation for supercharging culture. These principles will literally change your life and leadership.

—AMY CUDDY, PHD, *New York Times* bestselling author of *Presence*, and top-ranked TED speaker

Solid and comprehensive. *Brave Together* provides super clear and effective strategies to manage very complex stories in our lives. Stories of ambition, of loss, of struggle, of success; not only in our professional lives, but in our personal lives as well. Chris and Ian's book clarified some of the more complex struggles of how ego gets in the way of just about every stage of growth in our lives.

—RYAN WOODWARD, Story Artist for blockbuster films including *Iron Man*, *Spider-Man*, *Captain America*, *Thor*, and *The Avengers*

We have entered a new age of leadership. The principles of co-creation in this book will become guideposts for the next generation of leaders and cultures. The time is now for us to be brave enough to create a different future together.

—RONELL HUGH, Vice President at Qualtrics, former Head of Product Marketing at Adobe, and former Lead Global Product Manager at Microsoft

Leadership is about taking responsibility, making sacrifices, building harmony, and pursuing freedom for all views and expression. *Brave Together* shows us the path to get there.

—JOHN ONDRASIK, Grammy-nominated lead singer of Five for Fighting and songs "Superman" and "100 Years"

This book will change the way you see the world. For leaders who want to shape the future in a more hopeful and creative way with others, this is required reading.

—CHIP CONLEY, Cofounder and Chief Executive Officer at MEA and former Strategic Advisor and Head of Global Hospitality at Airbnb

Those who use rules-based thinking won't lead the future. It'll be those who embrace the singularities. Misfits who find ways to be *Brave Together*. Chris and Ian have created the guidebook for the rising generation of future shapers.

—NOLAN BUSHNELL, Founder of Atari and bestselling author of *Finding the Next Steve Jobs* and *Shaping the Future of Education*

Full of wisdom and gripping stories, *Brave Together* is an imaginative, inspiring, and genuinely mind-opening book. Chris and Ian offer the tools to break out of fear and ego and show how success can be powered by integrity, collaboration, and empathy.

—AMY CHUA, Yale Law Professor and author of *Political Tribes: Group Instinct and the Fate of Nations* and her debut novel, *The Golden Gate*

Building the right team to support a mission is crucial. *Brave Together* provides a creative framework for the leadership and team to use as they progress toward a successful outcome.

—JOEL PETERSON, former Chairman of JetBlue, former Professor of Leadership at Stanford, and bestselling author of *Entrepreneurial Leadership*

What a remarkable book—insightful, inspiring, and groundbreaking. *Brave Together* will become the leadership guidebook for our time, and Tier 3 Leadership will become the operating system for leaders today. *Brave Together* compels us to see things differently and then co-create the future together.

> —DAVID M. R. COVEY, bestselling author of *Trap Tales* and former COO of FranklinCovey

Deaver and Clawson have created a multidimensional leadership courage map. It will help you shift from going it alone to innovating together.

> —LOUISE MURRAY, CEO of Lemuria Dreamer, former VP Creative Entertainment at The Walt Disney Company, and former VP at Cirque Du Soleil

Leadership is about inspiring others, building the culture, and creating an unstoppable team. *Brave Together* is a must-read playbook for doing that!

> —SANYIN SIANG, CEO Coach, Duke University professor, Google Ventures advisor, and Executive Director of Coach K Center

Being brave is no longer about going it alone, flying solo, or building our own empires. It's about doing it all together. This book can power you in your life and leadership to do just that!

> —JONAH BERGER, Wharton professor and author of *Magic Words* and *Invisible Influence*

Brave Together offers us a path to building intentionality into our lives. It shows us how to shift from self-focused success to design better leadership habits.

> —NIR EYAL, author of *Indistractable*

This book will reshape how you think about leadership and culture, with all its complexity and potential. It's a road map to collaborative success that is profound and practical.

> —DORIE CLARK, author of *The Long Game* and faculty at Columbia Business School

Brave Together is about how co-creation reinvents people and organizations. Great insider stories coupled with profound messages and relevant tips make this book a source of co-creation for anyone wanting to have a positive impact.

—DAVE ULRICH, Rensis Likert Professor at Ross School of
Business, University of Michigan, and Partner at The RBL Group

It's impossible to read *Brave Together* and not have your beliefs about personal and business success challenged. Using examples from their own work with the world's most creative companies like Apple and Disney, the authors make the powerful argument that co-creation with others is a far superior strategy to working harder alone. In the end, it will feel like you just heard a sledgehammer slam into a bell pealing the message that there is a better way to live and succeed. They provide all the advice you need to change your fortunes. The rest is up to you.

—WILLIAM PASMORE, PhD, Professor at Columbia University and
SVP Center for Creative Leadership

BRAVE
TOGETHER

BRAVE TOGETHER

LEAD BY DESIGN, SPARK CREATIVITY, AND SHAPE THE FUTURE WITH THE POWER OF CO-CREATION

CHRIS DEAVER AND IAN CLAWSON

NEW YORK   CHICAGO   SAN FRANCISCO   ATHENS   LONDON
MADRID   MEXICO CITY   MILAN   NEW DELHI
SINGAPORE   SYDNEY   TORONTO

Copyright © 2024 by Chris Deaver and Ian Clawson. All rights reserved. Printed in the United States of America. Except as permitted under the United States Copyright Act of 1976, no part of this publication may be reproduced or distributed in any form or by any means, or stored in a database or retrieval system, without the prior written permission of the publisher.

1 2 3 4 5 6 7 8 9   LCR   28 27 26 25 24 23

ISBN 978-1-265-38667-2
MHID   1-265-38667-6

e-ISBN 978-1-265-38710-5
e-MHID   1-265-38710-9

Design by Lee Fukui and Mauna Eichner

Library of Congress Cataloging-in-Publication Data

Names: Deaver, Chris, author. | Clawson, Ian, author.
Title: Brave together : lead by design, spark creativity / Chris Deaver and
    Ian Clawson.
Description: New York : McGraw Hill, [2024] | Includes bibliographical
    references and index.
Identifiers: LCCN 2023033702 (print) | LCCN 2023033703 (ebook) | ISBN
    9781265386672 (hardback) | ISBN 9781265387105 (ebook)
Subjects: LCSH: Leadership. | Organizational behavior. |
    Management —Employee participation. | Creative thinking. | Diffusion of
    innovations.
Classification: LCC HD57.7 .D47125 2023 (print) | LCC HD57.7 (ebook) |
    DDC 658.4/092 —dc23/eng/20230809
LC record available at https://lccn.loc.gov/2023033702
LC ebook record available at https://lccn.loc.gov/2023033703

McGraw Hill books are available at special quantity discounts to use as premiums and sales promotions or for use in corporate training programs. To contact a representative, please visit the Contact Us pages at www.mhprofessional.com.

McGraw Hill is committed to making our products accessible to all learners. To learn more about the available support and accommodations we offer, please contact us at accessibility @mheducation.com. We also participate in the Access Text Network (www.accesstext.org), and ATN members may submit requests through ATN.

To the Brave leaders of the future.
Culture isn't what happens to us. It's what we co-create together.

CONTENTS

CONTENTS

FOREWORD

*The future is already here—it's just
not very evenly distributed.*
—William Gibson

Pioneer of cyberpunk, deep thinker William Gibson is many things, but don't call him a futurist. He said, "I'm not trying to predict the future. I'm trying to let us see the present."

Throughout my career, my present yielded some remarkable glimpses into the future. Most of that opportunity came as the result of working for Steve Jobs at NeXT, Pixar, and Apple. At NeXT, I taught object-oriented programming. At Pixar, I ran education and training as the Dean of Pixar University. At Apple, I was a member of the Apple University faculty.

In those organizations—at times—I saw something different. What Chris and Ian would call co-creation. A way of working together, of being valued while creating value. An individual-centric approach to being team-centric. A fierce interest in creating experiences for themselves and others that required making new things in new ways, never for the newness, but because getting the thing right mattered so deeply to every person on the team. Not only their shared expertise, but their shared beliefs stood out on every facet of the finished product.

The artifacts that were produced, like NeXTSTEP, still in the heart of Apple's products today, like Pixar's collection of characters and stories, like Apple's family of surprising and delightful devices, are memorable and have lasting impact. But it wasn't innovative products that evidenced the future I saw in glimpses. No, it was the organizations themselves, their beliefs and behaviors in action, their culture. The people.

These were organizations—NeXT, Pixar, Apple—that in their best moments were seeking to see—and be—what comes after collaboration, when it isn't the labor we need to share, or even the thinking. They were about creating amplifiers out of human beings, amplifiers that the humans themselves intrinsically take pleasure in being part of, that make their processes and products and themselves all geometrically better. What Steve called, "Insanely great."

This book will help you look for and identify bits of future in your present. In the everyday of your work and your home, as well as in the privacy of your hopes and ambitions. Places where what you are doing may already contain a bit of that insane greatness, if you can just get to see it from the right point of view. This book's perspective will prepare you to recognize and thrive in environments where creation is shared.

I found the book to be broad and descriptive. It has something to offer to a range of readers because anyone who works with other people has dreamed of better ways to work together. It speaks to varied experience and roles, because being brave together allows us—and requires us—to show up whole and complex, to be ourselves. Co-creation works because of, not in spite of, our differences. This is the kind of book that could help leaders to explore their creativity and creatives to expand their leadership.

I think the work is dense, in the sense of rich, thorough, thoughtful. I don't think you'll read it on the plane and be ready to put co-creation into action at your next meeting. I read it slowly. It took me some reflection to digest each chapter. I enjoyed the contrast and compare from my history that the reflection brought about. It gave those memories of past success and failure some clarity. I hope you'll enjoy the book in the same way, sharpening your recollections with fresh perspective.

This book is Chris and Ian's story. So it is personal, it unfolds, it isn't a manifesto, more a really well-documented journal. This journal, itself, created through their co-creation: an example for the book is the book itself. Their observations rang genuine and authentic to me. You'll hear both voices, and I hope sense the discovery as their shared experiences with co-creative environments brought them together and deepened their desire to share what they've both seen.

Enjoy the book, and get ready to take your place among those stirring things up, to make sure the future is more evenly distributed. Welcome to the team.

Randy Nelson
Boulder Creek

BRAVE TOGETHER

WHAT DOES IT MEAN TO BE BRAVE TOGETHER?

Be brave. Things will find their shape.
—Erin Bow

tanding on the grass in front of the glassy campus, which looks like a spaceship freshly landed on Earth, Tim Cook smiles. "We're excited to introduce the next generation of AirPods Pro, our most advanced AirPods yet."[1]

Music starts pumping and the camera zooms in, showing the silhouette of a man dancing, and then Tim says, "To tell you more about AirPods Pro, here's Mary-Ann . . ."

Wait, did he just hand over the virtual stage? And who's Mary-Ann? Where's the rock star magician, waving at the starstruck crowd, promising the next best thing? Not this time. Now it was about the most innovative teams presenting the best new products and sharing the spotlight. It was a perfect example of how Apple's culture had transformed from "think different" to working "different together."

Mary-Ann highlights the brand-new chip in AirPods Pro, which upgrades performance for breakthrough audio experiences, as well as the beloved active noise cancellation and spatial audio that makes it feel like we're on stage performing with our favorite band. Mary-Ann isn't the head of marketing or SVP of product. She's a senior firmware engineer who is part of the collective of industrial designers, architects, and project managers who've made this new iteration of AirPods possible—which included people like Jerzy Guterman, who led his antenna team through the phases of "this is impossible; it can't be done" to "this is the future of audio."

In short order, AirPods have not only surprised and delighted hundreds of millions of people but become a $24 billion business of their own—seemingly overnight. And the story of how this came to be is more than a technical treatise on innovative features. It's a story we were involved deeply in shaping with senior leaders and teams at Apple. It started with a directive from Apple when they hired me (Chris) with this extraordinary challenge: "Seventy percent of our people have been here five years or less. We can't teach them Apple culture fast enough. Can you help?"

The most valuable company in the world was asking me to take it to the next level by focusing on culture. But this was not a company in decline or a toxic fixer-upper. The leadership team wanted to keep what made Apple great and make things even better. What started as a small braintrust turned into a grassroots movement, and grew organically with the help of brave leaders, timeless principles, and the promise of co-creation. We began by asking a different question: "How can we shape the future culture together?" We needed to involve the new people and learn from those who had already made an impact. It became a massive cultural shift at Apple, from "think different" to working "different together" that powered over 100,000 people to move the future of innovation forward. We witnessed an iconic company with a venerable history transform. In some ways, Apple was not so different from any organization that experiences growing pains. It had to deal with struggles on how to handle secrecy, the usual infighting, and friction when it came to collaboration.

This is about the power of co-creation, about being brave together, especially in moments when we're confronted by fear. Apple was part of a beta test for how to approach culture shaping. We've gained broader insights in our careers for how to apply co-creation to any domain. As a leadership coach in the tech industry, I (Chris) have identified the correlation between timeless principles and culture, while I (Ian) offer unique perspectives based on world philosophies having pursued an education in international cultural studies, and as a leader in healthcare. Together, we've established BraveCore to help leaders lean into the co-creative future. Bringing *Brave Together* to life has become our true calling. We offer this new framework to enable us all to become co-creators in a world in desperate need of it.

A REDEFINITION OF SUCCESS:
FROM SELF-MADE TO SHARED

Great things . . . are never done by one person.
They're done by a team.
—STEVE JOBS

When I (Chris) was young, I believed achievement was everything. I joined the Boy Scouts, and earned every merit badge to become an Eagle Scout by the age of 12. In school, I worked hard to get the best grades. To me, these achievements brought not just accolades but validation: I felt successful. Most of all, I felt worth. I meant something. I was someone. What could possibly go wrong? Everything.

I kept pushing myself for years, pursuing every dream. But something happened along the way. I got tired of it all. In college, I'd written a letter to Roy Disney, asking for a job at Disney animation. Later, a Disney recruiter called me. "Hi! This is Lisa. Roy said to talk to you."

There was pixie dust flying everywhere! This was my big break! I'd wished upon a star, and it had actually come true! I felt my dad's words of advice ringing in my ears, "Never give up your dream."

But something strange happened next. "Thanks," I replied. Then I felt compelled to say, "But . . . no, thanks." And I hung up the phone. Why? Why do we sometimes skip certain dreams, as painful as it seems?

I realized something was missing in my life. I'd been on a treadmill chasing solo success. I felt empty and alone. That dream job, at that time, was not the answer for me. I found myself wanting more in life. Everyone around me was telling me that "success" was about grinding out the hustle, building my own empire, and running full speed toward my dreams. I watched them frantically chasing their own, but never looking satisfied. In their minds, they never had enough followers, never enough likes on posts, never enough of anything. I didn't want to be stuck animating someone else's ideas or obsessing about building my own empire. I wanted something different.

At the time, I couldn't pinpoint what this all meant. Meanwhile, the world was changing. Work was changing. Companies, once titans of industries, were fading overnight. Self-made celebrities were quitting, disappearing, and deleting their accounts. Others were getting canceled for insensitive things they'd said or done. The culture wars were heating up, characterized by extreme political divisions and tribalism. The world had changed. We have a heightened awareness that we need each other now more than ever before—and yet, we've never felt so disconnected, distanced by distractions. How will we define our future? And what first principles do we need to apply to get there?

Instead of going to Disney, together with some Albanian and Brazilian friends, I started the nonprofit International Mentoring Network Organization, which brought together aspiring professionals from around the world to meet their dream mentors—people like Stan Lee and Stephen Covey. We were featured in *Fast Company* and *Entrepreneur*. We didn't make any money, but we reached millions of people in more than 70 different countries. And I learned something during this experience: the future isn't self-made; it's shared.

Fast-forward, and I eventually joined Disney. But I came in as an HR business partner most passionate about shaping culture. Before Disney, I had reinvented my role at Dell by forming a team to reimagine their leadership to become better listeners who empower innovation. This brought me into the boardroom, consulting with founder Michael Dell on how to transform the culture, which took his team to a $100 billion future.

When I joined Disney, they were acquiring Pixar and wanted to expand the "braintrust" mindset, which we did, across businesses. At that time, I wrote a book proposal and got an agent (who represented the *Shark Tank* stars). That led to a book deal that I felt compelled to turn down. Why? "How could another book about next-level personal habits add to anything?" I wondered. Having seen and read a lot, I'd become skeptical of the self-help hacks offered in the marketplace—everything from 4 a.m. wake-ups to freezing cold showers, atomic email batching, and firewalking our way to rapid success. None of it had created a revolution in my life. Why would anyone need a new book with more of the same?

I also realized I was writing a book alone. It's not unusual for authors to do, but I felt the future was meant to be shared. I needed a team. I pressed pause on publishing and, following my success at Disney, took that job at Apple. Right out of the gate, they challenged me to improve their culture.

In an upcoming chapter, we'll share how we discovered the first principles that powered the culture change at Apple from "think different" to working "different together"—enabling teams to be more collaborative and to build innovative products in new, co-creative ways. This was a reflection of Tim Cook's words: "If I share my idea with you, that idea will grow and get bigger and be better because you may have a different viewpoint on it. . . . You might add something to it. And, if I share it yet somebody else, it gets even bigger. That process is how Apple creates products. It's not that somebody goes off in a corner or a closet and figures something out by themselves. It's a collaborative effort."[2]

I skipped the dream of publishing a book on my own. In the back of my mind, I knew I needed to first be brave enough to build a future with others. I needed to experience co-creation—something I'd been yearning for but didn't know it. It would change my life forever.

I met Ian Clawson in 2017 in Gilroy, California, the garlic capital of the world. We weren't interested in buying garlic (as tempting as that garlic ice cream was). We wanted to build worlds. We shared a passion for creative work. We got vulnerable and started sharing story ideas we'd developed for decades but had never brought to life. I'd designed some comic strip characters that had never taken off, and Ian had a powerful storyline. We brought them together and saw something special start to take shape, a world of its own.

We flew to LA to pitch our movie concept to a Marvel story artist who'd worked on *The Avengers*, *Iron Man*, *Spider-Man*, and *Captain America*— the classics. The clock started ticking on our 30-minute pitch meeting. We jumped right into our story, world exposition, and characters. We didn't have answers for all his questions but remained hungry for and open to learning. He could see we'd thought about this world layers deep and that we'd poured our souls into it. We explored with him where the story could go. From the glass windows of the conference room, we saw his coworkers leaving for the day. The energy in that room was special. Shared flow. We hadn't looked at a clock the entire time. When our meeting reached the three-hour mark, he paused, looked us in the eyes, and said, "Guys, this is epic! This will get made."

This was pure validation for us, not only of the power of our idea for "The Vigilant" world that's now in development but of the power of co-creation— and the potential to transcend solo success and shape the future with others by being *brave together*. Beyond just a movie concept, Ian and I realized we'd co-created something insanely great. That's when we zoomed out and began to articulate what we'd experienced and why co-creation is the future.

THIS IS THE WAY: WORKING TOGETHER

We've been told that if we just work harder and smarter, we'll reap our dream rewards, but this promise has failed us. It's created silos, selfishness, and a lonely work life. It's made fear or going it alone feel like the only options. It's caused burnout and pain because we are so divided and struggle to work together. But the future is calling. People are searching for a better, more elevated way to work and live.

Brave Together challenges the traditional approach to work, workplace culture, and leadership. In this book, we share how to break free from the baseline fear we all experience—the dread of the unknown, the fear of missing out, the pain of going it alone—to be brave enough to co-create the future with others in any domain. The journey of co-creation (Figure I.1) involves the Mirror Test, which reimagines our experiences based on the real versus the ideal; the Hero's Sacrifice—the most critical, and most underrated, part of the Hero's Journey—which offers us the path out of ego and ignites a selfless power that binds us together; and Become the Future, which creates a synthesis that brings out the best of our mind, heart, and spirit. Co-creation becomes a new way of life and a better approach to our work, giving us hope.

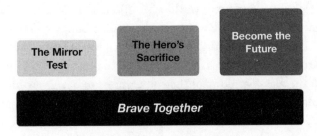

FIGURE I.1 **The Journey of Co-Creation**

But co-creation isn't possible without the application of a set of guiding meta principles that are especially valuable during uncertain times:

- **Lead with questions** to provoke a culture of curiosity, where anyone can imagine and express a better future.

6
▲ ▲ ▲

- **Turn pain into power** by creating gains, letting your sacrifices become the building blocks of your success.

- **Make others the mission** by setting aside ego and pursuing work based on one measure: how it inspires the lives of others. Help others feel seen, respected, and understood.

- **Define the situation** by the actions you take. Your efforts must be connected to value systems that bring out the best in you and in others. Change things and contribute to a mission larger than yourself.

- **Create context** by focusing on the deep work that not only is different but makes a difference. Be inspired by your future story and who you need to become. Be that now.

- **Follow true north** by building alignment of principles, collective courage, and creative energy to achieve the best outcomes.

We've pressure-tested these meta principles not only as patient observers but as practitioners and coaches within our teams. We've witnessed their power to ignite life-changing and business-transforming solutions beyond Apple. This same framework helped Disney build their NextGen platform, which received *Fast Company*'s "Innovation by Design" award, and Dell transform into a more customer-centric culture by expanding innovation.* Ian experienced its power in the culture work he did in healthcare, leading teams to give their all and creating conditions for people to work together during the Covid-19 pandemic, with all its challenges.

You may wonder what the difference is between first principles and meta principles. They serve different but complementary roles, providing us with guidance as we shape our lives and cultures.

- **First principles.** These are foundational values based on our own perspectives that influence our decisions. They can vary greatly for each person and are shaped by our own experiences. The best first principles are a creative articulation of who we are and how we live our lives.

---

* We've chronicled and shared these artifacts on our website BraveCore.co.

- **Meta principles.** These higher-level truths are drawn from collective wisdom and universal moral standards. Meta principles are a directional framework for us to define our first principles, providing the space and flexibility in which our first principles can evolve as we transform and grow.

We don't have all the answers or the solutions to every challenge, but we offer a foundation that prepares you to solve life's greatest problems with others. We help you connect the dots and discover deeper truths. We stand on the shoulders of giants. In this book, we honor and share what we have learned from others who inspire us, including Dale Carnegie, Stephen Covey, Ed Catmull (who wrote *Creativity, Inc.*), startup founders, movement makers, and leaders making a difference at Apple, Disney, Pixar, Burberry, and the NBA.

Applying the framework and meta principles of co-creation enables us to be brave together. It also helps leaders be more creative and creatives be better leaders. Ask yourself what you can do differently. What if you focused on working creatively with others? What if the question on leaders' minds wasn't "How do I keep my people?" but rather "What do they want to feel?" and "How can we shape a creative work life we love?"

What if you co-created with your family, friends, and larger community? Imagine it. Be inspired and inspire others. Lean into bigger dreams that are shared. Shape the future. When you're in it together, anything is possible.

PART I

THE MIRROR TEST

The Mirror Test is a co-creative pattern with responsibility at its core. It reimagines our experiences with others based on how we see ourselves and the opportunities around us. It helps us become more aware of the distinction between what's real and what's ideal, and provides clarity that can fuel our future. We can feel overwhelmed by the world's push to achieve more and have more and allow fear to hold us back. But the Mirror Test challenges us to pause, reflect, and embrace our creative identity. Enabling a life of co-creation, to bravely approach the culture we dream of from the inside out and to change the world from within. As we look deep into our souls, we become brave enough to transform together, discovering that we don't have to go it alone. We can see a collective future powered by principles.

In the following chapters, we'll explore how the Mirror Test frees us from the status quo and mind control games. This pattern helps us understand who we are and how we can approach life in new and different ways with a co-creative mindset. By leaning into the power of questions, we no longer feel the pressure to be an expert. We can become expert listeners,

open to new ideas, changing our mind, and even embracing failure in the

name of growth. By focusing on first principles, we shift from survival

mode, changing how we look at leadership and culture. This energizes the

people around us. We see how being brave together helps us feel better

connected and how we can help each other evolve. Co-creation enables us

to access shared wisdom to imagine and build a beautiful world together.

CHAPTER 1

STUCK IN STATUS QUO

I find the people strangely fantasied,
Possessed with rumors, full of idle dreams,
Not knowing what they fear, but full of fear.
—PHILIP in *King John*,
William Shakespeare

D o you ever feel stuck? Trapped by inertia? Too comfortable with the devil you know? The status quo can often feel safe and familiar, but it can undermine our creative identity. The choice to remain stuck in the status quo is often driven by fear. The only path to a better place is charted one brave step at a time.

How do you build the unseen future together? How do we stop looking out for number one and start truly collaborating as a team? With collective creativity.

FEEDING OUR CREATIVE IDENTITY

You are not your idea, and if you identify too closely with
your ideas, you will take offense when they are challenged.
—ED CATMULL

As a healthcare administrator, I (Ian) faced a real challenge: I experienced growth in an operations role while leading great teams, but I had a creative side that lay dormant and unfulfilled. Not so much stuck in my job, but maybe stuck in my life, unable to be my complete self.

Over the years, my computer grew cluttered with countless files of original short stories, story treatments, and digital music tracks. Creative work was my outlet, but it was more like a hobby. Only my closest friends and family knew this side of me. Deep down, I always knew that my future would be tied to my creative identity. I just didn't know how yet.

In 2013, I was approached by Dave Arcade, a brilliant illustrator and friend, for a once-in-a-lifetime opportunity. At that time, Dave had direct access to pitch the then-CEO of Nickelodeon Studios. Dave said we had a window to develop a cartoon series. He considered only a handful of people he would even want to partner with in a project like this. I was both flattered and excited. We got to work. Even though we lived in different states, we were able to find a working rhythm.

Two years later we created an animated series called Spaceland. We developed a polished pitch deck. Eight completed episode scripts with fully baked artwork, character profiles, world design, and story elements. We couldn't stop dreaming and thinking about Spaceland. It was magical. It became a real place that took on a life of its own. It still holds wonder and magic for us to this day. Everyone we shared it with was blown away. The world we were building was something special (Figure 1.1).

When it came time to pitch, something strange happened. My creative partner went dark. It was hard to communicate with him at all. Until recently, I didn't understand the dynamics that would take years for both of us to comprehend. But at that moment, I was relentless. In my mind, we had to see this through. My creative identity was screaming for validation. But Dave was checked out. During a flight home to Utah from Burbank, California, Dave came to the realization that he didn't want to move forward with the pitch, even though we had an ideal situation.

Later, I learned that he was afraid. Sure, there was a possibility that Spaceland would be rejected, but his fear was tied to its certain success. Would we both have to move our families to LA to make it work? Dave had seen firsthand how other show creators were treated by the studios. A jaded insider, he didn't want a work life controlled by a studio. After learning he felt this way, it was hard for me to blame him. But I was still devastated. We had worked so hard.

Looking back, I too was motivated by fear. Fear of regret. To me, failure is when you stop trying, and I didn't want to stop. Not when we were so close to making Spaceland a reality.

ARTIFACTS / LOOT

FIGURE 1.1 **Spaceland Art**

I learned so many things back then:

1. Working with someone else can be incredibly difficult.

2. Co-creation is messy and painful.

3. I have my own strengths and weaknesses as a co-creator.

4. Co-creation makes the quality of our work so much better. Converging ideas, skills, and creative gifts made this project stand out in ways that neither of us could have pulled off on our own.

5. I resolved more than ever to find someone I could work with.

Dave and I have since reconciled, and I continue to admire and respect his creative mind and his work. We remain good friends. We both feel that one day Spaceland will come to life, but on our terms. The timing wasn't right back then. In retrospect, I wasn't ready either. If I hadn't experienced that setback, I wouldn't have met Chris. I also wouldn't have had these unanswered questions and a burning desire to understand co-creation at a deeper level: how it all works, what it takes to powerfully work with others, and how to be brave together.

FACING OUR FEARS

Everything you want is on the other side of fear.
—JACK CANFIELD

When we're truly honest about what affects our work life most, it's fear. Most of our anxiety is tied to fear. Ask anyone if they've *ever* had a bad boss or been in a toxic workplace, and 100 percent will tell you they have. Sadly, it's the norm. And it needs to change.

We could categorize bad bosses as evil. But how most bosses lead is a direct response to their own fear: fear of performance issues on their teams, fear of how they're perceived, fear of the unknown, fear they don't have all the answers. What if they're wrong? The closer you are to a bad leader, the more insecurity and fear you see in them.

Most new leaders never get proper training. Most copy-and-paste a fear-based leadership style, creating fear in others. It's all they know. But how did fear become so widespread in our work life? And how do we break free?

Fear is our baseline. It's where we start, whether we know it or not. It's ever-present and all around us (Figure 1.2).

FIGURE 1.2 **Move Beyond Fear**

We face three types of fear:

1. Fear we feel from others.

2. Fear that is self-inflicted.

3. Fear tied to our growth.

Fear We Feel from Others

Some people use tactics to purposely create conditions of fear. They induce fear to gain control or because they see others as a threat. This may cause us to believe that these people have power over us.

- **Fear of rejection.** When we're afraid of being rejected, we shy away from building relationships. Some people are hard to read and don't have open or agreeable personalities. Fear of rejection prevents us from moving forward, whether we're hesitant to ask our boss for a raise or to ask that attractive person out on a date. But if the idea of rejection hurts, it won't hurt as much as regret. When we give in to the fear of rejection, we talk ourselves out of taking risks that could improve our lives.

- **Fear of being judged.** We like to feel accepted. And feeling judged can hold us back. But some people will always hold a negative opinion of us. This is why it is hard for people to show up as their creative selves at work. They're afraid that their ideas will be mocked or ridiculed. But you can't let others shake your principles. Be brave enough to be yourself.

> *Instead of worrying about what people say of you,*
> *why not spend time trying to accomplish*
> *something they will admire?*
> —Dale Carnegie

- **Fear of being micromanaged.** At work or at home, we can feel boxed in when we feel disempowered. Working with others takes structure and process, but not at the risk of losing our creative voice. Controlling environments hurt us. Controlling bosses and performance-obsessed cultures go for short-term gains while killing our motivation. We need to set boundaries to escape toxic scenarios, or we need a change of scenery.

Fear That Is Self-Inflicted

Self-inflicted fear is like a mental prison that pulls us down, affecting our moods and our lifestyle. Only we determine the duration of our sentence, and we hand out our own punishments.

- **Fear of failure.** This is one of the most common fears. Sure, failure is embarrassing. It can give us a negative self-image, show us how we don't measure up, and make us guarded. This fear makes us avoid new experiences and opt for the "safe and sure thing" in life.

- **Fear of inadequacy.** This is the fear of not being good enough, that we don't measure up. This manifests in negative self-talk, perfectionism, and deep insecurity. The aim should be for progress over perfection, being comfortable in our own skin, learning from our mistakes, being centered in humility and patience, and forgiving ourselves.

- **Fear that something bad could happen.** There is nothing you can do to completely prevent bad things from happening. Ruminating on what could go wrong can make us overly cautious. Allowing this type of fear keeps us from enjoying life. We face this fear by making better choices, identifying our guiding principles, and taking action.

Fear Tied to Our Growth

This kind of fear can actually be positive. We may feel anxiety, but the discomfort can power our growth. We can tell if this kind of fear is healthy or not by checking our stress levels. Temporary discomfort is one thing; however, prolonged discomfort may not be healthy.

- **Fear of uncertainty.** There are no guarantees that doing something new will make your life better—but it can. Don't be paralyzed by a fear of what you can't control. Build a foundation for your life with what you can control. Being brave isn't about being fully prepared; it's about trying new things, getting unstuck. Whether accepting a new job or moving to a new place, stay open.

- **Fear of change.** Change is hard. It's scary. That's why so many people resist it. Yet change is happening all the time. You can lose out on a lot of incredible opportunities by avoiding it. Take it one day at a time.

BRAVE ALONE: GOOD, BUT NOT ENOUGH

Being brave breaks us free from fear. It creates new opportunities, builds new relationships, brings new work, inspires new ideas, and leads to a new life. Being brave is about moving into the discomfort zone, confronting fears, and tackling our challenges. It's about developing the best habits, getting the fundamentals right, and building courage.

As you lean into this newfound power, your potential converts into kinetic energy, and you begin to see yourself as a force of nature. How good do you think you can get?

Most people don't know what to do with us when we are brave. Brave people are willing to swim upstream against all the naysayers. With grit, determination, and courage, we stay on mission and see things through. We stand up for principles and challenge the way things are done. We may gain a handful of enemies: coworkers who don't like to be called out, and bosses who don't like to be questioned.

You may face dilemmas and risk being ostracized. The status quo doesn't like to be challenged. You may receive passive-aggressive reprimands or formal punishment at work. Being brave might put a target on your back. You may have to deal with unfair gamesmanship by people in power, but don't let it break your spirit. Being brave is hard, especially when we're fighting against everyone's natural fears. The more we live our principles, the more power we unlock within ourselves.

Once your work life trajectory is moving in the right direction, what's next? When you achieve what you want, how will you maintain life at this level? At times, we may feel stifled, bumping our heads against the ceiling of success. Nothing is ever good enough. We continue looking for ways to be different: the next self-help trend, another 5 percent of our lives to optimize. Being bold becomes an addiction.

Maybe we haven't reached where we want to go yet? Does braving it alone have its limits? It's easy to let fear enter our lives unannounced like a repo man, looking to reclaim the courage we momentarily took out for a spin.

You could be scared about what's next. What if I succeed even more? Braving it alone comes with that risk, and all the messiness and hard work that inevitably follows. We've seen people hit a breaking point when it all becomes too much to handle and unravels. Will that be me? We can no longer carry the full load and wear all the hats. It all starts to fall apart—not for lack of trying, not for lack of sacrifice. Maybe it was too much? Or maybe you've lost your way?

Braving it alone comes with self-imposed pressure and moments of loneliness. Social media becomes a window into what we're missing out on. We endlessly scroll to make up for a lack of face-to-face connections, and we may post just to give the appearance that we're happy and thriving. We may even start to feel empty, like we're living an online version of ourselves, rather than the real thing.

Being brave is good, but it's not enough. Neither is building strong habits. Optimizing everything makes for a good life, but we can lose sight of what truly matters. If brave alone is not enough, then what is? Brave together. Building with others. Any team that's achieved lasting success knows this. For every Michael Jordan, there's a Scottie Pippen and Steve Kerr who also shot crucial baskets and made big plays. Together. For every Bono, there's an Edge, Larry Mullen Jr., and Adam Clayton who harmonized and prayed as a band before every U2 concert, turning their focus away from individual performance and toward each other and their audience. Together. For every Steve Jobs, there's a Laurene Powell Jobs who bursts open the universe with challenging questions and insights that make hearts sing.

The dark truth of success is that if we make it all about ourselves, our own egos, our individual performance, it eventually breaks down. It won't have staying power. Most of us have experienced the reality of bosses or corporate cultures that go it alone, pushing agendas on us rather than building with us. Startups know this feeling. People running full speed toward their dreams know this feeling. But it's fleeting. It doesn't last if it's not built with others, co-created. And when things fail, like 80 percent of startups do, we ask why.[1] Not enough money? Not enough product-market fit? What if it has little to do with any of that and everything to do with not building the team that is doing the best work of their lives together? Why do teams fail? Maybe success has less to do with the right communication or getting the perfect culture fit, and more to do with being willing to be brave together.

Yet we've found ways to strive, despite it all. To get things done. But our heart and soul are telling us there must be more to life. Doing more of what we love, with others doing what they love. What if we lived that every single day?

Why do leaders, teams, or companies fail? They fail from within. Same with relationships. Being brave *together* is the foundation for success. If we don't learn that, we'll find ourselves burning out. We'll miss our larger purpose on this Earth. We may even become a version of ourselves we don't like or recognize. Then what? Where do we go from there? How can we make the changes we need?

FROM A ROUGH LEADER TO A CHANGED ONE

Imagine you've started a company that's gone from $0 to millions in revenues. Now you've got fancy cars and find yourself flying across the country. You've figured out the formula for success. Everything you touch turns to gold. You take pride in creating an effective performance culture. Being tough on the team works—until it doesn't. It all starts hitting the fan, with an economy collapsing and clients leaving. The company is on the verge of bankruptcy, and employees are exiting in droves.

As a business leader, what do you do next? Find someone to blame? Call it quits for lack of product-market fit? Investors start calling, looking for answers. Do you ask for more money? What's your plan for the future?

Mohammad Anwar found himself in this exact situation. Softway had succeeded for 13 years, but now it was on life support. It was a dark existential moment. He'd done a massive layoff to save the company. Afterward, he asked 100 people in a town hall meeting if they still trusted him. Only two raised their hands. Facing his new reality, he felt completely and utterly alone, a total failure. He had to make a choice: blame other people and circumstances or take responsibility.

Mohammad went to a football game at the University of Houston, his alma mater, to clear his head. The team was undefeated, looking for their tenth win. By the fourth quarter, they were down by 20, heading for their first loss. He'd come to see the game to feel better, but now he felt even worse. He got up to leave, but for some reason, he decided to stay. The team rallied to win the game with 30 seconds left. The next day, Mohammad watched the press conference, wanting to learn the secret to their incredible comeback. What he heard changed his life forever. Head coach Tom Herman said the key was love—the love players had for one another, the kind of love that builds cultures that win championships.

He made a choice right then and there: to become the leader he knew people needed. He took responsibility for his actions and sought forgiveness for how he'd behaved. He took the time to build relationships and transformed himself and the business. Mohammad even wrote a book with his team called *Love as a Business Strategy*. People at Softway now feel more energized, knowing they have hope in a Rough Leader who grew into a Changed Leader. Together, their team inspires each other and they've created a culture of love and innovation. How did Mohammad start to face his demons and change? The Mirror Test.[2]

THE MIRROR TEST: CONNECTING TO YOUR CORE

What gives shape to your thoughts? How do you see yourself in the world? Why do you do what you do?

Data gives us a snapshot of the past. Principles influence the present. Creativity helps us imagine the future. How many of us search for answers to who we are and who we need to be everywhere but inside ourselves? Many people travel the world trying to find themselves when all they need to do is be brave enough to go deep inside their soul, do the hard work, and create new patterns.

Patterns are different than habits. Patterns are about our connection to others, not just ourselves. The best place to start is within. Be honest with yourself about the changes needed to put your life on a better path. Those who desire to change the world start by changing the world from within.

> *It's easier to change yourself than to*
> *change the world. . . . Live the life you want*
> *other people to live.*
> —Naval Ravikant

The Mirror Test helps us reach a deep understanding of ourselves. It can also help us find the first principles in our lives and work. To the extent we live these principles, we manifest the best future.

Start by asking yourself: "Are you managing an image? Or are you trying to build your future identity?"

The Mirror Test is an active wrestle between the real version versus ideal version of ourselves. People who only dream ignore their reality and never seem to achieve their dreams. Some are stuck in the past or entangled in their reality to the point that they're afraid to experience the ideal. We must be brave enough to face our reality: the good, the bad, and the ugly. The Mirror Test is all about clarity. Most people focus on making the ideal real and struggle to do so. The secret is to focus on making the real more ideal. What's right in front of you? What is a reasonable first step you can take?

The real benefit of the Mirror Test is the power to stop looking for something or someone external to change your circumstances. Take responsibility. Stop avoiding what you fear most. Are you afraid of how others will judge you? Of failure? Are you overwhelmed by change and hard work? No more excuses. Start changing your life by embracing accountability.

For a full synthesis, we need to bring together the past, future, and present to help us make the real more ideal.

Past. What first principles have worked for you? Can you build on them? What negative stories do you tell yourself that are holding you back? Can you rewrite these stories?

Future. Imagine yourself 10 years from now: What do you see? What do you feel? What are the biggest sacrifices you need to make to achieve that? What do you need to let go of? Which new principles are you embracing to align to that future? What are your hopes and dreams for others? How will you bring it all to life?

Present. What is your greatest pain that stands in the way of shaping your future? What is your struggle? What plagues your mind? Notice your daily and weekly routines. What gives you energy? What are you excited to work on? What activities are distractions or time wasters? Who inspires you? How can you be more inspiring?

The Mirror Test reminds us to take ownership, to not be a victim, to not blame others. Be kind to your past self. Make peace with your past to reconcile your future. Be brave now by allowing your future self to inspire you. How can you make the real more ideal to create progress in the present? If you take the first step to do that, you won't feel so stuck.

Consider the New Golden Rule: *Treat yourself how you want others to treat you.* Deep reflection is key. Focus on what you can do, who you can be, and how you can make a difference in the lives of others. The Mirror Test experience can help unlock this mindset shift and sequence of growth: self-awareness leads to self-care, which turns into self-love, which helps you understand self-worth. Getting things right at your very core positions you for a life of co-creation.

REFLECT THE FUTURE: BRAVE TOGETHER

Our divided world is like a broken mirror, making it hard to see the future. Each person can hold up their broken shard, representing their own unique voice, truth, and creative ideas. Brave together is the way to establish a frame in which to start assembling this mirror. Every single piece matters.

Here are some valuable ways to see your situation differently:

- **Don't go it alone.** Be brave enough to create something better together with others. Make changes now where you are. The more you exercise bravery, the more resilient you will become.

- **Return to the Mirror Test to skip feeling "stuck."** Ask yourself: "What can I do differently?" Reconcile your past. Learn from your future self. Be present in the real.

- **Reflect on how you can help others feel less "stuck."** Think about how you lead. What holds team members back or keeps them quiet? What can you do to create a better dynamic within your team? How can you empower people? Here are some ways to disrupt a culture that is stuck:

  Break out of your data fortress. Stop swimming in spreadsheets. Be less of an auditor. Spend time with your team. Immerse yourself in meaningful work with others. Involve them. How can you add value to your team?

  Change the way you see people. Don't treat people like a commodity, chess pieces, or an expense item. Invest in your relationships. If you connect genuinely, your culture will improve as a whole.

  Focus on experiences. Don't agonize over performance. Being critical of every detail undermines the work experience. Instead, be intentional. What are your meetings like? How do people feel? Improve the employee experience, and performance will amplify organically.

  Lean into creativity. Avoid the temptation to control everything. Manage systems, not people. Lead with questions. Create an environment where people feel free to flourish and share ideas. How can you be more inspiring?

  Embrace empathy. Create an environment of respect, compassion, and empowerment. Share, listen, and invite.

CHAPTER 2

NO MORE MIND
CONTROL

If you don't control your mind, someone else will.

—JOHN ALLSTON

She was tired: of graphic design programs that took students months to learn; of trying to teach them fast enough to no avail; of linear, rigid, closed systems with learning curves that felt like mountains, even for creatives. She was also frustrated with working in a controlled system. She'd had it. She would break free by building her own design program, something the world needed more than it knew.

What if she could create a platform that would simplify it all for everyone? And, with its ease of use and accessibility, become a challenger to a more complex Adobe Photoshop experience? Melanie Perkins partnered with Cliff Obrecht to launch Fusion books. They gave students the power to design yearbooks with a simple drag-and-drop function. But Melanie dreamed of doing something bigger. She wanted to build a platform that would democratize the process for non-designers—literally anyone—to shape their brand on social media.[1]

But that dream felt too big. She lacked resources. There was too much competition from companies she figured would try to squash her. When Melanie and Cliff set out in earnest, looking for investments into their big idea in Perth, Australia, she got rejected. She wondered if her dream would ever be realized.

Enter Bill Thai. Bill had already faced his own existential dilemma: tired of the traditional by-the-book investing world, he was able to successfully build and sell his own businesses. He craved something different from the transactional world of investment. Once he reached the pinnacle of exits and had a nice financial cushion, he discovered a passion for kiteboarding, a sport that involved a great deal of risk, challenge, and vulnerability—the same conditions for launching a startup. He started visiting Australia on a regular basis to kiteboard.[2]

When he eventually pivoted back to the investing world, he had an idea. What if he could liberate the old model of investing? Break free from sharky boardrooms to create a brave space where entrepreneurs could come together and—instead of a typical pitch and posture session—people could experience the raw elements of the beach to connect naturally as humans first. No agenda, no status. Just a shared experience kitesurfing, looking out for each other while doing something amazing—together. Getting vulnerable in the ocean could lead to sharing ideas, maybe even turn into builds as teams.

Bill joined forces with pro kiteboarder Susi Mai, and they started MaiTai Global. Together, they created an informal retreat, inviting entrepreneurs, investors, and interesting people. They even took this experience to Nekker Island with Richard Branson. There, they tested a new videoconferencing platform from one of their attendees. It brought people from all over the world together virtually. It was called Zoom. And Bill was the first investor.

When Melanie was invited to MaiTai Global, she hoped she'd get the attention of the right investor. But the yearbook builder wasn't enough to convince people it was the future. Melanie kept showing up anyway. For years. Even after she wiped out in the middle of the ocean on a kiteboard, waiting for hours to be found. Persistence. She had become it. She had pitched to 100 investors and failed. Bill saw her startup struggles and connected her with the right people, which led to the right developer. Together, they reimagined the platform and Canva was born. It has since become the answer to common design challenges. Now anyone can become a creator. Canva is now a multibillion-dollar company—all because a small group was willing to break free from the tyranny of traditional systems, learning how to go beyond braving it alone and forging lasting connections by being brave together.

UNPLUGGING FROM THE OLD

Do you ever feel the need to unplug from the old system? Start from scratch and reimagine it? Like there's a chip stuck in your brain, killing your best ideas—that, if removed, would change everything? Why do businesses kill creativity?

The world of work today tells us that results are everything. Our productivity and output are monitored, along with everything else. Performance on display. The quality of our work is tracked with constant reporting. Our compliance is judged and enforced. We let work determine our identity and self-worth.

Even the great Google is now telling its employees that there will be "a comprehensive review of performance," and if the results are not good, then there will be consequences.[3] Is this the same company known for its utopian culture? Now the guru of business storytelling, Malcolm Gladwell, is saying it's not in people's "best interest to work from home." Is this the same guy who's worked remotely, quite successfully, since 2005?[4] Is control the goal? None of us wants to feel mind-controlled by hierarchy.

TRADITIONAL WORK EXPERIENCE

CONTROL MINDSET	DEFAULT CULTURE
Micromanaging	Controlled environment
Results focused	Performance driven
Job title importance	Climb the ladder
Risk averse	Protect status quo

A traditional work life approach has led us from deep disengagement (70 percent of workers were disengaged *pre*-pandemic, per Gallup[5]) to the Great Resignation, Quiet Quitting, and whatever's next. We want something better. How can employers transform to become a career partner? How can employees be brave enough to challenge the status quo? We need to reimagine work. Perks are nice, but they have become toppings on a rotten salad. Higher wages help, but they don't make up for a controlled work experience. It's time for employers to be brave enough to shape a different work life with their employees. Together.

Leaders facing broken cultures and work experiences they've shaped have failed themselves and their people. The toughest news is, there's no quick solve for it. It's been built over years and decades. So, what should leaders do now? Take the Mirror Test. Get clear on how uninspiring and complacent they've become. Take responsibility for never being intentional about shaping a work life experience that benefits all.

HOW WILL YOU LEAD THE NEXT WAVE?

Dance with the waves, move with the sea,
let the rhythm of the water set your soul free.
—CHRISTY ANN MARTINE

We feel overwhelmed by the uncertainty of the future of work and anxious at the thought that things may stay the same or get worse. What do we see in the future? We find ourselves living in a time when artificial intelligence can answer most any question. Knowledge workers are bored or, worse, afraid they're becoming obsolete. Yet the greatest requirements for the future are empathy, collaboration, and co-creation. Just one look at job descriptions today shows us that companies are starving for creative, collaborative solutions. Consumers want products and services that speak directly to their hearts, that are intuitive, surprising, and delightful. They want to be understood and supported. They want tools not only to help them solve their current problems but to help them face challenges in the future. The next wave of work will need to meet the shifting expectations of consumers. This isn't our parents' market anymore.

A post-pandemic world has challenged employees to change the default work life we've been living, which has left us with a need to feel inspired again.

We all feel the world transforming. It's scary not being in control. Things are moving faster than ever. There's a macro shift going on all around us, and companies are ill-prepared for it. They're fighting to remain relevant. The corporate culture and leadership playbook of the past have expired. The good news is that we can choose what remains as building blocks for a new work life. But to better grasp what's happening now, we need to understand the past. How did we get here?

The working world can be envisioned as three successive waves, beginning with the eighteenth century Industrial Age (Figures 2.1 and 2.2).

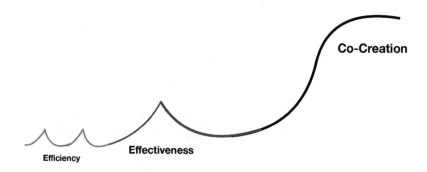

FIGURE 2.1 **The Next Wave**

WAVE 1: THE INDUSTRIAL AGE
(EIGHTEENTH CENTURY—EARLY 1900s)

The Industrial Age gave us the manual worker, the focus on "working hard," and efficiency. The gains were production lines that created most of the products we enjoy today, but it also led to the exploitation of people and the environment in the pursuit of profit.

The Progress

- A push for efficiency with a focus on skilled and technical work.

- The rise of capitalism.

- Urbanization and the growth of metropolitan areas.

- New technologies (the transcontinental railroad, the cotton gin, electricity, etc.) and factories.

- An emergent middle class.

- The ascendance of materialism and consumer goods creates new opportunities for the working class.

The By-Product

- The standard of a 40-hour workweek. The era of performance-driven workplace culture began. An emboldened management attempting to control everything.

- Authority became concentrated in the hands of the wealthy while factory workers suffered. There were few to no rules or regulations to protect workers.

- The working-class neighborhoods were desolate, congested, filthy, and polluted.

- Minimal opportunity for recreation in the first 60 years of this new age.

- Child labor, slums, disease, and death.

- Unions represented a disenfranchised working class.

WAVE 2: THE INFORMATION AGE (MID-TWENTIETH CENTURY—EARLY 2000s)

The Information Age gave us the knowledge worker and a focus on effectiveness. We figured out how to "work smarter." With the proliferation of data came the challenges of security, privacy, and other struggles. In our pursuit of knowledge, academic expertise, and quantitative data, we built massive silos that encouraged us to compete against rather than collaborate with each other.

The Progress

- The era of the knowledge worker and data collection.

- A 24-hour news cycle and an increase in movie and TV show productions.

- Computer processing and access to a connected internet.

- Smartphones and social media platforms unleashed.

- The popularity of continued education and advanced degrees.

- The trend of entrepreneurship.

The By-Product

- The need for data security, privacy concerns, consumer exploitation.

- The formation of silos and competitiveness in the workplace.

- The expansion of the expert model.

- Monopolies that aim to control the market.

- News conglomerates that attempt to control messages in society.

- In theory, human resources are meant to represent employees, but in practice, they protect corporate interests.

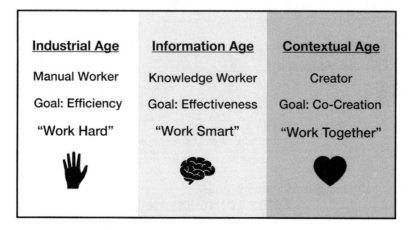

FIGURE 2.2 **The Contextual Age**

WAVE 3: THE CONTEXTUAL AGE (CURRENT)

In the Contextual Age, the best results can happen when people are better connected, engaged in creative work, and powered by principles. They are working together to create better solutions for humanity. Work and life are blended, more decentralized, and designed for compassion. The future of work will thrive if wisdom is shared in the pursuit of deep empathy.

The Potential

- The era of creative work. A demand that grows based on the limitations of artificial intelligence (AI).

- A shift from organization charts and hierarchies to an intentional focus on work culture.

- Horizontal collaboration that innovates by connecting dots.

- Leadership that evolves by embracing timeless principles and co-creation.

- Not a work life balance, but a work life blend.

- The promise of new technologies like Web3, decentralized blockchains, and decentralized autonomous organization (DAO) smart contracts to empower co-creation.

- Better alignment of passions and purpose when it comes to work experience.

> *The ultimate measure of someone is not where they stand in moments of comfort, but where they stand at times of challenge and controversy.*
> —Martin Luther King Jr.

EMBRACING CHANGE

Most leaders are asking themselves a familiar set of questions: "Who can I hire to fix this?" "How much more do I have to pay my people?" "How can I get greater productivity out of everyone?" This results in only incremental change, if any. Problems recur and grow bigger over time without solving for the future. Companies stay stuck in the status quo or are viewed as mediocre by their employees and consumers.

What can leaders do to make the shift and succeed?

- **Lead differently.** Too many leaders believe they need to double down on the same practices, sticking with the way it's always been done, squeezing more out of their employees. They get caught up in the wrong battles: execution, P&L tunnel vision, image management, and a brand strategy bent on sending out the right virtue signals. However, they've missed the core issue: their people are starving for more than a growth strategy. They desire more empathy. A new type of leadership is needed to unlock lasting change. Leaders must start with the question: "What do I need to do differently?" Maybe instead of showing how smart you are in a meeting, show your team deep compassion.

- **Be transparent.** Some C-suite leaders and company owners have no idea what isn't said in meetings. They have no way of taking an accurate temperature of the room, much less of the whole company. Meanwhile, middle managers are held back by fear. They apply smoke and mirrors to control optics for self-protection rather than empowering people to have brave conversations. It's time to be brave enough to talk about the good, the bad, and the ugly.

- **Go beyond execution.** CEOs have been focused on the "executive" part of their title for far too long. "If we'd only execute more, we would hit all our targets," they say. Really? Is that why their people are leaving? Is that why their employees feel that the culture is terrible? As the company's growth and ambitions are stunted, their best people are left wondering, "Why am I still here? Why do we keep doing this?" We can all agree that execution is important, but it's not the only button to press when things go sideways.

  If you tried to inspire people on the street with a vision of "pure execution," 10 out of 10 of them would walk away. So, why are we surprised they're leaving to find something better? They don't want to hear more about performance and results. They want to feel the power of relationships and what it's like to truly work together. Yes, continue to build the best products and services. But build the best work life for employees, too. It's time to loosen your iron grip on control.

Insanity is doing the same thing over and over again and expecting different results.
—ALBERT EINSTEIN

- **Set boundaries.** Building solid teams and the best work life experience will take more effort from all of us. No more fear tactics. No more retaliation for speaking up. No more turning a blind eye. No more normalizing bad behavior. These boundaries start with leadership teams in any organization. Toxic bosses weaponize fear. Brave leaders help dispel fears.

We can no longer tolerate selfish behaviors in our leaders. With many of us working remotely, we've invited work into our homes, and we expect this "guest" in our home to be compassionate enough to be welcomed.

Toxic bosses drain any joy or creativity out of work. They detach themselves from others and are devoid of empathy and trust. They rely on gaslighting, passive-aggressive talk, fear tactics, and silent treatments. These narcissistic behaviors come from a place of fear. Being brave together helps us create true, lasting connections. Not every bad boss operates like an extreme narcissist, and not all the best leaders consistently live their principles. This summary helps us see where we can improve as leaders:

NARCISSISTIC BEHAVIORS	PRINCIPLE-POWERED BEHAVIORS
Sense of entitlement	Respects others
Manipulates others	Creates autonomy
Need for admiration	Gives recognition
Lack of empathy	Shows compassion
Arrogant	Humble

If we want revolutionary shifts, we need to change the trajectory of our work experience. We must be brave enough to lead differently, be transparent, go beyond execution, and set boundaries. We must measure ourselves against higher standards. Principles can hold leaders accountable.

Next, we will introduce a framework to help us see the best future and develop a brave new mindset, one that will enable us to reach our full potential with others. This model not only offers a path forward for leaders, but for anyone looking to shape a better life.

CHAPTER 3

THE GREAT REALIZATION

But life at its best is a creative synthesis of
opposites in fruitful harmony.
—MARTIN LUTHER KING JR.

Studies tell us that creativity will lead the future and relationships are the key to it all. Then why haven't companies gotten the memo? Instead, the power struggle between employers and employees continues, toggling back and forth between a hot job market and looming layoffs. Meanwhile, not much has changed in terms of culture and work experience. Companies still want results, and they're still squeezing the creativity out of people to get them.

We can't solve these problems with the same leadership styles and tools that created this mess. We need more from leaders who believe that performance solves everything, more from teams trying to collaborate in Zoomland. People are "quiet quitting" or "rage applying" to escape broken work cultures. If traditional leaders can't be trusted, how can we lead the future? If expertise, hacks, and results alone are no longer the path, then what is? Co-creation.

How does co-creation work? And how is it different than the alternative? A great way to see the potential of co-creation is to look at nuclear fusion versus nuclear fission. Former NASA physicist Chris Jones, who ran for governor of Arkansas, shared:

There are two kinds of nuclear power. The one kind of power is you take a particle, matter, and you split it. And energy is released. That's the politics of division. When you take a community, and you separate them, you split them. Energy is released. That energy drives things. It's driving our current political discourse. But there's another kind of nuclear power. It's nuclear fusion. When you take two atoms, it could be any atoms—carbon, hydrogen, nitrogen, hydrogen. And you combine them. When you combine those atoms, energy is also released. When you combine communities through love, when you get folks to work together in an inclusive way, when you go beyond the destructiveness and division to solve problems, that energy that's released is far more powerful than the energy of division.

Now, in nuclear power, nuclear fusion—bringing atoms together—is far more powerful than nuclear fission—separating atoms. It takes more work to get to nuclear fusion. It's harder to get there. It's more complex. And you go back and think about communities and our political discourse, bringing people together is far more powerful than separating people. It takes more work to get there. And the research shows that diverse teams lead to better outcomes. But it's far more complex. It takes longer to get there. But when you get there, the outcomes are far better. Put in the hard work, bring the folks together. And we'll get the power we need.[1]

THE DEBATE: EMPLOYEE OR ENTREPRENEUR?

On the one hand, employees stick with employers that offer a regular paycheck and benefits, a steady career, and a dependable way to support themselves and their loved ones. They argue that it's the safe bet, and they don't seem to be wrong. But what happens when they hear that nagging feeling telling them that their passion, what makes their heart sing, can build a business that provides them with enough income? Could they pursue the work they love without risking it all, maybe even in the context of their same job, at the same company?

Within companies, leaders push their expertise and titles. Status rules supreme. People say you've got to play the game if you want to get ahead, but everyone ends up becoming some form of a politician, whether or not you definitively pick a side. Employers feel the pressure to have all the answers. HR programs masquerading as "for the people" are influenced by the higher-ups to enforce productivity, performance, and compliance. At work, "executive presence," once the revered aspiration of all would-be leaders, has been replaced with the realities of informal work and the need for real, brave leadership. Employer-employee relationships are broken. Where will this lead?

On the other extreme, entrepreneurs are telling us we need to break free from traditional employment to find freedom, that this is the only way. Start a business. Build an empire. Make our mark in the world. They espouse the daily grind and hustle culture as a template for success. Are they wrong? We know that 80 percent of new businesses fail. But why? Does this reflect entrepreneurs who weren't "all in" to be successful, or is there something else at play? What's missing?

Maybe the obsession with lifestyle is what's off? Perhaps it's making us self-centered. We're seeking shortcuts and hacks, thirsting for material things and short-term results—now. We're seeing others as competition. Influencers are everywhere. So is the lust for personal branding and self-promotion. Lifestyles on display have created a fear of missing out. Everyone is trying to be seen and heard. There's a constant push to get followers, get likes. It can often feel like a dead end.

At the core of employee, employer, and entrepreneur problems, we find an absence of guiding principles. The meta principles in *Brave Together* are designed to help people who desire to be change makers and creators. Our hope is that you return to these meta principles time and time again to help you break out of the default settings for business and work. It all starts with a simple, yet massive shift in our thinking.

The ongoing debate over work life experience has accelerated. The business world presents us with two tiers. Take your pick. Each claims to be better than the other.

Tier 1: The Employee-Employer Model (Traditional)

This is the safe option. Make a decent living wage, with health insurance and some perks. Gain experience. Get promoted. Employers protect the status quo to produce consistent results. Decisions are taken up the chain, mitigating risk. Creativity is seen as a threat. Do more with less, meet the budget, stick to the process. Employees try to keep their heads down—they don't want to make waves. But they have a burning desire to be seen. They want to do meaningful work. Yet they often feel stuck. There are no growth opportunities. They are underpaid and undervalued. Better-than-average employees learn how to navigate the system. Unless you are progressing, you start to despise it.

Tier 2: Entrepreneurship (Alternative)

Entrepreneurs take pride in their lifestyle. It's a badge of honor to break free from traditional work life oppression. They value freedom, building an empire, and taking risks, but the rewards can be even greater. Entrepreneurs thrive in a DIY playground. They don't want to waste years of their lives working for someone else. Building a business is hard. Sustaining a profitable business is even harder. This can be a lonely path, but it can also be filled with adventure and growth.

THE CO-CREATOR MINDSET

The debate about which tier is better is ongoing. What if we stopped framing work life in these extremes as either-or? We need a new approach for the future, one that is co-creative (Figure 3.1). We need an "and" answer.

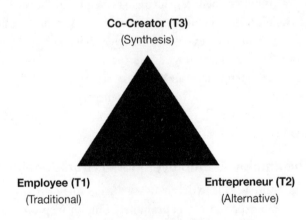

Co-Creator (T3)
(Synthesis)

Employee (T1)   Entrepreneur (T2)
(Traditional)   (Alternative)

FIGURE 3.1 **Framework for a New Mindset**

The binary debate of Tier 1 (T1) and Tier 2 (T2) leaves little room for building the future, causing a divide. We believe people can build on the best practices of our past while solving for gaps. Out of this tension, Tier 3 (T3) is born, not to replace but to see beyond the other two tiers. While not everyone will choose T3 as an operating system, this framework gives us better building blocks for the future. T3 is an "and" answer.

We can learn from the flaws found in T1 and T2, while harnessing a T3 mindset to build on the good we have already gained from the previous approaches. Employees don't need to leave an employer to practice co-creation, and entrepreneurs can become co-creators now.

These tiers are not meant to categorize people. They are default mindsets, characteristics, and modes of operating. There are building blocks and exceptions in each category—no one fits neatly into one tier. This framework can help us see how our life and leadership approach match up:

T1 EMPLOYEE MINDSET	T2 ENTREPRENEUR MINDSET	T3 CO-CREATOR MINDSET
Dependence	Independence	Interdependence
Fixed working hours	Flexible work hours	Shared time
Guaranteed income	Risk + potential rewards	Building social capital
Work hard	Work smart	Work creatively together
Boredom	Exploration	Co-creation
Order	Chaos	Meaning
Controlled	Freedom	Creative influence
Survive	Strive	Thrive
Blame others	Course correct	Build with others
Secrecy	Being open	Being transparent
Play it safe	Take risks	Shared journey
Money is everything	Time is everything	Contribution is everything
Accountable to others	Self-actualized	Responsible for others

T1 EMPLOYEE MINDSET	T2 ENTREPRENEUR MINDSET	T3 CO-CREATOR MINDSET
Efficiency	Effectiveness	Shared empowerment
Results focused	Lifestyle focused	Relationship focused
Job titles	Expertise	Transcendence
Logos/logic (mind)	Pathos/emotion (heart)	Ethos/principles (spirit)

Our friends have studied the Blue Zones, places where people live the longest, and discovered common elements unique to these regions, combining them into the best natural healthcare products for people.[2] As we've studied the most innovative leaders and teams in the world, we've asked, "Is there a zone of co-creation that tells us how the most innovative teams work?"

We have identified these "Purple Zones," characterized by the most connected team environments, in places like Pixar, teams at Nike, and even startups. We've learned from these cultures over the past few decades, working alongside co-creative leaders. We've witnessed how innovative teams co-created products together and how the best experiences emerged, digging into what makes them so insanely great—how they inspire, excite, and delight people.

Teams in the Purple Zones, no matter their size, focus on amplifying innovation through *zero ego teaming*, are open to *creativity* from diverse voices, build a *rock tumbling culture* of the best ideas through honest (and healthy) debate, and inspire the pursuit of a *shared mission* (rather than individual rock stars getting the spotlight).

One example of how the best teams create and sustain this culture is a common practice during their interview process. They don't pursue candidates if they hear them use the word "I" too many times during interviews. They refer to it as "I strain." While still searching for technical depth, these companies tend to hire people who see themselves as part of the "We" collective. They want to invite people to their team who show up with humble confidence.

By building with Purple Zone ingredients, companies can drive co-creative momentum that delivers impactful work. If leaders are willing to sacrifice ego, people can be brave together. Teams can transcend the "superhero" trap of highlighting solo success by creating a selfless force, giving themselves prime positioning to win on every front—in the market, in the workplace, and in life. They don't have to obsess about competition because they pull people into what they're creating.

When observing teams in these Purple Zones, we asked: "What do they experience as they co-create?" Here are just some of the benefits:

Co-creation unlocks lasting joy in our work and our lives. We unlock change when we co-create. Brave moments spark change in our lives as we connect what we love with what others love. We gain a fresh, childlike view that inspires us with a sense of play again. Researchers Tim Hughes and Mario Vafeas found that contrary to what most advertising tells us, it's not the consumption of goods and services that drives our happiness, it's co-creation.[3] They studied people learning guitar and playing country blues music, and discovered that performing co-creatively with others was key. But contrary to prior studies, the act of co-creation among artists was not enough. They found that it was critical for performers to co-create value by engaging an audience (in a co-creative way) to amplify happiness.

Co-creation frees us from feeling alone. In a world burdened by mental health crises, we find strength in working creatively with others. We can find freedom from ego and the energy to move the world forward. We create connectedness by getting in the zone together, starting with how we collaborate. In a study of 308 employees at a German university of applied sciences, researchers dug into the question of whether collaboration impacted well-being.[4] They explored how coworkers who own a culture of collaboration made a difference in how people feel, and how it affects "presenteeism" (coming to work when you're sick). They found a significant positive relationship between health-promoting collaboration (reducing presenteeism) and both well-being and work ability.

Co-creation reframes our approach to leadership. When we build with others, we expect more of ourselves: to be more compassionate, more generous, and more gracious with others. We become connected through a shared hope, seeing what is possible together, and turning shared dreams into shared direction. Co-creation unlocks our true potential with others. Research tells us that most senior leaders say that co-creation has transformed their organization's approach to innovation (57 percent). Co-creative leadership has enabled them to produce more successful products and services and new commercial opportunities (61 percent).[5]

Co-creation shapes products and services that drive business growth. Leaders, teams, and companies that do co-creation well drive 10×+ growth. Nike did it by building co-creative teams into the DNA of their culture ($30–$50 billion in sales), while Asics and Skechers have struggled to do so ($2–$5 billion). Teams that deliver co-creative experiences help customers feel more belonging with a brand and more connected to companies that have thriving cultures. We've found that even with just 10 to 20 percent more co-creation and inclusion than their competitors, company cultures can earn 10×+ revenue growth over time. Companies that shape inspiring cultures with a co-creative mindset show us the future of customer service.

CO-CREATIVE MAVERICKS

The *Top Gun* movies have entertained us with Tom "Maverick" Cruise and team taking flight and getting the best of the enemy, battling it out in the skies, with ego and boldness in the face of fear. But they don't show the real story of the TOPGUN program.

In the 1960s, the United States and allies had superior air combat technology—more agile airplanes, better weapons, better-trained pilots—but they were losing more aircraft and lives than ever. The US Air Force chose to invest more in and optimize their technology. The Navy took a different approach. They saw silos across teams, that—in their view—were causing battlefield losses, disconnects between organizations, broken strategies, and unfortunate deaths. They had a people problem.

The new battlefield couldn't be won in the air alone. Given the ground troops, the command center, and other aircraft in the sky, the game had changed. The Navy chose to invest in teams—horizontal leadership, not just deep vertical abilities. This was the origin of TOPGUN. Like in the movie, they recruited the best of the best, the top 1 percent, for the program. But the real TOPGUN wasn't composed of cocky or egocentric pilots. "We are not looking for someone who is arrogant or overconfident. We are looking for aircrew who are humble and approachable, traits that will make them effective teachers in the end," Hill Goodspeed, historian at the National Naval Aviation Museum, said.[6]

Their teams had an extraordinary amount of camaraderie and esprit de corps, and far less of the typical Hollywood egos and craving for competition. There weren't any trophies, and pilots were encouraged to work together to achieve successful missions. The school's slogan is "excellence without arrogance." TOPGUN graduate Guy Snodgrass said, "Being a part of an elite military unit like TOPGUN is a genuine team sport. Points aren't awarded and rankings don't exist. Instead, it's about iron sharpening iron. Setting the conditions where everyone is allowed to achieve their fullest potential."[7]

TOPGUN is all about people sharing with others the best lessons they've learned. Navy Lt. Joe Anderson, a TOPGUN instructor, said, "We can't be everywhere at once, so the idea is that we teach the students here, and they move on and teach what we've taught them to the rest of the fleet."[8]

"Their job is to make sure that, top to bottom—CO all the way down to the brand-new aircrew—are trained in the latest tactics developed by TOPGUN," explained Navy Cmdr. Dustin Peverill, a 20-year Navy veteran and two-time TOPGUN instructor. "The payback that the fleet gets from a TOPGUN graduate isn't just an individual investment; it's a community investment—a Navy investment."[9]

The results? Not only has the program continued to thrive for decades, but the US Air Force has copied this template, giving up their strategy of doubling down on tech. They created conditions that brought silos together and amplified collaboration. The TOPGUN approach has inspired "Ice Men," "Mavericks," "Roosters," and "Phoenixes" (women, like Becky Calder, who joined the program) to shape the future of what the best military could be. They've built a team of co-creators, inspiring teams to lead with a new mindset and be brave together to shape the future of the Navy.

What if every leader, instead of looking to invest in more technology, cost-cutting strategies (like layoffs), or other fast answers first looked inside, and asked: "How can we better connect our people? What if we broke down silos and built stronger, cross-functional teams?"

When people approach work vertically, they remain within their areas of expertise and end up growing silos, staying inward focused instead of connecting horizontally to empower others. They feel insecure venturing beyond what they know. Siloed organizations get stuck putting the "parts" before the "whole," creating a fragmented culture where people feel disconnected. This leads to confusion, pointless conflicts, and politics. Organizations like these are more prone to live in the past, protect the status quo, learn less, and drive people away.

In a meta study of 290 academic studies on high performance, Andre de Waal, Michael Weaver, Tammy Day, and Beatrice van der Heijden found silos to be cancerous to success. In their research titled "Silo-Busting: Overcoming the Greatest Threat to Organizational Performance," they found that the highest performing organizations not only break silos but are intentional about it. They discovered that when companies performed the best, they were silo-busting and driving collaboration in the culture.[10]

We break down silos in our lives and work as we pursue shared wisdom. This goes beyond knowing. It converts ideas into practical tools and frameworks. This means moving from talk to action and leading by example. It means sharing our skills and talents with others and learning from theirs. It means having an open heart and a willing mind. It means being bold and building co-creative muscle into everything we do. And it means starting from wherever we are and then watching the growth.

Wise leaders don't just swim in information. They experiment with experience. They break free from the self-imposed pressure to "have all the answers," to be the smartest, most authoritative expert on any given subject. Shared wisdom creates better connection and more collaboration and leads to co-creation. When we're connected with others on a shared journey, we go beyond the trap of self-actualization, becoming givers instead of takers.

How do we reimagine how we work together? Where do we start? Meeting people where they are: in meetings.

DESIGN MEETINGS AS BRAVE CONVERSATIONS

One of the best ways to change work life experiences for the better is to reimagine our meetings. We should rethink their purpose, goals, and desired outcomes. We should focus on the experience itself—not the organization, but the minds and hearts of the people.

Why are most meetings so terrible? Most are downloads sessions, data dumps, with no real listening. They offer nothing inspiring, just a loaded or directionless agenda. Are we surprised that more than 70 percent of us are disengaged? Meetings were already boring before the pandemic. Now we all feel stuck on Zoom, more alone, isolated, and frustrated. People want to feel more connected, not less.

Why do meetings exist? If it's not to connect and inspire us, then what's the point? Meetings should be designed with intention, as a time and space to build things together and not just part of a mundane routine. Remote work has made collaboration harder, but it's also created new opportunities. What if leaders reimagined meetings? Instead of ensuring "execution" and attempting to keep communication going, what if the experience could be more fluid? What if meetings included questions that inspire, conversations that connect each other and empower people to collaborate and even co-create?

Most leaders who once thrived by having a presence in the office are now having an identity crisis. How can they influence as virtual leaders? How can we make meetings that surprise and delight us and others? Here's how to get started:

Reimagine meetings as co-creative conversations. Meetings were never meant to be boring, one-sided info dumps or download sessions. How do we change that? Turn it into a conversation. Make it fluid. Like Bruce Lee said, "Be like water." Share personal feelings and stories, and make the focus on connecting. This will help challenge the status quo. Design meetings to ideate and build strategies together. Give space for people to contribute and upload. Brave conversations can be uplifting to your team.

Email a conversation-starting question before the meeting. Set the stage with a powerful question prior to a meeting, a prompt that sparks creativity. Don't just send an agenda. Send a question—and watch the team come together.

Lead yourself and others with questions. Questions have underrated power to transform our thinking and the quality of our conversations. What questions should you be asking yourself that challenge your assumptions? Open yourself up to better questions. Leading this way anchors people's work experiences in the future, powering their journey with questions that bring people together.

Take egos off the table and put building blocks on the table. It's not about being the smartest person in the room. It's not about defending ideas. It's about building bridges and connecting dots. Don't let ego suck all the air out of the room. Build psychological safety, brave space, and routines for people to share experiences and shape new insights.

Let the best ideas win. It may feel unnatural to build this way, but it invites courage and strength. The best cultures do this well. This approach changes everything. Being guided by the greatest question: "How do we want people to feel?" This puts empowerment at the center of workplace culture, not just adding it as a "nice-to-have" or short-lived HR program.

We've all been on Zoom meetings that have gone 30 minutes or an hour (painfully) too long. You find yourself checked out, staring at the "Leave" button, and counting down the minutes. How do we change this?

One team of senior leaders in a mature Silicon Valley tech company was planning a virtual offsite. We were working with them to design the day and the experience. They wanted to do an eight-hour session. That would test most people's energy, attention, and sanity in an untenable way. We designed the day with three simple exercises:

1. **Personal storyline.** Share definitive personal experiences based on work life highs and lows. This gave people the chance to make new connections within their team they didn't know were there.

2. **Retrospective.** Share what they've learned from prior projects, reflecting on what works and what doesn't. This gave people a voice they don't often use.

3. **Futurespective.** Shape a shared vision of the future using pure imagination.

Each exercise took about one to two hours, and we kept things fluid. This gave people permission to create together.

Having the courage to share and deeply explore personal experiences (such as, "You lost your dad to cancer? I lost mine years ago, too.") as part of the conversation set the stage for the day. Then they got real about what had worked and what hadn't in the past. The leaders posed thought-provoking questions, and employees had a valuable seat at the table. By the time they got to the last exercise, people were ready to jump boldly into the future. Together, they imagined what the future of their work could be. They got creative, collaborated, and wrote exciting and aspirational "team dreams." They designed futuristic headlines in the *Wall Street Journal*, reflecting the work they were doing now with the imagined outcome it would have three years into the future: "Upstart Tech Company Inspires Innovative New Technologies with Tesla." They were sharing and building on each other's ideas on how to do just that. Magic was happening.

They got serious about building on this idea of designing new software technologies that could be integrated with Tesla, how they could partner together, the core elements required to kick-start their innovative efforts, and concrete actions each of them could start taking now. This meant regularly scheduled weekly co-creative sessions where they could share updates and bring the work together. They were mobilizing as a team to focus on the next steps to bring it all to life. By the end of the eight hours, surprisingly, people were so engaged in the experience that they wanted to stay on the call. It had awakened a new kind of energy. The senior leadership team felt the event was a success. It was unlike anything they'd ever witnessed.

The employees loved it. They felt connected to each other. We helped them see that, with a co-creative mindset, they could reframe their approach to shape an entirely new experience. They discovered how to work creatively together.

BRINGING CO-CREATION TO LIFE

This Silicon Valley team bravely designed their conversations in ways that amplified their people with a co-creative mindset. Here's how you can do the same:

1. **Make meetings personal.** Studies show that people are feeling burned out, more alone, and exhausted. The last thing they need is to be bouncing from one meeting to another, "getting right down

to business" at every turn. The best approach? Give them space. Start with two questions: "How are you doing?" and "How are you really doing?" Give them the opportunity to check in, share their dog story, let their five-year-old daughter wave at the camera. Bonding is one of the best ways for people to feel part of a team and want to stay. "Anything but work" check-ins are great, highlighting what we're grateful for. Ask people to share personal stories and experiences. Sharing these experiences can set the tone for great conversations.

2. **Give people permission to build.** Your people aren't as much interested in random rewards as they are in challenge, or the dearth of it. They want to tackle big challenges, disrupt the status quo, and build the future together. They want to be trusted so they can expand the impact of their work. Let them loose on an important challenge and give them permission to connect with whomever they need to make it happen. Bust the barriers for them, and they'll raise the bar themselves.

3. **Get real with deep retrospectives.** Look back, for the sake of learning and sharing. Create the context for people to get real about what worked, what didn't, and what they've learned. Keep judgment out of it. Look for ways to improve and ideate together. Stay open to growth with a co-creative mindset. Address and reconcile the factors that are holding your team back. This deepens bonds that go beyond just "report outs" and starts building the conditions for better innovation.

4. **Inspire the ideal with "futurespectives."** Get creative together. Focus on the future and imagine what is possible. Give people prompts and activities to encourage creative expression, and let their ideas flow. How do they want to feel about their work? Frame simple, powerful steps together to get there. Organize a creative strategy together. These can turn into actual building blocks that could shape the future, becoming the patterns, or team habits, it will take to bring it all to life. Let the team establish a reasonable timeline and assignments. As a leader, express your confidence and trust in them to unlock their ability to build.

5. **Turn "boring work" into inspired co-creation.** If people don't feel inspired by their work, they'll leave. It's that simple. They want to be part of something big and feel that they belong. It may not be your job to keep their work from feeling boring, but you can create an environment where the work feels and is co-creative. How? Connect the dots with them. Tell people you want them to "co-create" solutions. Show them by getting in the trenches to see what they see and feel what they feel. Provide a template of co-creation by how engaged you are with them. The more you involve the team, the more collective progress you'll have. There's nothing like leaders who build purpose as they shape products and solutions as one.

Co-creation is about embodying principles. It's about reimagining meetings as conversations versus downloads and building bridges across teams versus more islands and silos. It's about giving people a sense of joy and work that energizes them. It's when leaders care about them personally and where the word "love" may even emerge in all its simple yet powerful ways. Isn't this what every single one of us wants? A beautiful future we can imagine and shape together, a future every leader can start building now—by design—by sacrificing our own ego for the greater good of others, knowing that people will feel the truth of our motives deep in their hearts by how we make them feel, not through pithy memos. People experience the strength of shared purpose, building success for each other and a meaningful experience for customers. This results in a joy that has staying power, weaving itself into the fabric of our personal lives with our loved ones and shaping a future where we not only show up better in work, but far better in life.

We stand now at a critical moment in leadership: What will you do? How will you lead others into the future? And how will you design it to inspire others to dream of being part of it?

Brave Together.

Lead with a Question

Turn Pain into Power

Make Others the Mission

Define the Situation

Create Context

Follow True North

CHAPTER 4

LEAD WITH A QUESTION

The Wisdom Principle

*You're never going to learn as profoundly as
when it's purely out of curiosity.*
—CHRISTOPHER NOLAN

s it possible to create a perpetual motion machine, one that could work infinitely without an external energy source? Science tells us it's impossible, that it would violate the laws of thermodynamics. But could it be done anyway? Leonardo da Vinci took a stab at it, sketching designs, using fluid mechanics, for a "self-filling flask." But ultimately, he failed to produce a working machine.[1] Centuries later, Nikola Tesla put his powerful mind to the task. This was a mind that had produced volumes of innovative texts and inventions, including 80 US patents that revolutionized entire industries.[2] He became so adept at harnessing the power of his mind that, rather than first building models of machines, he preferred to iterate everything in his head. Blueprint, build, and test, again and again—in his mind. He could see which parts of his machines would fail or succeed, and then he'd build accordingly. Having saved all the time he would have spent prototyping, he'd have a working model of something insanely great.[3]

When Nikola attempted to tackle the problem of perpetual energy, he developed a concept he'd tested in his mind with enough iterations to share it with others. He then brought the idea to a former professor, a mentor he trusted, who criticized it as impossible, a waste. But Nikola didn't give up. He went back and forth in his head, retesting the schemes, the design, and all the parts. And he concluded that, even in the face of the opposing forces of academia, he was right—and the professor was wrong.[4]

Tesla created most of his inventions in isolation. He worked alone. He had an incredible work ethic and unique way of looking at the world, and he captured the details in what are known as the Tesla papers. In January 1943, after Tesla was found dead in his room at the New Yorker Hotel at the age of 86, the American government swooped in and took possession of his papers, fearful that the secrets could fall into enemy hands. What exactly happened to Tesla's papers? It remains shrouded in mystery—and speculation. Should genius be kept to oneself and taken to the grave?[5]

There is a different path, one that offers an energy source with the power to fuel the perpetual motion of our future work life forever and to guide us toward the greatest innovations. We've not only iterated it in our heads, we've manifested it across multiple domains. And we've witnessed its power in the best leaders, most inspiring teams, and greatest companies of our time.

Being *brave together* harnesses the power of asking great questions and our ability to co-create with others. It can produce the kind of energy that's endless, the kind that doesn't rely on a single person because it's built on an activated team leading with questions and working creatively together.

EXPERTISE IS NOT THE ENDGAME

For decades, people have flaunted their intellect and knowledge as the ultimate superpower, obsessed with inserting their "expert perspective" into everything. Companies claim to be the main authority in their market, stacking teams with experts to one-up everyone else and hiring a thought leader to share their "one solution to rule them all" with a rollout promising to "transform their organization" immediately. Experts are here to save the day! Leaders do this so they can skip critical thinking. Plus, they're off the hook if it doesn't work. They can say, "See, I told you we shouldn't have hired that guy." Often, people in the organization will reject a new program, like antibodies defeating a virus.

From creative control to shared flow:

T1: Organization—Centralized Authority (The Industrial Age)

T2: Expert—Knowledge Worker (The Information Age)

T3: Co-Creators—Shared Wisdom (The Contextual Age)

In the Information Age or knowledge worker tier, some experts try to build a career or a business dedicated to helping others with their deep knowledge, yet many use knowledge to gain an edge over others. They think they need to build an empire and be the smartest person in the room to demonstrate their value. If employees don't consider themselves experts, how do they get ahead? By being submissive. They obediently check all the boxes and adhere to what their expert leader imposes. Employees jeopardize their good standing if they question the expert, give feedback, or act independently.

Experts outside an organization position themselves as "thought leaders," constantly looking over their shoulders to see how many followers their closest "influencer" competitor has. Experts can spot silos in organizations, yet they struggle to see their own silo they've built.

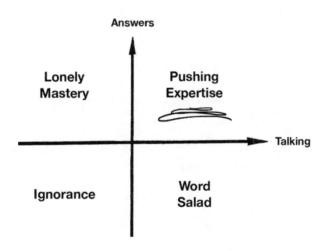

FIGURE 4.1 **The Expert Model**

The expert model (Figure 4.1) closes off connection with others. Experts see the one answer they offer and assume that others will be impressed by it. Rather than collaborate in a meaningful way, they tend to view others as a threat. They cling to their one answer as the solution to every question—which, of course, it isn't. "One idea to rule them all." Like Gollum in *The Lord of the Rings*, they cling to their "Precious" at all costs. Their ideas become their identity, and their pride and ego stand guard to protect these ideas at all costs.

Bad managers believe they should have all the answers. They're the ultimate "knowledge handyman." They have an experience to match every problem you're facing, and they've already done it all better than you. They react first with answers. Bad managers can't stop talking. Why do they do this? Who knows? Maybe they've learned all they know from other bad managers. Or they've been rewarded for all their good ideas in the past. The answers that have taken them this far have made them overconfident. Some even believe they know it all, convinced they have nothing left to learn. This kills co-creation even before it can begin. Here are some other negative effects:

- Focusing just on technical knowledge risks only leading with answers.

- Knowledge experts are quick to apply antidotes while shutting off listening.

- Going deep on a subject can create a silo, making it harder to forge connections.

- Instead of innovating with others, experts protect and defend their expertise.

- Experts can be blinded by ego, which makes them dismissive of others who could add value.

When we approach questions in this way, we don't pay attention when we're preparing our responses. These bad tendencies pull us away from the one thing that matters most for our health and happiness: relationships—they are the key to life.

Mental health challenges are rampant and on the rise. Yes, we're all connected online. We live in a world that can't stop talking, and yet we feel more isolated than ever before. Why? We're suffocated by answers. Everyone is telling us what to think, what to believe, what to do, and how to do it. We are given answers, answers, and more answers. But we're social beings. We want to feel connected and be heard. We're meant to explore. We want to be empowered.

What if we stopped pretending we have all the answers and started asking powerful questions instead? What if we were brave enough to open our minds in a way that inspired everyone?

THE POWER OF ASKING

Leading with a question is about harnessing the power of asking. Steve Jobs said, "Now, I've always found something to be very true, which is most people don't get those experiences because they never ask. I've never found anybody who didn't want to help me when I've asked them for help."[6]

Jobs went on to talk about the time when he was 12 years old and called Bill Hewlett, cofounder of Hewlett-Packard, to ask for some spare parts to build a frequency counter. Not only did Hewlett agree to young Steve's request, but he offered him a summer job assembling frequency counters. He said, "I've never found anyone who's said no or hung up the phone when I called. I just asked. And when people ask me, I try to be as responsive, to pay that debt of gratitude back. Most people never pick up the phone and call. Most people never ask. And that's what separates, sometimes, the people that do things from the people that just dream about them. You gotta act. And you've gotta be willing to fail, you gotta be ready to crash and burn, with people on the phone, with starting a company, with whatever. If you're afraid of failing, you won't get very far."[7]

The power of asking starts with *What if?*—being brave and taking risks.

One day, we were sitting in Ian's living room when we realized that we had to meet with Ed Catmull, founder of Pixar, author of *Creativity, Inc.*, and a leader whose legacy continues to inspire us. We didn't know him, and we didn't know how we'd meet him. After one week of pursuing a close connection, we were introduced to Ed. He was gracious in his response and agreed to meet us.

Here we were two weeks later, anxious to learn, at the Lazy Dog restaurant in Cupertino, California. When Ed arrived, he was wearing black-rimmed glasses and a T-shirt with an image of *Bao*, the short film hit from Pixar. His salt-and-pepper mustache curled up the corners of his mouth as he smiled. We'd thought, since he's the creative leadership Yoda, we would just tap the "wisdom dispenser" and he'd load our fertile minds. Instead, Ed asked questions and listened.

After 15 minutes of us sharing, we got anxious. When would he start sharing *his* wisdom with us? Realizing we'd been talking the whole time, we asked, "Ed, what's your leadership philosophy?" He said, "I lead with a question." He told us about his early days leading Pixar, as a PhD, answering every question people asked him. The pressure overwhelmed him. He realized he wasn't empowering anyone. His wife encouraged him to go on a meditation retreat for seven days to only ask questions and listen. After the first few days, he was ready to quit. But he stuck with it, and it changed his life. What if we led with questions? What if that's the future?[8]

In reading *Creativity, Inc.*, we were most drawn to the concept of a braintrust (which we'll explore more in a later chapter). Ed applied leading with a question to his braintrust teams. The questions focused on a challenge related to a Pixar project. Days prior to a braintrust meeting, Ed would send out a thought-provoking question to the team, giving people space to sort through ideas on their own. Team members would then come to the meeting prepared. It made for some "get your hands dirty" discussions where they would openly share ideas and challenge each other in respectful ways. A collective answer would emerge from these meetings, with everyone empowered to move forward. Even if there wasn't complete agreement, the braintrust provided support. All from the power of questions.

If you want to focus on improving relationships, lead with a question. Instead of "How are you doing?" try asking, "What's something exciting you are working on?" or "What do you recommend we do?" Watch people smile and light up when they feel connected. Next time you see someone is struggling, ask, "What's on your mind?" This could make the difference in their day. It could free up their emotional constraints, even if just for a moment.

When someone listens deeply to us, we feel seen. We were designed to listen (with the ratio of two ears to one mouth). Leading with answers creates anxiety. Without being heard, people feel deflated and alone. Why would we want anyone feeling that way, at work or at home? It's not complicated. People like to be heard. Here's why:

1. Being heard makes us feel like we belong.

2. Feeling understood connects us in life.

3. Connection to others empowers us.

LISTEN WITH AN OPENNESS TO CHANGE YOUR MIND

Changing your mind doesn't make you a flip-flopper or a hypocrite. It means you were open to learning.
—ADAM GRANT

Most of us don't listen well. And it's not (exactly) our fault. It's likely we were never trained to listen. Ever since we were toddlers, we were taught to talk. Then talk more. Raise your hand, share the answer. But what happens in a world where the distance between us and others can only be narrowed by connecting with them? Stephen Covey taught that we should "seek first to understand, then to be understood." People think differently, so it's good to be open to every perspective. What if we did more of this in life? In business? In politics?

Critical thinking involves more than just being inside our own heads. We need to listen, observe, and learn. Then we can make decisions and apply new insights. We can move our lives in a better direction through inspiration.

As he grew into the leader representing the best of Apple, Steve Jobs didn't just listen to understand. He listened with an openness to changing his mind. He'd sit in meetings, ask hard questions, and then if he became convinced to change his mind, he'd do it. Right then and there. Senior leaders at Apple say Steve could pivot 180 degrees in real time, disagreeing with himself. This shocked those who'd worked with CEOs who always stuck to their guns. When people asked Steve why he'd pivoted, he'd say the new take was more compelling—no matter where it came from.

The world is starving for empathy, openness, and unity. And we can only solve our greatest problems together. The next time you approach a conversation, try something different. Don't just listen to understand. Listen to change your mind. Now, watch how you feel and how the other person feels. Imagine the difference it would make if you did more of this.

META PRINCIPLE 1: LEAD WITH A QUESTION

What makes principles timeless? Not trendy ideas found in self-help or business books like waking up at 4:00 a.m., using an authentic voice, taking cold showers, developing super habits, doing extreme exercise, or following diet programs. These aren't principles; they're tactics—designed to lead people to believe they can hack their way to a successful work life. Timeless principles stick. Their power isn't based on a quick fix or happenstance but on having been pressure-tested over millennia. True principles move us beyond motivation to make up the core of an inspired life.

Most books, especially over the past few decades, focus on a singular theme or principle. Most principles featured are prescriptive in nature. But in his work (especially his book *The 7 Habits of Highly Effective People*), Stephen Covey established an ecosystem of principles, which we have found to be deeply useful. It's tempting for authors to establish a set of formulas and tactics that equal success. If you just do X, Y, and Z, you will be wealthy. When you attempt to apply it and don't become wealthy, they tell you, "Well, you didn't do Y and Z hard enough."

In *Brave Together*, we zoom out of the prescriptive weeds. People are tired of being told exactly what to do, and why, when, and how they should do it. Instead, we introduce six meta principles designed to be directional—leaving space for anyone to approach them with their own thinking, perspectives, and unique individuality. This allows anyone to enhance their experience by applying their own creative approach.

Meta Principle 1: Lead with a Question (Figure 4.2) points to the importance of exploration. It stems from a place of humility, openness, and curiosity,

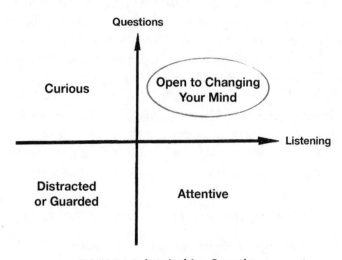

FIGURE 4.2 **Lead with a Question**

steering us away from a "lead with an answer" approach, which is all too familiar. We will provide a template of how and why solid questions have worked for us, including the Golden Questions that have given us direction as leaders, helping us connect the dots for ourselves and others. But we won't tell you what question or questions you need to ask. That's up to you.

Lead with a Question as a meta principle shifts us from being the expert to sharing wisdom. It's common for leaders to want to hoard insights, using the "knowledge is power" approach, fearful they'll lose their competitive advantage. Leaning on expertise makes them dependent on outside resources. But sharing wisdom with others doesn't diminish impact; it amplifies it.

Wisdom is the ability to discern and use good judgment. When it is shared, it can lead people to powerful transformations. All the knowledge in the world is useless if it isn't accessible and put into practice. Here are some things to consider in shifting from knowledge work to sharing wisdom:

- Sharing wisdom with others creates value.

- Better observations can enrich the lives of others.

- Learning from others helps us make better sense of the world around us.

- Sharing wisdom fosters a culture of resourcefulness and shared insight. It goes beyond knowing and enters the territory of application.

Shared wisdom isn't just about sharing answers; it's about asking questions together. It's about applying knowledge to experience and converting ideas into practical tools. It's about going from talk to action, leading by example, and sharing our gifts and talents with others. This kind of wisdom opens doors.

THE GOLDEN QUESTIONS

To kick-start how Lead with a Question can impact your work life moving forward, we'll share the "golden questions." These questions can direct us to wisdom. We have asked these questions in interviews and shared them in conversation with collaborative partners. We've tested them with family and friends. They have proven to be icebreakers and conversation starters that enable you to move past pleasantries by bringing depth and quality to inter-actions. Here they are:

1. At the back of your head and heart, what is something still unfulfilled in your life? This question is tied to learning. You can learn a lot by asking yourself this question. Answers that come to the surface will reveal certain truths. Pain from your past or pain in your present. Possibly both. The goal here is to acknowledge this reality. Get clear about this answer. Look past excuses you've used before and the lies you've told yourself. Get to the heart of it all.

Now, imagine posing this golden question to others with a sincere desire to see someone as they are. Know that this is a heavy question. It can take time and space for someone to respond, but it can be such a powerful experience when asked. Be patient and kind in the process.

2. What are you most excited about right now? This golden question is about things you love. It will either elicit energy you have bottled up or it will fall flat. This will help you see if you're living in fear or striving to be brave. It's the difference between a static work life or one that is dynamic. As you ask people this question, take note of how they light up (or not). Their body language and tone of voice will show excitement. See if their passion comes out. This answer doesn't have to reflect your current project, role, or company, although it may. It could be something you are building on the side, a hobby, or a personal pursuit. As you clarify what you are passionate about, what will you do with this insight? How can you help others after identifying their passion?

3. What inspires you to be your best? This question has to do with how you are living your life. What inspires you to improve? Is it your family or loved ones? Is it a vision of your future life? What is the source of your inspiration? Perhaps you are moved by a good book or a podcast. You might find solace and beauty in nature—by the way the sun warms your face or by watching a breeze ruffle the leaves on a tree—when your life feels integrated within a larger ecosystem. Maybe it is by serving a greater purpose. Or perhaps right now you feel stuck, and struggle to move the needle in your life. This question puts your values front and center. Can you identify your core principles? Do you need to rethink your values? By asking others this question, you can learn what inspires them.

We understand that the golden questions don't solve everything. That is not our claim. The golden questions help us understand what we can learn, what we love, and how we can live. They are foundational questions about your work life that you can return to time and time again as needed. The best use for these questions is in conversation. They can strengthen your relationships while empowering others. But these are just a guide. What questions will help *you* become a better leader?

Questions have the power to lead us to higher places. They anchor our future, unlock an endless supply of discoveries that can guide our lives, and give us hope.

Asking better questions can change our lives. How can you harness the power of questions? Exploring with curiosity could lead to better connections and better opportunities. In the next chapter, we'll see how questions help us develop our first principles and get us out of survival mode.

CHAPTER 5

GET OUT OF
SURVIVAL MODE

They tried to bury us. They didn't know we were seeds.
—DINOS CHRISTIANOPOULOS

A re you in survival mode? Do you look forward to the weekend and dread the Monday morning alarm clock? You may feel stuck in a job, misunderstood by your boss, or searching for a way out. You may be affected by a Tier 1 way of life. Are you frequently changing jobs? Wondering when you're going to catch the next break?

If you are in survival mode, every day can feel like a struggle just to get through. Even our favorite heroes from classic books and movies faced hard moments. A Hero's Journey doesn't start off with clarity. It involves a new experience, changing our dismal routine, and an openness to learn and grow. It takes courage to embark on our own Hero's Journey.

The Hero's Journey, derived from mythology, has three main parts:

1. **The separation:** The hero sets out on an unfamiliar adventure.

2. **The initiation:** The voyage takes place and the hero arrives.

3. **The return:** They returned to their home or to people they once knew; only now, after their adventure, the hero has transformed or gained a special skill, ability, or reward.

You are the hero in your own story. Maybe your journey has just begun, or you still need to take your first step toward a desired adventure. Perhaps you are in the messy middle, trying to make sense of it all. Most people covet the hero's return, when they are praised for slaying the dragon and showered with love, riches, and glory. If our story is just about achievement, life will feel lonely and empty. The best story is an adventure with others.

It's time to be brave. To go all in on your Hero's Journey. How are you becoming more compassionate? More determined? More inspiring? What principles do you use as a compass to guide your life? What could you build with others?

We are in survival mode when we feel the full weight of our struggles. A good friend of ours spent years in survival mode. We saw her pain from a distance. She was brave enough to tell us her full story. She doesn't mind us sharing it with you, but we will refer to her as Jessica to preserve her anonymity.

Jessica felt terrible, like a total failure. At best, she was barely able to function; at worst, she had long stretches where she would just go numb. She struggled to get out of bed, knowing divorce was inevitable. All that stinging guilt and the reality of a mountain of debt stacked up for years—how would she ever emerge from it all? Her pain was overwhelming. And she was just starting to pull back all the layers. What would she do?

Jessica's marriage shattered when she realized she was with someone who hated her. She felt it every day. Her husband would look at her with disappointment, say things under his breath, and put her down in front of their kids. It was unhealthy for everyone, but Jessica felt she had to keep it together. The kids needed parents who were together, right? That's what everyone told her. "Stick it out," they'd say. "Things will get better." How could she ever divorce? Her parents would never approve. What would people think? It didn't matter. The inevitable happened. She reached a point where she could no longer feel sorry for herself, but she felt like she was failing her kids.

She had to carry the emotional load of raising her young children while working to make ends meet. She had to fend off the angry outbursts of an ex-spouse, which made co-parenting even more challenging, all while paying off credit card debt and student loans. This was not the life she'd planned. She was embarrassed by overdraft fees hitting her bank account and the stack of bills labeled "Past Due."

Every day, Jessica felt like she was waking up to a nightmare. Life was suffocating, unbelievably hard. How could she move forward? Jessica tried everything to get it all back on track. She pursued "the next big thing," which turned out to be a pyramid scheme that never lived up to the hype, another letdown. She went all in selling stuff on eBay, but never made enough money and only ended up with leftover clearance items she failed to flip. She tried one online business after another, never making enough sales on social media, even though she put herself out there. Meanwhile, she couldn't stop spending on things that seemed to matter at the time but in the end didn't. It was retail therapy; she was searching for happiness by accumulating things. She was exhausted from trying. She questioned her abilities. She gave in to fear. Every shortcut she tried fell apart. Every tempting hack fizzled. Is this what life would become? Nothing but setbacks? She wasn't making any progress. She found herself in an endless loop in survival mode.

Have you ever had these thoughts or heard other people say:

- "I feel utterly alone and helpless."

- "Life's just too hard. Why does it have to be this way?"

- "Everyone has perfect lives on social media. Mine's so far from it."

- "I work all day, giving everything, collapse on the couch at night, spend hours on my phone or watching TV until I fall asleep—only to do it all over again the next day. What's the point?"

You might be trying to find a job in a tough economy, overcoming a health problem, or facing the breakdown of a key relationship. Maybe you're just hoping for something better, something more? But you're questioning what it takes to kick off an extreme life makeover because it feels like you're trying to climb Mount Everest during the worst of winter storms.

FIVE SIGNS YOU'RE IN SURVIVAL MODE

You Feel Checked Out

According to Gallup, more than 70 percent of people are disengaged in their work life. Since 2021, the term "quiet quitting" has described this type of disengagement: doing the bare minimum to not get fired. What leads to quiet quitting? Low pay, no growth opportunities, feeling disrespected, lack of flexible hours and benefits, childcare issues.

Most people feel checked out when they let life happen by default, not by design. It's easier to let someone else just tell us what to do, rather than figuring it out for ourselves. We end up sticking to repetitive tasks and a lackluster routine. Then we feel disconnected. We have surface-level relationships with no depth. For those looking to take life to the next level, this won't work.

> *Remember, some of the people you'll encounter this week*
> *with the biggest smiles, the funniest jokes, and most*
> *"friends" are going through the darkest, loneliest, and most*
> *painful battles. The safest bet is to be kind to everyone,*
> *regardless of the mask they're wearing.*
> —STEVEN BARTLETT

You Rarely Experience Joy

When we're in the midst of the chaos of life, bogged down in the day-to-day, we can lose sight of everything else. The truth is our personal growth is directly connected to the quality of our relationships. Relationships are joy-producing engines. But our focus on survival can get in the way. We may not let trusted people in on what's really happening because we don't want to "bother them," depriving ourselves of the positive effects they can have in our lives. If we want more joy in our lives, we need to invest in our relationships.

You Constantly Search for More

When we focus on what we lack, life feels unsatisfying. We're constantly searching for something more. We're plagued by what we need to do, where we need to be. We thrive on the need to complete our to-do lists, to feel busy, and to be entertained. We can get stuck moving from one thing to the next, which we call "nexting." It makes us feel important, yet we end up never arriving.

Think about your commitments. Why do you do what you do? Are your daily and weekly activities aligned with what's most important to you? Or are they more important to other people? Hit pause on nexting. Watch what happens. Literally sit and do nothing. No work, no internet, no TV, no music. The more we hit pause on what's next, the more we have a chance to reset, to breathe. Actor Brandon Kyle Goodman said, "I told my friend that I'm emotionally 'hitting a wall,' and she said, 'Sometimes walls are there so we can lean on them and rest.' I can't even begin to express how much I really needed to hear that."[1]

You Get Caught Up in Competition

As a leader, you may feel pressure to put results first, at the expense of others. You may see employees as a means to an end. Do you feel you have something to prove? Are you guarded around others? Like they're competition? Do you compare yourself to them? Do you see them as a threat?

Competition is born of a scarcity mindset. We fear that there's never enough. We can get fooled into believing we need to bring people down to get ahead, but by pulling others down, we also fall.

Maybe you have trust issues? Or you've been burned in the past? Perhaps you haven't healed from losing a loved one, a relationship, or an opportunity? Is it envy? Not having as much as someone else? Charlie Munger, billionaire investor and partner of Warren Buffett, says, "He's never cared about comparing his riches to that of others and that his focus has always been on securing independence, the freedom to do what he wants in work and life—and he wishes more people did the same. He sees too many people worried about how much others have, when someone else will always have more."[2]

You Reach for Shortcuts and Hacks

Deep work takes more than what hack culture offers. Show up. Be consistent. There are no cutting corners when establishing a foundation for your future. Seek support from those you trust and admire. Surround yourself with people who are striving to be better, who will push you and hold you accountable. There are no cheap elixirs for getting ahead.

Leaders may be tempted to cut corners. We've seen moral shortcuts. We must be careful. More than anything, we need to live principled lives. Integrity is core to the future. Doing what's right may be expensive and involve really hard work. Doing what's wrong will cost you a fortune and can set you back a lifetime.

THE POWER OF FIRST PRINCIPLES

How will we get through what we're facing? To solve the greatest questions of the future, we'll need to combine the magic of what's in our hearts with what's in the hearts of others. Principles can be the bridge to make better connections in life. We need to do the inner work if we are going to be effective co-creators. We start by noticing principles we already gravitate toward, wisdom we've learned from others—a family member, teacher, coach, mentor, or leader—that has left an impression on us. The best kind of principles are sticky. We enjoy saying them to ourselves. They anchor our actions as we share them with others.

In their book *Made to Stick*, Chip and Dan Heath share how sticky ideas are easily understood and remembered,[3] and they drive our best behavior. Using this framework, how do we create our own first principles?

1. **Simple.** It's concise and easy to grasp.

2. **Unexpected.** It gets our attention and keeps it.

3. **Concrete.** It's specific.

4. **Credible.** It's true.

5. **Emotional.** It's deeply felt.

6. **Stories.** They're shared, retold, and inspire us to act.

When we build with first principles, we get out of survival mode and start striving. First principles are foundational. They're the basic building blocks for creating our future (Figure 5.1). Those who design, invent, and build can't access pure originality and creativity without an understanding of their first principles. They can, at best, copy other people and products that exist, but copies are soon forgotten.

We can reframe first principles as anchoring questions to remind us of who we are. Let's explore why we need first principles in our lives.

FIGURE 5.1 **Build Better with First Principles**

First Principles Are a Source of Energy

When we build with first principles, we tap into a different kind of energy. It's not about going through the motions or trying to control or copy others. We're empowered to confront our past, be brave in the present, and become bold enough to face the future.

We worked with a startup founder who explored his experiences with the valleys in his life, deep struggles that challenged everything in his being. He emerged with a fresh first principle: "Clear the Deck." This meant taking the time every night to close out his day: going for a walk at dusk and mentally putting away the folders on each thing requiring his attention. This gave him the ability to rest. Then in the morning, he'd rise at 5 or 6 a.m., walk outside in nature, breathe deeply, meditate, pray, and open himself up to the possibilities of the day. This pattern gave him the courage to start a business, raise millions in funding, and create a team. This one principle gives him the recurring energy he needs to accelerate on a path of possibilities that didn't exist before.

First Principles Are Most Powerful When Designed Together

We've seen the future take shape in real time as people design and live first principles. But it's surprising how often leaders don't get it. They fail to realize they need to take an active part in shaping their first principles and not just rely on conventional wisdom or half-heartedly follow a company's mission statement, as good as it may be. First principles help us take responsibility and live from our core.

An executive friend of ours was struggling with a situation. He'd started a business that was already producing tens of millions in revenue, but he had a cofounder he couldn't stand anymore, and he felt the majority of his team of 150 was uncommitted to and unprepared for the growth he wanted. They had a backlog of accounts that hadn't been serviced, operational issues stacking up, and logistical problems growing.

When we asked him what he wanted most, he said he wanted to become a $50 million business, and then sell and exit the company. In his mind, he was living the dream on a beach in Key West, sipping a piña colada. Meanwhile, his people were watching. He wasn't involved enough. If he wasn't committed to the culture, how could he expect his people to be?

He told us he wanted to explore doing some team building work. Based on where things stood, we didn't feel that was appropriate. We steered the conversation in another direction. He was already living in a future where he'd exited the company and made off like a king, and he was showing up that way while he expected his team to be fully committed to helping the company get there. It was a gross misalignment. He couldn't have both. We told him that all the most innovative companies made their entire existence not about a specific financial goal but about building a meaningful culture. Their goal wasn't to sell their company but to build a lasting impact. To change lives, maybe even change the world. They were feeding the goose that kept laying the golden eggs. We asked him:

- "What if you started shaping the culture, instead of executing an exit strategy?"

- "How can you shape your first principles of culture with your core team?"

- "How can you lead them to love their work and do their best work?"

These questions became the guideposts of their future. A year later, he called us, excited. They'd gone from being an uninspired culture with infighting among the cofounders and executives to becoming a high-growth talent magnet. People wanted to be part of the magic they were making.

Successful companies design first principles together. They are focused on building a culture people love and where they can do their best work to make a difference.

BUILDING CO-CREATIVE MUSCLES

Everything about us—our brains, our minds, and our bodies—is geared toward collaboration in social systems. This is our most powerful survival strategy, the key to our success as a species, and it is precisely this that breaks down in most forms of mental suffering.
—BESSEL VAN DER KOLK, MD,
The Body Keeps the Score

Pandemic, wars, economic devastation—there will always be something that triggers our survival mode. Our default is to survive, but we have to learn how to strive. How? By determining and being guided by our first principles, which will empower us to tackle the sudden challenges life throws at us and help us to become better humans.

Let's return to our struggling friend Jessica. She didn't give up. She didn't hack her way out of it. She dived deep into her life to identify her first principles.

What did she discover? She wanted a better direction for her family's future that only a principle-powered life could provide. She reframed her story from that of a victim. She pursued her best options in brave new ways. She joined a company and led a team on new projects. She rebuilt her life while helping her team deliver lasting results. She co-created a mantra with her team to "Build the Best" products that would have an impact on people's lives for years to come.

Jessica applied integrity everywhere. No more shortcuts. No more complaining. Another first principle emerged: "Trust the Truth." Where others would lie, cheat, and steal to gain business, only to have customers leaving them later, she would be honest—even if it cost her in the short term. Her customers loved her candor, and it paid off. She applied this first principle at home. She would be honest with her kids. From now on, they would face their challenges together.

All of this led to her ability to pay off her debts. Not all at once, but in increments. For her finances, she lived by the first principle "Beat Debt to Death." She made time and patience her greatest warriors. She stopped buying things. She spent quality time with her kids, building better relationships with them and focusing on their needs, so she could "Be Their Best Guardian."

Jessica no longer felt destitute, no longer a train wreck. She even attracted a new love, someone she began to fully trust, who admired her with full devotion and care, and who would go to the ends of the earth with her. This love carried over into all her relationships. She even forgave her ex-spouse, and they were able to be on speaking terms again, which helped their kids adjust to all the changes. Her family's life was powered by her first principles.

She survived. But most of all, she learned how to co-create her future with the people in her life, where love could thrive every day, despite the challenges.

Jessica told us, "I used to look for quick fixes for everything. I'd get distracted every day by something new, and I'd go after it for a while, change my habits, or hustle in some new way, just to be disappointed. But now I have my first principles. They never disappoint me. It's the long game, and I'm good with that."

Breaking out of survival mode is one of the best feelings in the world. It's like leaving a stifling, dark valley and breathing fresh air as we move up the mountain of life and gain a new view. Our problems get smaller as we ascend, putting things into perspective. Some problems fade with our past. However, the view off in the distance makes us eager and excited: a higher mountain. New challenges help us grow. Taking life to the next level means asking ourselves, "What do I need to sacrifice?"

What does this look like in the collective sense? In teams and within organizations? Change is difficult. Leading a team through a transformation and helping people navigate culture is even harder. We invest effort and energy beyond the personal into powering others. It starts with a clear view of not only what we need to do differently but how we can be different—together.

PART II

THE HERO'S SACRIFICE

The Hero's Sacrifice is a co-creative pattern rooted in humility. The world tells us that to succeed we need to beat others, build an empire, or become a self-made celebrity. But what if that feels empty? Humility is not a sign of weakness but a powerful path forward, helping us break free from the trap of ego. The Hero's Sacrifice is the most underrated part in the Hero's Journey. It turns selflessness into our greatest superpower, binding us together.

In the coming chapters, we'll explore how Apple made their own Hero's Sacrifice to take their culture to the next level, and how any leader can too. We highlight lessons from the NBA, and how people can break the rock star curse to build a team that rocks. We explore how a change of heart allows us to put our bad habits to rest, so we can make real changes. When we're willing to place others first, we start to see the promise of co-creation. We share principles tied to sacrifice that help us remake ourselves into more inspiring, caring, and empathic people. We discover the possibilities that come from turning our pain into power, shattering the shark tank, and making others the mission. It takes letting go of griev-

ances and turning toward others. These are small steps that can make a big

difference.

The Hero's Sacrifice pattern gives us a path to recalibrate our thoughts

and emotions to keep our focus on what's core. It creates a foundation for

culture, connecting hearts and minds. It makes it possible to co-create a

work life experience that is people-centric, where respect and compassion

are the norm, with leaders who inspire people to innovate the best work.

This leads to genuine engagement and a shared passion for shaping a beau-

tiful future.

CHAPTER 6

THINK DIFFERENT TO DIFFERENT TOGETHER

(An Untold Apple Story)

> *Give your difference, welcome my difference,*
> *unify all difference in the larger whole—such is*
> *the law of growth. The unifying of difference is the*
> *eternal process of life—the creative synthesis,*
> *the highest act of creation, the at-onement.*
> —MARY PARKER FOLLETT

For years, people have wondered how Apple does it. How does the company innovate the way it does? How does it create such insanely great products that surprise and delight? Few people know the struggle that it's faced to get there. Like the great Michelangelo, Apple might say, "If people knew how hard I worked to gain my mastery, it would not seem so wonderful at all."

When I (Chris) joined Apple in 2015 as an HR business partner, I marveled at the technical depth of its genius-level engineers. There seemed to be no problem they couldn't solve. In a magical way, Apple had somehow brought together the best minds to create the best products in the world. But beyond the focus on innovating, it had a fundamental premise to the work: secrecy. It held this value dear, to preserve the "surprise and delight" for customers. The kind that arrives on the day of launch when nobody, not even most employees, know how insanely great new products will be.

But this culture of secrecy had its dark sides: hoarding of critical information, pushing personal agendas, and infighting. As a new HR business partner, I was often pulled into these escalations. And it was usually about "that team not sharing."

I started to wonder what this all meant. I'd hear one new employee after another, brilliant people, asking: "How do I operate like this? If I can only share information with certain people, how do I know who and when? I don't want to end up fired or in jail."

For those who were new to the company—including the vast majority of engineers—these dilemmas felt paralyzing. Meanwhile, with the product ecosystem growing and the technical challenges increasing, the need for collaboration grew. What could we do?

I wrestled with this question, looking everywhere for answers until I saw an interview at Startup Grind with Harvard Business School professor Clayton Christensen, the same Clayton Christensen who'd written the book *The Innovator's Dilemma*, which had inspired Steve Jobs to crack the code of disrupting one's own company (which resulted in the iPad). The interviewer asked Christensen what he thought about Apple. He said he worried a lot about a lot of companies, like a mother worries sometimes. Then he said he worried particularly about Apple. But he added that Apple would be just fine, if it could do this one thing that Steve did: spend time staring in the mirror, essentially asking, "What do I need to do differently?" This hit me hard. And it prompted this thought: *Yes, but what's that mirror?*

Apple was a company that had historically innovated as small teams of engineers who had built long-standing relationships, but times had changed. The company's growing workforce increased the demand to accelerate connection, convergence, and collaboration. Secrecy was getting in the way. It was happening with the development of AirPods. Teams were innovating for months in silos, only to finally converge in the eleventh hour before launch, in five- or six-hour-long daily meetings that caused tremendous friction and burnout. People were frustrated. They wanted to leave or to "never work with that one person again."

If we were to give the world the best AirPods Pro, how could we do it in a more seamless, relationship-building way?

Customers don't know those behind-the-scenes struggles, just like most engineers who developed the first AirPods didn't know they would be such an explosively successful, meme-worthy product for the public, selling millions and creating an entirely new category.

FROM COVEY TO CATMULL

At this time, Ian and I wrestled with the current climate of workplace cultures and the deficiencies found in leadership development. We've always had an affinity toward the ecosystem of timeless principles that Stephen Covey once presented to the world. We were both drawn to his seminal book, *The 7 Habits of Highly Effective People*, and the way its conclusion focused on synergy and interdependence—a refreshing shift from self to selflessness.

While Covey inspired people in their personal growth, we realized co-creation doesn't belong at the end of the journey. Given the challenges cultures now face, co-creation must be front and center.

We've also been captivated by this notion of the braintrust that Ed Catmull shares in *Creativity, Inc.* Most people feel they don't have creative license to make decisions at work or the ability to contribute without express permission. While Pixar is a creative brand, it offers a template for channeling collective genius by encouraging the creative voice. Why don't other companies do this? Most work cultures are loaded with bureaucracy and politics that squash creativity at first sight.

At the core, we wondered: What could principles tied to co-creation do to help bridge the silos found in companies like Apple?

Perhaps this was our own "garage build moment" (Steve Jobs and Steve Wozniak famously started Apple in Steve's garage). We were faced with the burden of trying to understand problems emerging in workplace cultures. We both were at a point in our careers where we could be brave enough to figure out solutions. We knew that a leader could not control what a culture becomes, but we also saw that people can influence and contribute to culture.

How could Apple have avoided the internal turmoil we faced with the development of AirPods? How do cultures take the shape they do?

These questions and the inspired sessions with Ian led me to form a mini braintrust at Apple. As a small group of HR partners, we started to explore this by getting curious about the Apple culture. When we unpacked it all, we started asking: "Which leaders and teams innovate and collaborate best, and why?"

We gathered a short list of people and sought to understand the elements that were key to their success. We noticed a braintrust in the camera team that was a powerful example of collaboration. But no one outside of that team seemed to know much about it. It fascinated me that there was an organic braintrust at Apple, since I'd come from Disney and seen the power of the braintrust at Pixar—a collective team committed to, in Catmull's words, "egos off the table, building blocks on the table."

Most know that Steve Jobs impacted Pixar, but here was an insight we hadn't considered: Ed Catmull and Pixar had influenced Apple culture in a fundamental way. And here was a working braintrust that maybe we could expand and scale across Apple. But what made it work, and why? What were those key ingredients we could share?

OPENNESS WITHIN A CLOSED SYSTEM

As we met the short list of innovative leaders, what we found surprised us. While Apple had so clearly underscored secrecy as a fundamental value to the company, all these leaders highlighted the power of the one thing that made them so successful: sharing.

Of course, not a single leader suggested sharing externally, like Silicon Valley companies that released product road maps to the public. That would spoil the surprise. But what we found was a level of openness in a famously closed system that involved far more sharing than anyone was talking about, and far more than new employees knew. Yes, paradoxically, sharing could be done in the context of secrecy.

When we met with the "Camera Braintrust" (the team that develops the cameras in any hardware devices, including the iPhone), or "CBT," we learned that they applied these key ingredients: a weekly cross-staff transparency session, focusing on a vulnerable or open approach to sharing challenges they were facing. Each leader and team would share exactly where they were in their development and what they needed from the other teams. This led to cycles of innovation that accelerated camera technology to new heights, making it the gold standard of collaboration.

When we saw how well the Camera Braintrust was working together, we wondered what would happen if we applied that same approach to the

AirPods team: regular cross-staff sessions, transparency, and shared voices. What happened next was amazing.

We partnered with people like Randy Nelson at Apple University, the same person who'd founded Pixar University. His views on the power of sharing and collaboration were key to challenging assumptions of what could be shared at Apple. We spent time coaching, collaborating, and influencing key leaders and engineers involved in the evolution of AirPods. As teams converged, they became more open, connected, and in sync. This led to higher-quality collaboration. What emerged was a braintrust with regular sessions, openness, and connection that brought to life the insanely great, noise-canceling AirPods Pro. It was a testament to innovation but also to the power of sharing.

COLLABORATION BY DESIGN: APPLE'S PRINCIPLES OF THE FUTURE

Innovation is the calling card of the future.
—ANNA ESHOO

Next, we wondered, what if we expand this notion of the braintrust everywhere else at Apple? Collaboration was happening, but it seemed to be by default. We needed Collaboration by Design.

People on the outside were questioning the innovation Apple had to offer. Where would it go next? What would teams at Apple do to build insanely great products to chart the future?

The most innovative teams and best collaborators at Apple applied some amazing work patterns. We needed to heat map the entire organization and learn what was working and find ways to amplify it. We had to get clear on what could drive innovation further in the future. We got in the trenches and observed, witnessed, and interviewed teams that were the best of the best to co-create these first principles of the future culture at Apple.

Follow the North Star and Have a Vision

This was the filter for everything the best teams at Apple did. They took a deeper view, looked at the future horizon, and connected every conversation to the core purpose. It put all smaller tasks into perspective. At the core, the teams that were co-creating shared the North Star of making "the best _____ in the world," all in the service of enriching people's lives.

The Beats team had been doing this when Apple bought their company and absorbed their engineers, designers, and managers into Apple. But there was friction. The Apple bar of quality was high. Could Beats meet it? Apple engineers weren't so sure, and they made it known. The Beats engineers fired back, saying Apple's products weren't cool enough. The battle lines were drawn. We realized fast that this friction had only one answer: vision. If they focused on their shared North Star, we'd get through this.

We brought together the teams to build relationships and focus on their common vision for bringing the very best products into people's lives. The Apple engineers insisted the Beats folks would have to raise their bar of quality to meet the demands of the most valuable product ecosystem in the world. The Beats engineers agreed, but demanded fair treatment as part of the team—not as second-class citizens.

We moved Apple engineers over to Beats to learn from them and share insights, and we moved Beats engineers over to Apple to gain perspective and enhance their view of Apple's rigorous quality standards—all while protecting the Beats brand and bringing it to the next level. Matthew Costello, the humble leader of Beats and Apple's Home ecosystem, brought zero ego to the table, which made everything that much more seamless. Amazing for a guy who rubbed shoulders regularly with Dr. Dre, Jimmy Iovine, and Tim Cook. Matthew's North Star was built on valuing *every* person on the team. His vision played a powerful role in bringing everything together.

We have opportunities to shape the future all around us. But they start to emerge when we have a grounded point of view of what's possible and a brave trajectory that can inspire us. It happens when we see the future together.

Don't Wait for Perfection, Share Early

Within a culture of secrecy, this was a different kind of challenge. Jen Edwards and her wireless team partnered with other teams, becoming a template for this principle. No waiting for perfection. They designed team meetings to share early with partners, giving open updates and making transparent asks. Their meetings were never downloads. They became revelations, inviting surprise and delight, opening hearts and minds to possibilities. They went beyond the data to where intuition and reason converged beautifully to produce the best products.

Priya Subramaniam, head of operations, captured the spirit of this principle when she had to share critical information. She didn't have the time to wrap it up in perfect slides, so she told her VP, "I know this information doesn't look good, but you need to see it right now." The VP appreciated it. Priya gave her entire team this same gift. The power to tell each other whatever difficult news needed to be shared. For her, it wasn't about building the perfect deck or the perfect meeting. It was about brave conversations.

The most innovative teams at Apple do this by setting frequent cross-staff conversations, supporting each other, and giving enough context to understand breakthroughs in the work and what's needed to move builds forward. As humans, we like to guard our ideas. But the more we share, the better the builds. Let the best ideas win.

With so many engineers locked in Apple's secrecy mindset, it proved challenging to share new insights in early innovation territory. With senior leaders, we launched the IDEA program: a rapid-development think tank where cross-functional teams throughout the company came together, ideating and iterating demos of new products. We established new relationships and connected the dots across hardware, software, and design. New technologies and better product road maps emerged. Best of all: new co-creative muscles formed across teams and across the culture. Senior leaders saw the power of co-creation amplified.

Take Ownership and Be Authentic

We partnered with the Retail Strategy team as they led 60,000+ Apple Retail employees and "geniuses" across more than 500 stores. Head of retail Angela Ahrendts' mantra of "Don't sell. Serve!" was core. It was a mantra that proved powerful enough to guide them in their work of framing the best experiences for customers everywhere. As team members embodied it, we witnessed the impact with thousands of people each day in retail stores in the United States and the tens of thousands per day in places like Shanghai, China. They felt empowered enough to make Apple stores feel like the digital Disneyland for customers who walked in, as they focused each conversation on serving, inspiring people with authenticity.

The Retail Strategy team also knew the power of authentic feedback from team members. What could they shape next? They created a channel for team members to share. They launched Loop, a feedback-sharing portal for everyone. It became a grassroots way of upvoting the best ideas. Team members loved it. Ideas quickly populated, and tens of thousands of votes started pouring in.

This first principle also helped launch "Today at Apple" classes offered at Apple stores designed to help customers learn how to use Apple products and applications and level up their creativity. The Apple stores endeavored to learn and understand the communities' needs, which helped the culture of each retail store by region feel authentic to the people they serve.

When the product teams were building the next iteration of the iPhone, they faced seemingly insurmountable challenges. The level of complexity required to solve the technical problems led to a moment when they held a prototype that "without antenna capability, would be a really nice iPod." They refused to place blame. They only asked what they needed to do differently. The antenna team knew they had to allow the product design team to encroach into sacred antenna territory to make the antenna work. But how would it fit into the new iPhone? The display and touch flexes would have to do turnaround at the bottom, with flexes in contact with the primary cellular antenna and the front camera. Also, Face ID modules would need to be embedded into the antennas. They had almost no room to work with. But they took ownership and designed a high-powered antenna that worked beautifully in the limited space. Collaboration by Design brought the impossible to life.

We have opportunities every day to own things: the story, the work, the outcome. Those who do this well put their egos aside, and do not place blame. They care only about how problems are solved. Building the future together is about connecting silos, collaborating across teams, and taking more responsibility, not less.

Build Trust (and Braintrust)

When new problems arose, the most innovative teams understood that building trust is core, and it takes time. It's hard to be vulnerable.

We worked with Graham Townsend, head of the Camera Team, to inspire a deeper culture of co-creation. The team already had a working camera braintrust meeting. Now they expanded it to other teams across the organization, bringing together hardware, software, operations, and other groups to have brave conversations to shape the next iterations of products. Graham became an evangelist for co-creation. Standing on stage in front of 250 senior leaders at Apple, he shared their success story of building with braintrusts. He invited them all to join forces in applying this first principle to the future culture of Apple.

Another leader told us he was focused solely on his work and didn't see the value in one-on-one time with cross-functional partners. But he wondered why other teams weren't responding to his email requests. We asked, "When do you sync up with them?" He saw the irony and started connecting with key partners each week, building relationships and creating trust, which made all the difference. These leaders started sharing more than ever, and their builds got better.

The most innovative teams at Apple build partnerships. Steve Jobs said, "My model for business is The Beatles. They were four guys who kept each other's kind of negative tendencies in check. They balanced each other, and the total was greater than the sum of the parts. That's how I see business: Great things in business are never done by one person. They're done by a team of people."[1]

Share Freely Within the Circle

We worked with the Industrial Design teams, who saw that amplifying sharing was the only way to make it work. Give and take. Challenge and debate. Aligning the best ideas. They told us the best answer in a debate is not an argument but an inspiring demo. This proved true. They got into a rhythm of sharing that made it easy to build together. Their meetings became places to blend points of view into a whole, which would ultimately result in a product worthy of the Apple logo.

It starts with establishing the circle. Who's in it? How big is it? And then encouraging a trust-sharing context. This was difficult, given Apple's focus on secrecy. We worked with the Human Factors team. During development of the Apple Watch, when no one on the outside even knew Apple was working on it, nurses were hired to test it. They would come to Apple in street clothes, and once inside, would change into their nurse uniforms—for over a year. These teams established a circle of trust. They shared data and insights. Then they expanded the circle, sharing across teams, protecting secrecy while ensuring the flow of ideas and relevant information.

The most innovative teams become one in purpose. They can be themselves inside the circle. They don't look for a yes or no answer. The ideas they share become building blocks to co-create solutions to seemingly impossible questions. Questions like, How do you develop diabetes glucose tracking with Apple Watch? The only way to answer that was to do so together.

Take Smart Risks Together

We worked with teams across 26 different countries running tests on all Apple products: iPhone, Watches, AirPods, MacBooks, and more. We partnered with Xinjian Zhang and his team across Asia to build a stronger culture of taking smart risks together. The global teams realized they needed to share information faster. But how could they do this in an environment where the conversations felt more like deferring than debating? How could they navigate Apple's culture of secrecy? Sharing anything felt like a risk, especially anything technical. What if they got in trouble? With Apple? With their governments?

Apple University tried to foster more healthy debates with the teams in China—to no avail. They brought in the experts, heavy hitter PhDs who'd studied China and all its intricacies. But no amount of history lessons or prodding about the benefits of "debate culture" or "rock tumbling" could change people there from staying mostly silent and deferring to the senior leader in the room.

After working with Xinjian Zhang for months on this challenge, we launched work sessions with 30 leaders, without knowing exactly what would emerge. The focus was to empower each other through co-creation. We shared what was emerging across the company as Apple's future-oriented principles. It ignited the conversation. Xinjian got brave and shared his insights, and the energy in the room changed. We all felt it. Their leaders opened up. They shared like never before. They took risks. They were brave. And it changed the way they would work together as a team moving forward.

We continued to partner with them to break down the methods for sharing. We clarified what people "Need to Know," "Need to Share," and

"Need to Spread." This gave the team in China direction to act accordingly, which became a smart risk that paid off.

For the most innovative teams, taking smart risks means jumping in the pool at the same time. It means people become so aligned that the impossible starts to seem practical. This new energy can take builds and teams to amazing places and enables them to create something that surprises and delights even its creators.

Be Biased Toward Others' Ideas

Out of all the first principles that emerged during this memorable work, one of our favorites came from the VP of touch, display, and camera technology, Lynn Youngs, a Jedi-level genius who told us he considered himself a "coach." When we asked him what the key to Apple's future was, he said: "I come to the table with my ideas, and they come to the table with theirs. If we consider ideas 'our kids,' I have to care as much or more about 'their kids' as I do about mine for something magical to happen." Then he added, "A lot of people hate bias. But bias can be powerful if we harness it. It's about being biased toward others' ideas."

The most innovative teams don't just listen to understand but listen with an openness to changing their mind. Great teams focus on the blending of ideas. They stay open, create space for sharing, and raise the level of empathy to the point where the best innovation can happen. They are willing to metaphorically "sit on both sides of the table" to get into other people's minds and hearts long enough to understand every perspective and every possibility that can be combined to create the best solutions.

DIFFERENT TOGETHER

Apple's first principles resulted in a culture shift that we called "Different Together" (Figure 6.1). Combining the power of Apple's historic culture of "Think Different," which highlighted the strength of an infinite variety of voices, with the power of doing it all "Together."

Most people are familiar with the "Think Different" video, but what emerged from this incredible culture work was a new artifact. As we partnered with Greg "Joz" Jozwiak and the Apple Marketing team, they helped

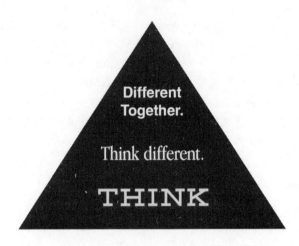

FIGURE 6.1 **Different Together**

capture the spirit of Different Together in a video called "Join Us. Be You."[2] It is an ode to everyone, including the brave people at Apple who are willing to co-create and shape the future with others.

Apple is heading into a future where it's far better prepared to innovate together. With a co-creative lens and braintrust teams, people are better positioned for challenges like distributed workforces, economic downturns, and even global catastrophes. Now Apple can continue with collective confidence as it hits the gas on innovation—because "Different Together" now means the culture at Apple is making a difference together.

Apple was our beta test for culture shaping. We believe co-creation can be applied to any domain. Any company can transform its culture (especially when a lot is working already) and can break free from the cultural norms that are holding it back from shaping the future.

Now that AI can do what knowledge workers have done in the past, the world is at a tipping point. The future belongs to the brave ones who can unleash the power of co-creation in their culture.

How can you and your team take "together" to the next level? Start here:

- **Ask an anchoring question.** "What should the future culture be?"

- **Ignite the power of diversity.** Being different is making a difference with others.

- **Pivot from silos to connections.** Share. Grow inclusion with brave conversations. Lead horizontally, not just vertically—from Thinking Different to Different Together.

- **Look to your people for insights.** This inspires people, creates better work experiences, shapes more innovative products, and amplifies results.

In helping shape the future culture at Apple, we saw how powerful change starts with a clear understanding of pain. For Apple, it was the pain of navigating the tension between secrecy on one side and collaboration and teamwork on the other—while looking to amplify co-creation. We had to shake things up with surgical care, ensuring the best experiences for all, which led Tim Cook to say of the culture shift, "We are a secretive company. But we've rewired ourselves on the values side. Think about the environment— we talk about what we're going to look like in 2030. We talk about our road maps to get there. We want those to be stolen."[3]

What about everywhere else? In teams, companies, or families that struggle to keep it all together? How do we lead by design when failure seems to be our constant companion? How can we shift negative energy, even all-consuming anger, into world-changing strength? We're going to explore how to do exactly that next.

[

Brave Together.

Lead with a Question

Turn Pain into Power

Make Others the Mission

Define the Situation

Create Context

Follow True North

CHAPTER 7

TURN PAIN INTO POWER

The Passion Principle

The pain of yesterday is the strength of today.
—Paulo Coelho

What do you do with a dying business model? Revenues were negative and the bleeding continued, but Clint Schaff didn't let that stop him or his team. He had been tapped to lead LA Times Studios, the first in-house revenue-generating content studio of the *Los Angeles Times*, a newspaper business that had been completely disrupted. It was in the red. But deep down, he knew he and his team could innovate their way out of it. He set out to do just that, brainstorming a list of the craziest world-changing ideas they could think of, among which was #47: start a podcast. Simple enough. That one idea turned into a $10–$15 million business and became a shining light for the *LA Times*. Clint and his team went on to produce podcasts such as *Dirty John* and other hit shows, pulling in 50 million plus listeners. They continued harnessing their shared passion for storytelling, explored partnerships to expand their reach, and landed deals with Netflix. They did all this by turning their pain into the power of co-creation.

Clint and his team focused on some key things we can all do. Teams can flip their script of a failing business or a culture in decline by joining forces to create momentum with gains. How? By focusing less on external sources for solutions and more on unlocking the shared passion and creativity in your people and creating the space for people to be passionate together. Passion fuels co-creation.

But what do we do when the pain cuts so deep we can't even see a path out? What if a business is so broken that there's no end in sight? How can we build an unseen future with the hope it takes to make something great? We must face the hard truths about our work life and reconcile what is holding us back. To unlock our power and co-create the future together, we need to break free from seeing loss everywhere and instead recognize the gains all around us. Building gains with others brings out the best expression of our shared passion.

SEEING LOSS EVERYWHERE

Studies tell us that we interpret 80 percent of what we experience every day as negative, or as a loss.[1] Eighty percent. This is rooted in how our brains evolved to react to threats: fight, flight, or freeze. Imagine someone gave you $100. How do you feel? Pretty good, right? Now imagine you had that $100 bill disappear from your wallet. How do you feel? Terrible. You can't stop thinking about it. Studies show we feel the loss of something far more than an equivalent gain.

Fearing loss is motivating when it's of an existential nature: when it comes to providing for our families or fighting for our lives or our freedom on the battlefield, but it's not helpful in our day-to-day lives. What's worse is that we are confronted with a 24-hour news cycle, social media that permeates every corner of our awareness, and political discourse that divides us into "have" and "have not" camps. We are fed a steady diet of negativity and loss, which leads to sadness and then to anger (Figure 7.1).

FIGURE 7.1 **The Loss Equation**

Pretty soon we find ourselves between strong emotions that keep us in a negative state. Just one look at Twitter confirms this. People are angry. Can we become more self-aware? What's within our power? How do we break this cycle of negativity and loss?

What do you do when faced with a sudden tragedy that crushes your soul? I (Ian) witnessed this unfolding with one of my nurses in my time as a healthcare administrator. Her name is Belle Ang. Everyone on the team loved it when it was her shift. She had an infectious smile, and she was upbeat and enthusiastic around patients and her coworkers. Belle's zeal for life rubbed off on the people around her. They could feel her presence.

Then one day, during the middle of her shift, she approached me. The color was gone from her face. She said, "I have to leave!" The phone call Belle had just received would change her life forever. Her nine-year-old son had been rushed to the emergency room with severe flulike symptoms. Seventy-two hours later, Tristan Michael Ang was pronounced dead. His cause of death was undiagnosed. The experience devastated Belle.

Belle took a 10-month leave of absence, and her husband remained unemployed. The bills were flooding in. She felt the pressure to return to work, even though she was not emotionally ready. Talking about death is taboo in the workplace, yet I felt inspired to share with her the principle of Turning Pain into Power. We connected at this vulnerable moment, a human connection that touched us both. As she described the current state of her family, I could hear the pain weighing down her words. Belle spoke in a somber tone. She looked defeated and tired. Her spirit was broken.

This tragic loss consumed her life. Her anger ate at her soul. I no longer saw Belle as an employee or one of our beloved nurses. I saw her as a mother in indescribable pain. I told her, "You have one of two choices. You can become bitter over something that indeed seems cruel, unfair, and inexplicable; or you can get better and take your life back, one day at a time." I shared a simple visual with her (Figure 7.2), written in pen on a piece of paper.

I saw Belle again two weeks later. She told me that she had shown her husband that visual, which represents turning pain into power. She said that it was now framed in their living room. She explained how this one principle had changed her life and had given her and her husband hope for the future. She showed courage in her ability to move forward, get back to work, and make a difference in people's lives again—with a renewed focus to be an anchor for her family. This is what Turning Pain into Power can do.

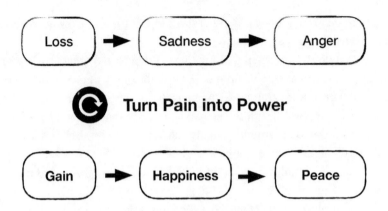

FIGURE 7.2 **Turn Pain into Power**

THE POWER FLIP

Turning Pain into Power is more than just a mindset. It's a way to navigate our difficult emotions. Loss can be a vicious cycle that hijacks our subconscious minds, and we end up addicted to anger. How do we change this cycle? We become empowered when we can look at our circumstances in a different way. We start to see ourselves with compassionate eyes.

Choose to see gains. When we start to recognize gains, our life fills with gratitude. Gains lead to happiness. Happiness helps us experience peace. Others begin to see we are grateful, that we're peacemakers building joy with them.

Why don't we do this every day? There may be baggage holding us back. Perhaps there's an experience that haunts us to this day, something someone said or did that hurt us, something we're fearful of. We need to reframe each day with gains, and no longer let loss rule our thoughts or feelings.

Make the choice to never play the victim in your life. Turn Pain into Power. Flip the script. It's possible to reverse engineer your old mental model of loss by redirecting your thoughts and actions to focus on the small gains you can achieve. You will see the gains all around you. Gains make happiness possible.

Part of winning this battle is staying coachable. How can we do this? Michael Jordan was once asked what he thought his best skill was. Did he say it was his ability to dunk from the free throw line? Nope. His scoring ability?

No. His answer? "I was coachable. I was a sponge and aggressive to learn."[2] The easier you are to lead, the further you'll go.

THE TRUTH ABOUT PASSION

Author Mel Robbins shared in some of her social media posts the truth about the power of passion:

> Passion is not a person, a place, or a thing—it's a state of mind. It's how you feel when you're doing what excites you, what energizes you, and what expands you. Your passions will change as YOU change, and that's okay! What excites you in your 20s is probably going to be different than what does in your 30s, 40s, 50s, and throughout your life. Instead of stressing yourself out over finding that one thing you think is your passion, focus on what you can do TODAY that will expand, energize, and excite you."[3]
>
> Passion is another word for energy. When you are "passionate" about something, it just means that when you do that thing, it energizes you. Your passions in life bring you joy and make you happy. That's why passion is not something you find, it's something you feel.
>
> Your passion is for you. You don't "find" passion, you just feel it. It could be literally anything that brings more energy into your life. If you want to feel more passion, spend time doing things that make you feel energized.[4]

FROM ANGER TO
WORLD-CHANGING ENERGY

We've all felt it before, the pain caused by others. There are feelings we try to avoid—the hurt and betrayal—and memories that haunt us. They linger, squeezing our hearts. The pain never seems to stop, burning inside us like a wildfire. How do we avoid going past the point of no return? Anger can take us down dark roads if we're not careful. From one moment to the next, we can get so enraged, become so bitter, even callous in our life, without even knowing how we got here. One harsh word or a breach of trust can trigger the worst in us. We might abandon our principles in the name of "getting back at them," thereby losing ourselves.

For many people, revenge doesn't happen right away. They let venomous thoughts erode their relationships and, worse, their character. They're flooded with negative emotions that dominate their behaviors, leading to brutal consequences. It's been said, "Don't get mad, get even." When will we stop thinking of this as a strength? When will we see it for what it is, a weak-minded version of uncontrolled passion? How many outbursts by a leader, road rage deaths, or acts of domestic violence do we need to witness to prove this is a failed approach to life?

Chasing revenge is a fractured and unforgiving path. How deep does this desire for revenge go? Is it rooted in our core nature?

In *The Count of Monte Cristo* by Alexandre Dumas, Edmond Dantès is an ordinary man, doing his best to make a better life in the shipping trade, preparing for marriage to his love, Mercedes, and being a good son to a father he cares for deeply. What happens next is unexpected: Edmond is betrayed, torn away from his family and fiancé, and thrown into the prison of Chateau d'If for 13 years. While in this island prison, he hears about a treasure on a nearby island. Edmond learns from books about business and finance and learns how to fight. He also plots his escape and his revenge.

After acquiring newfound riches, he crafts his persona as the Count of Monte Cristo. Now with enough resources and resolve, he can exact revenge on all his enemies. Precise, perfect revenge, distilled in doses and designed to make them suffer the way he had all those years.

There's a powerful allure to this story. Karma, gaining the upper hand, crushing one's enemies—what's wrong with any of that? We've all felt that surge of confidence when the tables turn, and those who hurt us eventually start hurting. When the universe finally delivers justice, Edmond's story ended there. Or did it? In the book-turned-movie he marries Mercedes, buys the prison, and reconciles with God. Then he walks off into the sunset a new man. But was that really the end?

I've (Chris) always loved that story. I've had experiences in my life when people have betrayed me, burned me so badly I wasn't sure I'd ever come out of it. They say, "Success is the best revenge." That story gave me hope for a future when I'd succeed despite them all. And largely, that's happened for me. Those people's influence in my life has faded, but that led to questions like, "Where will this pursuit of 'revenge success' take me if they're no longer a part of my life?"

I found myself pondering that question one day, walking in downtown Gilroy, a small Northern California town near San Jose. As a few cars drove by, I realized this downtown isn't much, just a shell of a business district. There were streets lined with antique shops everywhere. I stepped into one and looked around. There were old toys, chairs, tables, and paintings stacked, with dust collecting on them. I was about to leave until I noticed some books. I love books, especially old ones. There's something magical about them. I foraged through cookbooks, encyclopedias, and classics. Nothing interesting. I was ready to leave. Then something caught my eye. I picked it up and opened it: *Edmond Dantès: The Sequel to the Count of Monte Cristo* by Edmund Flagg.

As I held it in my hands, thumbing through the pages, I felt a surge of excitement and interest. What's next for the Count? How would he move forward? Some of these questions were subconscious, yet deeply personal, as if I were asking: "What's next for me? How will I move forward?"

The story begins where the original left off. Edmond became wildly rich and successful and achieved his ambitions for revenge—only to find himself feeling empty, in need of a deeper purpose. Edmond shared his plight:

> But the deepest wound will close; the heaviest grief, the bitterest woe, becomes assuaged. Time, the comforter, soothes and consoles. From this stroke of bereavement I at length awoke, and, at the same moment, awoke to the conviction that my whole past had been an error; that my life had been a lie; that the years which had succeeded my imprisonment had been more utterly lost than those passed within my dungeon itself; and there came to me the conviction that time, talent, power and wealth had been worse than wasted—that the wondrous riches, undreamed of save in the wildest flights of oriental fiction, and by a miracle bestowed upon me, were designed for nobler, holier purposes than to subserve a fiendish and blasphemous vengeance for even unutterable wrongs, or to minister to the gratification of pride, and the satisfaction of selfish tastes and appetites, however refined and sublimated.

I looked around me—the world was full of misery—and the same disposition which had plunged me into a dungeon was crushing the hearts and hopes of millions of my race. My bosom softened by bereavement yearned toward my suffering fellows, and the path of duty, peace and happiness seemed open to my desolate and despairing heart. Resolution followed conviction; the world was my field; liberty, equality, and fraternity were my objects.[5]

A NEW PRINCIPLE-POWERED PURPOSE

Rather than stay hidden any longer behind his alter ego of the Count, Edmond used his real name and committed himself to his family and community. He became a changed man by lifting his voice to inspire people with a vision of what could be. He created a braintrust of like-minded people with shared passion to shape fiction and nonfiction that could become a movement of ideas, a shared journey that could change the circumstances of others. This became his new purpose on Earth. No longer weighed down by the burden of pain caused by others or his relentless pursuit of justice, he freed himself from his past by empowering others in the present to shape the future together.

Edmond was transformed. He became a catalyst for change. With a burning passion for a shared revolution, he gave people a reason to hope again. He saw the gifts in others and created the conditions for things to converge. He gave them a sense of ownership. Through a shared story, they were able to join forces, moving forward to pursue impossible things and shaping new experiences by embodying this change together.

What if we took our unresolved pain and turned it into power, converting it into fuel for the future? Not with a massive goal to change the entire world but with a focused goal to change our part of the world that we experience every day—changing it for the good with the people around us. This is how we build our life with gains. Being brave enough to face our challenges head-on, and letting go of our own toxic behaviors, bad habits, and unhealthy patterns. Instead of feeding a vengeful heart, we can amplify our adventurous soul. We have a choice. We can stay in the pain, grieving our losses like most, or we can create gains and build new momentum for a better future together.

ONCE UPON A NEW MINDSET

*Most folks are about as happy as they
make up their minds to be.*
—Abraham Lincoln

I (Chris) was stressed. The company I was with at the time was being acquired. What would that mean for me? And everyone else? I knew things were about to change, big-time. Layoffs would be coming. My way, too. So, what did I do? I took the kids to Disneyland. I took a break, got them out of school, and gave us all a "mental health day" with the Mouse and friends. And guess what? When I heard my daughter Faith say, "This was the best day ever," I knew she was right. But something else happened.

As Faith and I walked into the art of animation building, we had to immediately leave so she could use the restroom. When we came back, we walked in through the exit. Written on the wall in beautiful font were the words, "And they lived happily ever after."

I stopped and stared at those words. This was a strange moment. Walking into the ending of the story. But we were just starting. Or did we just walk into a possible new mindset? Little did I know this would change everything for me. In that moment, another phrase struck me: "And they lived happily even before."

I felt inspired to enjoy this experience with my daughter and to start from a place of happiness. It felt different. The pressure was off. The joy was easy to see. I wasn't looking at how a walk-through of this animation building would make me happy. Instead, I chose to be happy and be present with my daughter. We shared funny moments together, and I watched her light up. Our smiles carried on throughout the day. What if we all did this in our personal and professional lives?

How often have we heard those words, "And they lived happily ever after"? The magical end to all those classic stories. But the phrase is also a hopeful magical end to our pursuits in life. We find ourselves waiting for something off in the distance, wondering what it'll feel like once we've finally arrived and landed that dream job or promotion, or launched that business, written that book, or sold that company. *Then* we'll be happy. *Then* we'll be able to spend more time with those we love. But then never comes. Or if then comes, it's never enough. We've moved on to the next thing, fixated on the "ever after." Always wanting more: money, stuff, vacations, you name it.

We've been duped, lied to, fooled. We've seen the trend of YouTubers interviewing billionaires on the streets of a big city, asking the same question: "Does money make you happy?" Here was one particular answer: "Nope. No amount of money can make you happy. It's not designed for that. It doesn't change anything about your level of happiness. You decide that. Period."

Why do so many leaders carry on believing that if they just hit those financial results, everything will be perfect, only to discover that it isn't? Why do some people bounce from one job to another, assuming the grass will always be greener, only to find it's the same exact hue?

It's time to rethink our relationship with happiness. What if happiness isn't found in perfect results or the approval of others? What if we looked at the people in our lives differently? What if happiness is a close companion who's been right there with us through the thick of it all along? It's time for us to see happiness for what it is.

Did you know that Apple execs don't ever lead with financial results first? They care about the impact of their work. They focus entire all-hands and planning meetings on how they can make the best products that enrich people's lives, and they know that happiness is part of that journey. They're not happy because they're a multitrillion-dollar company. They're happy because they're pursuing greatness. They believe what they are building each day will surprise and delight customers. They create joy while on their journey.

Start with happiness. Be fulfilled in the moment, rather than looking for external forces to make you fulfilled. You won't regret it. Think: And they lived happily *even before*. Create patterns of joy before the next promotion. Before that vacation. Before the startup succeeds. Before changing the world.

SEE THE "FULL BENEFIT"

How can we do our best even in situations we hate? The Navy SEALs have a saying. When something sucks, they look at each other and say: "Full benefit." The SEALs see the good in every situation. How can you do this too? Don't dismiss difficult emotions or avoid them. Start by framing the good in the situation. See struggles as opportunities right out of the gate, and create gains with a grateful attitude.

It's a deliberate mindset shift. Walking and it starts pouring rain? Full benefit. Driving and you get a flat tire? Full benefit. Working on a project and the computer crashes? Full benefit. Trying to build a team that doesn't get along? Full benefit. Every challenge is an opportunity. Every moment is a gift—to learn and grow, to stretch us, to build. What if we welcomed it all? Turn loss into gains. See the full benefit of each moment. Turn Pain into Power.

Power. Few words carry such diverse definitions and evoke such intense emotions. Most of us want more of it in business and in life. But what does it really mean? For some of us, power carries the historical connotation of the few controlling the most resources, knowledge, and people. But real power today is being redefined as more than money, fame, and title. Power today is personal. It's about fulfillment, connection, and well-being.

Those who pursue a more powerful life think, talk, and act in different ways than everyone else. They put serving others first and look for ways to share inner power by being kind, generous, and empathic. When people extend their power, they receive more. They boldly lead with new ideas and new business models that become life-changing experiences. "Full benefit" living.

This is true for aspiring leaders, entrepreneurs, and anyone else searching for next generation success—for all people willing to be brave together. This is about reimagining our basic life patterns: the way we think, talk, and act. It's about going beyond our current limitations, choosing to be more connected, and looking to be inspired. It's possible to turn things around. Anyone can develop a "full benefit" or "live happily even before" mindset. With a little effort, any person can become a creative force, and inspire others to create gains in their lives. The key to power is to become part of something larger than ourselves and to share our passion with others.

CREATING GAINS FOR YOURSELF

How do we actually do this?

Change the World from Within

Open your heart. This can be the hardest part of your growth. And yet, it's worth it. Give yourself the permission to feel again. Be brave enough to change your routines. Go somewhere fun. Get out in nature. See the beauty. Visit with a friend or family member. Be present. Choose happiness. Give yourself that gift. If you're feeling squeezed by bosses, consumed by the numbers, feeling pressure from the demands of others, step back. Consider what's core. What is fundamental to your life and to your work? Recalibrate your focus on what matters most to you.

Fill Your Mind and Heart with Gratitude

Gratitude beats anxiety. Every time. It grounds us in a life of abundance. Acknowledge the positives instead of pointing out the negatives. See today's challenges as an opportunity or a lesson learned. Little minds focus on comparing and competing. Big minds focus on creating, rather than tearing down. Little hearts obsess about what is lacking or what is missing. Big hearts are grateful, focused on what can be done to unlock new possibilities. When we live with gratitude, we grow and can amplify our impact 10× to 100×.

Focus on Clearing the Deck

We overreact when we're tired and stressed or feeling lonely, unappreciated, or uninspired. Being aware of our energy levels helps us ensure the right self-care. Get proper rest, eat high-energy foods, talk through our stressors with friends. It all helps us feel seen and heard. Saying no to unnecessary commitments and pausing to create space each day helps us clear the deck. Don't hang on to burdens like an emotional hoarder. Treat each day as a chance to reset. Every day is day one.

Create Gains with Others

We can amplify our gains in connection with those around us—breaking out of broken moments of the past, building peace into our lives, and becoming better at lifting others.

Let Go of Past Grudges

Don't dwell on them. Don't chase the snake that bit you. Get the poison out, heal, and move on. Give yourself the "full benefit" of a peaceful life filled with joy. You can't have that if you're holding on to anger. We learned this from the Count of Monte Cristo's transformation. Create gains with the people you love and care about. Simple acts: a phone call, a quick visit, a meal together. Make the focus about them and watch the walls come down. Create gains by moving on from people or scenarios that hold you back. Sometimes moving on is about letting go. Forgiveness can deliver powerful gains.

After he got fired by his CEO, Matt, our talented friend Dave Arcade turned disappointment and anger into life changing power. Here is what he shared with us:

> I let that anger burn me up. They talk about hate burning you up inside. I got to the point where I said, "I want to punch Matt. That's how mad I am." This was month three of fury.
>
> Then I was talking to a friend Kyle who said, "Just frankly forgive him."
>
> And I was like, "What? But . . . everything he's done." Kyle said, "Doesn't matter. Has he tied you up to the mast of a ship? Has he tried to kill you?"
>
> "No." And so, I thought about that, and I took his advice, and it was as simple as that. And I realized, I don't want to be mad anymore. So, I called Matt up and told him, "I forgive you." And he started to cry. And we had a really good conversation.
>
> We live in a tough time when people believe forgiveness is weakness. But it takes far more strength than we know. You want to talk about Turning Pain into Power? Forgive somebody.
>
> Do you want to become more powerful than you can ever imagine? Forgive somebody. And it takes all that fire out of the tissue of your innards and puts it into a battery that you can then take and use however you want. It's an enormous amount of energy to redirect. And if you don't do that, it's like Chernobyl.[6]

Dave forgave his former boss and found new power to reinvent himself as Dave Arcade, creating his own freelance illustration business, making mind-bending murals for Disney, Pixar, and Nickelodeon. When we're willing to drop our ego, we free ourselves from pain that holds us back. Our gains enable us to move forward in life and co-create with others.

*I'm not going to allow my trials to defeat me, I'm going
to let them build me up and learn from them and take as
much wisdom as I can from each trial.*
—Maddie Marlow

Be a Peacemaker

The next time your buttons get pressed, choose to be a peacemaker. This might feel unnatural at first, especially if you tend to get provoked by contention. Peace doesn't show up on its own. It needs an invitation. Instead of framing peace as something you seek, be someone who creates peaceful experiences. Create gains by setting the right tone. Find ways to invite calm. Show compassion. People will appreciate your intentions. Don't wait for others to do the right thing. Be a peacemaker now.

Drop Expectations of Others

We tend to expect others to improve our work or life situation. "My boss needs to give me that raise." "My spouse needs to make me happy." We project our needs onto others, wanting to see them change before we do. We expect them to behave in certain ways when we ourselves may fall short. Most of our relationships get complicated because we don't communicate clearly, we don't set boundaries when necessary, and we make things worse with assumptions. It's unfair to place high expectations on others. This invites disappointment and friction in our relationships and can turn others away.

It's better to be the change we want to see in the world. We can create gains by focusing on how we live and following our first principles. This inspires others to make changes in their lives. Hold high standards for yourself and lower expectations of others. Then be pleasantly surprised when others go out of their way to make a difference.

*Don't forget to love the way you want to be loved,
listen the way you want to be heard, speak the way you
want to be spoken to, give the way you hope others will give,
care the way you want others to care because change
doesn't start with them. It starts right here.*
—Madeline Beck
in Mary Pope Osborne's *My Secret War*

Become a Better Friend

Happiness is all about relationships. A study of well-being among 1,600 Harvard undergraduates showed that social support is the greatest predictor of happiness.[7] Create gains by initiating a new relationship or strengthening at least one relationship every day. Doing so can help you build a vast network you can rely on to shape an insanely great career and a deeply meaningful life. Not everyone will become your closest friend. That's OK. You can still create better relationships by showing interest in others, asking great questions, and listening more than you talk.

Rewrite your life and leadership story. Start now. Convert any pain holding you back into life-changing power to live out a better future. See where ego may have contributed to the pain, and where it's causing friction now. It's time to confront ego. This is where we're headed next.

CHAPTER 8

TRADE IN EGO

Try to be wrong once in a while, it'll do your ego good.
—KEANU REEVES

magine being told you're "the best" at your favorite sport all your life. Everyone sees you playing at a level far above anyone else. You're faster, better, stronger. You're destined for greatness. You rise to the pro level, signing a massive dream contract to play with an amazing team—only to find yourself in your new reality. You're no longer told you're the best. Now it's made clear that only one or two people on your team are considered the best. They're sports royalty, rock stars. Everything revolves around them. It's assumed that if they play well, the team wins. If not, you lose. Plain and simple. But is it?

The NBA has plenty of "rock star" players grabbing the microphone to proclaim their dominance as "the best in the world" while their teams struggle. Does the decades-long obsession with having a top-performing player translate into championships? It has contributed to inflating the self-importance of "star" players as they maneuver for more back-office power, trying to influence trades "or else."

There's no way around the fact that a great player can lift a team to greatness (see Michael Jordan). But is it the only factor? Is it always the case? And when most players reach the highest level of sports because they were once viewed as the best, is it even helpful? How would you feel being part of the NBA just to warm the bench and be told that the only guy that matters is the star "franchise" player? What effect does this have on the making of a team? Is it a good idea to build a team around a "rock star," rather than focusing on building a "team that rocks"?

It seems to make for better headlines and greater market power. Big names sell. But do they always deliver the best results? Let's take a look at the NBA team the Memphis Grizzlies, playing without Ja Morant, their second-team All-NBA performer. Ja is a scorer. He can shoot. He can seemingly do it all with a smile. He is their shining star. But how did the Grizzlies fare without him? John Hollinger of the *Athletic* said:

> In 27 games: 21–6. That's the Memphis Grizzlies' record without Ja Morant this season, including the playoffs, and it's not exactly in line with our expectations for how a team might play without a second-team All-NBA performer. Included in those wins are a 73-point beatdown of Oklahoma City and Wednesday night's 134–95 disembowelment of Golden State in the Western Conference semifinals . . . The issue isn't just that the Grizzlies have managed to avoid playing worse without Morant. It's that they've actually played significantly better.
>
> The Grizzlies outscored opponents by 4.1 points per 100 possessions with Morant on the floor this season and by 6.4 per 100 when he was off. In the postseason, it's been the opposite—at plus-5.3 with Morant and plus-2.2 without—but that's also a much smaller sample.[1]

What about with a star like LeBron James? Surely, this idea couldn't apply to someone whose name is mentioned in the same sentence as "the GOAT," right? Of course, the Lakers need LeBron to win, right? Wrong. Of the 2022 season, sports journalist Jason Reed said this:

> Are the Los Angeles Lakers better without LeBron James? As crazy as this question sounds, the numbers say that Los Angeles absolutely has been better without James this season. It is a small sample size, and the quality of opponent definitely has to be considered, but it goes deeper than just the win-loss record with and without him.
>
> The Lakers have played better basketball when LeBron is not on the court this season. The on/off numbers tell the entire story. When LeBron is on the court, the team's offensive rating is 10.4

points higher. The defensive rating is 5.2 points worse, but that still means the Lakers' net rating with LeBron on the bench is 5.2 points higher.

Just to put that into context, a 5.2-point difference in net rating was the same difference between the Golden State Warriors and Charlotte Hornets in the regular season last year. That is a tangible difference.[2]

Surprising? Maybe. But what exactly does it tell us? In a *USA Today* article titled "Why Do NBA Teams Keep Winning Without Their Superstars?," Martin Rogers said:

> Nowhere in sports does star power exude more sparkle than in the NBA, which found a formula for marketing individual excellence a generation ago and has ridden it to global success. Basketball's small collection of most celebrated deities sell tickets, boost ratings, alter franchises and are rewarded with extraordinary wealth and fame. But they're not magicians, and losing a front-line standout, to injury for a day or a week, is far less catastrophic to the balance of the win column than you might think.
>
> On Saturday, the Houston Rockets beat the Golden State Warriors, a noteworthy result simply because it's news whenever the Warriors lose and even scarcer when it happens at home. It wouldn't have caused so much head shaking, except that it came without James Harden, who sat with a neck injury and flu symptoms, following his incredible run of 32 straight games of 30 points or more. With Harden, whose ongoing scoring exploits put him in the rarefied company of Wilt Chamberlain, the Rockets had surrendered three of their previous four games, despite him twice topping 40 points and averaging 36.3 points per game. Without him, they built a team that is in the midst of a dynasty and was at full strength. Go figure.[3]

What if our perception of "rock star" players is the problem? What if it's been getting in the way of building a "team that rocks"? The highest-scoring players may have reasons to brag and draw more attention to themselves, but this may not improve the team.

What if we've followed the same "rock star" model in business? Investing all our money, focus, and time on "rock star CEOs" who can "save" the company, while they fail to build winning teams (see Marissa Mayer at Yahoo and Jack Dorsey at Twitter, among many others). Why do we put so much focus on one person to do it all? And as individuals, why do we put pressure on ourselves to be the "rock star"?

We call this the "Rock Star Curse." It's a hard one for organizations, much less businesses, to break. But they have and we can too. Yeah, but how?

> *People are always debating: Who's the Greatest of All Time?*
> *Dumb question. It should be:*
> *Who's the Greatest Team of All Time?*
> —MICHAEL JORDAN[4]

On my (Chris') high school basketball team, our highest-scoring player, Jake, was a jerk. He berated the other players, calling us names and swearing at us during practice. We put up with it. After all, we needed him to win, didn't we? But Coach Zimmerman had different plans. Despite being five foot two, this guy was pure resolve. When he said something, that was it, end of story. So when he pointed at the gym door and warned Jake that if he insulted his team members again, he'd have to leave and never come back, we knew he meant what he said. When practice resumed, and someone missed a pass, Jake started up again, shouting and blasting us with vulgar names. Zimmerman called to Jake, and then pointed at the door. It was over.

What would we do now? No one expected what happened next (except maybe Zimmerman): We pulled together as a team, started winning games, and got to the division finals. All because our coach had the courage to shape the culture, even if it meant "sacrificing" the rock star. Great leaders and cultures are willing to do exactly that.

The best movies and most inspiring books reflect the importance of the Hero's Journey. Most people fantasize about the hero's return, when they're praised for slaying the proverbial dragon and rewarded by love, riches, and glory. The world has propped up self-made heroes who seemingly "have it all." It doesn't help that we live in a time when most products and experiences are designed to be "on demand." We want instant growth. No hard lessons required. We even feel entitled to a life we deserve. But a life worth living has to be earned.

We need to seek and do the deep work of the future: not getting caught up in titles, rewards, or accolades; not messaging the boss in the middle of the night just to show we're the hardest worker ever; not fixating on plastering our personal brand everywhere to become a self-made celebrity; not manufacturing a facade that feels empty.

When we watch our favorite movies, we see a pattern in which the main character suffers, which leads to their growth and lessons learned. They face the tough stuff, and then they emerge victorious. But in our own lives, we do our best to skip all the suffering. This is understandable. Who wants to suffer? But the best moments happen at the heart of the Hero's Journey, when, as the hero, we're willing to sacrifice, and we become our authentic creative self.

CUTTING THROUGH IMAGE MANAGEMENT

Some people are real. Some people are good.
Some people are fake.
And some people are real good at being fake.
—Anonymous

Why do people struggle to understand their identity? Too many are preoccupied with image management. This devolves into a life of competing identities to meet the expectations of others, never being satisfied as we fight to manifest our authentic self. How can we continue our brave journey without splitting into different versions of ourselves? The struggle to become our true self affects our mental health, our happiness, and our future. In many ways, everything hangs on how we do this.

Erving Goffman shared the concept of impression management in his book *The Presentation of Self in Everyday Life*. He said it not only influences how we are treated by other people, but it's also essential to social interaction. As a social psychologist, he observed people in public places: shopping malls, sporting events, and restaurants. Goffman shares that when we are born, we're thrown onto the stage called "everyday life." Part of life is learning how to play the roles we've been assigned by other people. We play our parts as others play theirs in conversation. Social life is a "performance" carried out by "teams" of participants in three places: "front stage," "backstage," and "off stage."[5]

Front Stage: Life's a Play

People act out different roles. We behave in different ways depending on the context. Whether or not we're aware of it, most of us behave differently in our private lives than we do in our professional lives.

When we are aware that others are watching, we act in a "front stage" manner, giving a "performance" that is deliberate and intentional, habitual, or subconscious. Front-stage behavior is shaped by cultural norms. Waiting in line, getting on a bus while flashing a pass, and chitchatting with coworkers about the weekend—all routine and choreographed front-stage acts.

Interviewing with a potential employer, conducting a meeting at work, and hosting a party with friends are larger "performances." We've created mental scripts to make our surface-level roles appear "normal" and consistent, depending on our audience. Bumping into a childhood friend while with your spouse means navigating two roles. It can be awkward, difficult to manage, and anxiety inducing.

Backstage: When No One Is Looking

We are free from the expectations and rules that govern behavior on stage when we are backstage. We are more relaxed during private moments when we can be ourselves and do what feels comfortable in private spaces. The pile of laundry on your bed, the cluttered bathroom countertop, the stacks of dirty dishes in the kitchen sink, a quiet interlude in the car, a private moment with a friend, or a candid conversation with a coworker during a lunch break—these all take place backstage. Backstage performances are still performances with others, but they tend to be less polished, raw interactions.

Why should any of this matter to us? Upon closer inspection of our daily interactions, we can see how we get caught up in image management. Our socialized roles and others' perceptions make up our reputation, an outward representation. Yet, we feel disconnected to who we truly are, an inward experience. We can build on Goffman's framework in *Presentation of Self in Everyday Life* to understand our identity better in these ways.

Aim for a Blended Life, Not a Balancing Act

We experience the tension and demands of a balancing act among all our responsibilities and relationships. Much of our success and sanity is determined by how well we toggle between the various roles we play in life—as a parent, spouse, sibling, child, friend, church/temple/mosque member, community member, employee, colleague, boss, etc.

We often struggle to balance these roles, and when things get "out of whack," we question our abilities and even our self-worth. Our identity can be clouded by it all. The phrase "You can't be everything to everyone" comes to mind.

Instead of the constant juggling act, consider a blended approach. The Hero's Sacrifice may be surrendering to your core identity and not checking all the boxes as a people pleaser. Be more intentional with your roles. Eliminate or upgrade existing roles where possible. We can get distracted playing different roles for different people, but the life best lived is integrated. We don't have to feel pulled in every direction, trying to be everything for everyone. That leads to exhaustion. We can lean into a more authentic self—not as a default but as a direction. How do you add value in your relationships? By being powered by principles and what you care deeply about. This brings out your best self with others.

Get Clear on Your Identity

Are you feeling stuck in your routine? Perhaps you feel trapped living someone else's dream? Somehow, you've let the audiences around you define your life. It's time to flip the script. What do you want to be known for? What would you like to accomplish? How do you want to be? To gain this clarity, you need to be honest with yourself.

Using the Mirror Test in the context of your Hero's Journey is key to understanding your roles better and what's within your power. If you want to improve the quality of your journey, make the Hero's Sacrifice. Rather than reaching a point in life that's full of regrets, look in the mirror now and focus on what you should do, what you could do, and what you will do. Here is how you can approach your Hero's Sacrifice:

> **What should you do? (should = value system).** What do you value? This makes up your moral compass and beliefs. Why do you do what you do? What are your boundaries? What principles guide the direction you are heading or your pursuits? Now shift your thinking. What should you value to progress toward the person you want to be and achieve your goals?

What could you do? (could = capabilities). Start with what you can do. What are your current talents? Now shift your thinking to what you could do differently. What skills or knowledge could you add or amplify?

What will you do? (will = willpower). What have you done? What's holding you back? It's time to address your surface-level excuses. Go deeper. Be braver. Now shift your thinking. What will you do to get different outcomes? What are you willing to sacrifice (Figure 8.1)? What are you willing to see differently?

> *Ego is its own worst enemy. It hurts the ones we love too.*
> *Our families and friends suffer for it.*
> *So do our customers, fans, and clients.*
> —Ryan Holiday

FIGURE 8.1 **The Hero's Sacrifice**

What makes one leader or team 10–100× more inspiring and impactful than another? What brings us closer to our own brave truth? Angela Ahrendts knows. As CEO, she led Burberry from being a stock retailer to a digital force, creating inspiring artifacts with her team. One was a book that told the storied history of Burberry, with an incredible chapter that envisioned the future of the iconic luxury brand. Angela went on to inspire change at Apple, bringing joy to people visiting the "digital Disneyland" locations throughout the world with 60,000+ employees, as she embodied and shared one simple but powerful charge: "Don't sell. Serve."[6]

Too many people obsess about selling themselves or what they're doing. What if we focused far more on how we serve and sacrifice? When we met with Angela, we shared our white paper ideas about our purpose and asked her, "How can we best inspire others?" She replied, "Show me what I love. Tell me what breaks my heart." Her words rang in the air and resonated in our souls.

How could we do this? For her? For others? We went back to the drawing board and began to build. An artifact emerged. Something inspiring. A manifesto that changed us, and we hope will help you. We felt inspired to write a letter to ego:

A BraveCore Proclamation

Dear Ego,

It's over. We are tired of the lies. We have spent years protecting you, and, in turn, we have protected the status quo.

There was a time when you gave us a false sense of security. We were invincible. You convinced us we had all the answers. We thought we were experts. We valued hacks and tactics to get there the fastest. To be the best. You convinced us that to lie, cheat, and steal was part of the game. That to win we had to play at the expense of others. Every man and woman for themselves. We believed that another important title would help us climb the ladder, only to feed our greed. You made us crave competition. We will no longer play this game. Ego, our relationship with you has made us shallow.

You helped us get the last word while the people in front of us never felt seen or heard. As we've cut out most human interaction from our lives, we've become more guarded than ever. You've helped us go from eye contact to text messages. Genuine smiles to emojis. Hiding behind emails and afraid to speak our truth. At times, we have felt truly alone. In this isolation, we have questioned our worth. Ego, we can't do this anymore.

We should have seen the signs, how you've influenced other people. Those in power. Those in the spotlight. The pain of the political divide, the culture wars, the status wars. You've divided us in fear. We now realize we've always been at war with you.

We've lost loved ones. We've lost out on opportunities. We no longer want to be a part of this cycle of loss. This self-inflicted war.

We see the struggle in those we care about most as they suffer, staring at their bank accounts, hoping they don't go negative. Those who've held on but are now giving up their dreams. Who've found sadness turn to anger. You've helped them point the finger. Ego, you've made it feel good to blame others.

Social media emboldened us. We became self-made celebrities. We showed the world how great we are. "Look at our meals, look at our house." While ignoring our children and neglecting our spouse. A fictitious lifestyle became too much to manage. This gives us anxiety. It's affected our health. You turned us into judges and critics. We don't like what we've become. Ego, you've distracted us, and our priorities have turned upside down.

Deep inside, we know there is something more to our existence. Something missing. To see beyond the traditional experience of success and to reach for a life of significance.

Ego, we realize we have also made mistakes. We've fallen short of our highest ambitions. We've failed many times. We have been afraid to act. Scared to speak up. It's time for us to take responsibility. We no longer want to blame you. We believe there is a beautiful future within our reach. One filled with hope, kindness to all, and humility. One that inspires everyone to witness the humanity in each of us, and the collective power it takes to build life with a shared desire for change. Change that shakes us at the core. Change that rattles our hearts to the point of becoming different.

A future that is everything we've wanted: with zero poverty, no racism, actual unity, and total peace. Where each one of us sees and feels the strength of the selfless force we've become. Where we work together to solve our greatest challenges through deep connection, collaboration, and co-creation. Where we bravely follow our heart. Where people around the globe and families everywhere embrace this love in timeless ways. Where this future together becomes a movement that carries us into the light for the next millennia. This is no small task. We know. And yet, it's worth all of our time and energy.

From this day forth, we'll trade our image for identity. We will be brave at the core. Instead of the tireless pursuit of what seems better somewhere in the external world, we will go deep within ourselves and build from timeless principles. From truth that speaks to us. We will no longer be afraid to show our love. We will no longer feel unworthy to receive love.

In this tension between the real vs. ideal, we will replace Ego with We Go because we choose to move forward with others.

This is our declaration of interdependence. To become the future together, we must:

- Manifest wisdom through shared knowledge

- Create empathy by understanding the passion of others

- Shape character by living principles

We believe that the embodiment of wisdom, empathy, and character brings out the best in any culture.

The future is counting on us. To be better, to be more. We will no longer be subjected to continual suffering; we will choose to sacrifice. To shave off our personal flaws, to trade comfort for adventure. To choose We over Me.

We are united in principles. We embrace diverse voices and all the creative gifts of our human family. We desire to co-create. To lift one another up. We are open to change and to be the change. Together. We Are BraveCore.

What would you write in a letter to Ego? How would you say goodbye? What do you love most? What makes your heart break?

THE HERO'S SACRIFICE

Sacrifice is often considered primitive, an ancient tradition—as if people from the biblical era were ignorant. Sacrifice may seem hard to understand, but it is deeply sophisticated and powerful. The best sacrifice is giving away something of worth to achieve a higher state of living. How can we shift from the Hero's Journey to the Hero's Sacrifice?

What comes to mind with the word "sacrifice"?

- **Tier 1 response = sacrifice for results.** They believe they are sacrificing their dreams to have a stable living. They sacrifice for an employer or boss. One person, who had just become a VP, told us in a trembling voice, "I sacrificed everything for this promotion. My marriage. My family. All of it." Do we really want to sacrifice it all for so very little?

- **Tier 2 response = sacrifice for self.** They delay gratification and seek further education or jobs to get ahead later. They sacrifice now for a better future. They give up one marshmallow today for more tomorrow. But it raises the question: Do we even need more marshmallows?

- **Tier 3 response = sacrifice for others.** The hardest part is sacrificing your old self to help more people. You must become a healthy and whole person to make a real difference in the lives of others. This is the core work of life. All of our potential joy depends on it.

For it to be a real sacrifice, some people believe they need to do something they've always known they needed to improve. They may have put it off and made excuses. On the surface, sacrifice could look like giving up time for others. But the Hero's Sacrifice goes deeper than that. It helps us combat the extreme nature of our ego. Sacrifice is about doing more with our life. Or it could be stopping something deeply personal. It might be giving up an aspect of our lives or whatever is holding us back. It means being willing to Turn Pain into Power. Here's what a Hero's Sacrifice involves.

The Return to Integrity

Who are you when no one is watching? Do you do the right thing, even when it may work to your disadvantage? Do you keep your word, no matter the cost? Are you following that internal compass, even when everything around is pulling you in a different direction? Integrity is intentional. It requires preparation, anchoring principles, and action.

> *Integrity is when what you think and*
> *what you say and what you do are one.*
> —NAVAL RAVIKANT

Are your behaviors consistent? What are your patterns? What needs to change? Some people think reputation is the same thing as integrity, but they are different. Your reputation is the perception of your integrity because it's others' opinions of you, which may or may not be accurate.

Others may try to determine your reputation, but only you determine your integrity. It's better to shape your core values by focusing on what is internal versus managing an image and fixating on the external. Integrity is the foundation for reputation. It's progress over perfection. With it comes the peace of knowing that you're manifesting your best.

Humble Confidence

Some people view humility as a weakness or something they can exploit, but it's actually a superpower. The world is full of self-inflation, quick opinions, and easy answers. What if the heroes of the future have a different type of confidence?

Humility means being grounded in timeless principles. It takes emotional intelligence and an understanding of skills that are not formally taught to us. This kind of approach is only achieved through experience, with others in mind.

Steve Kerr, head coach of the Golden State Warriors, said this about his player Steph Curry, "He is incredibly arrogant on the floor and humble off the court. I think that's really a powerful combination."[7]

Humble confidence is the willingness to be brave, to try something new, to become better. Are you willing to live your principles? When life becomes difficult or you feel stuck, choose the Hero's Sacrifice. Don't think less of yourself. Just think less about yourself and more about empowering others. Choose humble confidence. Sacrifice can feel hard at first, but it turns into a pattern of humility. Doing so will enable you to have new experiences, create unbreakable relationships, and lead you in a better direction.

Don't Let Social Media Feed Your Ego

The most convincing sign someone is truly living their
"best life" is their lack of desire to show the world that they're
living their "best life." Your best life won't seek validation.
—STEVEN BARTLETT

Why do we get caught up in the battle to feel relevant? It only adds to the noise. We've all seen business moguls and celebrities being trailed by camera-wielding paparazzi. Another video clip drops. Another tweet that the 2.5 million+ fans like, comment on, or repost. Everywhere you turn, there they are. Packaged and sold as the embodiment of success. It gets old. It can even get depressing.

"How can I ever become that successful?" you may ask, as you continue to scroll on your device. It's easy to get sucked into voyeur mode and feel this way. Social media can feed our ego in the worst ways. Using it to compare lives or to signal that our life is superior to others is a waste.

You are more powerful than you can possibly imagine. No one has ever lived who's like you. You have unique gifts that can change people's lives. With a Hero's Sacrifice you can make the difference, since you know great things come to those who put in the work and are brave. Don't let ego or pride limit your progress.

If you connect deeply with the sacrifice part of your Hero's Journey, you'll find joy in your work and with others. Your work life will start to play out like a movie, manifesting Einstein's words, "Your imagination is your preview to life's coming attractions." You're the product of countless generations who've sacrificed everything for your future. You've been held in reserve for this moment. It's your privilege to fight against shortcuts, fake philosophies, and false principles. Be brave enough to acknowledge what's real, and be a warrior for ideals that matter: humility, generosity, patience, and love.

Your destiny is to win in your work life—not to build an empire and certainly not while bulldozing others. Your story can include others as winners. What's your larger story arc? It starts with the battles you face each day. Quiet your ego with co-creation. How will you power your life and those of others with inspiration?

CULTURE WARRIORS

How can we live ego-free? What does that even look like?

Over a decade, the Golden State Warriors set the bar by building something special—more than a championship team, more than a team built around rock stars. When asked to make a Chicago Bulls–like documentary à la *The Last Dance*, Steve Kerr refused, being very intentional about not allowing cameras behind closed doors. While they've faced struggles over the years, and their dominance may not last forever, they created something special.

What's made the Warriors so successful has been their ability to play with zero ego, and do so in simple, powerful ways. Coaches from all over have come to observe the Warriors' practices, trying to identify their "secret sauce." But they've left disappointed. They can't see the magic hiding in plain sight, what's embedded in their team chemistry and culture. Here's what has distinguished the Warriors at their best.

Take Crazy Shots

During each practice, they take crazy three-point shots. Not just from five feet back, but from half-court. These wild shots seem uncharacteristic of a disciplined team and puzzles visiting coaches. *Why start practice with this chaos?* they may wonder. Because it loosens players up and builds confidence in doing crazy things together.

How can we do the same at work? We can start conversations with powerful questions, and be vulnerable enough to share our bold ideas or crazy dreams, the long shots. This encourages others to dream big together. Then we get serious about how these big ideas can materialize by becoming an unstoppable team.

Be Humble

The Warriors are all about staying grounded. In interviews, they don't talk about themselves, but instead spotlight other team members. This selfless culture creates a shared desire to have each other's backs.

How can we do the same? Set ego aside. Share the credit. Stand together. Be a selfless force that gives our best for others.

Always "High-Five" Each Other

The Warriors have a powerful little secret: the "high five." Not just any high five either. This one is shared—every time. For a made shot, missed shot, or bad pass. It's about connection, reminding them that no matter what happens, they're still a team. They stay in growth mode together.

On observing the Warriors practice, decorated college coach Steve Green said, "You couldn't walk by somebody without acknowledging them or being acknowledged, and it wasn't just players. All the coaches, all the staff members—everyone. It sounds kind of crazy, but I'd never seen so many high-fives."[8]

How do we practice this in our work life? Praise each other whether things go right or wrong. Don't wait for a major success to congratulate each other. Don't wait for a failure to provide support. Make it routine to lift each other up.

Stick with the Fundamentals

The Warriors run the fundamentals in practice: shooting, dribbling, passing, etc. They don't consider themselves "too good" for the basics. This surprises coaches who watch their practices, seeing the Warriors repeating drills you'd typically see at a high school or college level. Scott Cacciola of the *New York Times* said of Steve Green's observations of the Warriors' practice:

> Beyond the emphasis on team building, Green was struck by the Warriors' focus on fundamentals: dribbling, shooting, passing. For a solid chunk of each practice that Green attended, the players threw dozens of passes against large pitch-back nets that were configured with targets. The Warriors love to pass, but Kerr wants them to be more precise.
>
> "You can see on tape if a guy is catching the ball at his shoelaces instead of in his shooting pocket," Kerr said recently. "There's a dramatic difference in his makes and misses when you get a good pass or a bad pass, so we're trying to work on that."[9]

What about us? How good can we get at collaborating? Share the work. Sometimes we feel we need to take it on all by ourselves. How can we involve those around us?

Find Joy in All of It

When they're at their best, the Warriors find joy in every part of the game. They're always smiling, cracking jokes, and laughing, even when a player from the other team is trying to antagonize them. There's power in finding joy in moments. It reminds us that we're already winning. But the Warriors aren't perfect. And when they've failed to carry that selfless joy and gotten overly competitive with each other, they've fallen short of their potential. We're all human. But we can learn from and be inspired by the Warriors at their best.

How can we bring more joy into everything we do? What if we paused more to find the joy in situations? We need to recognize when we are operating in automated mode. We can't forget to feel. We need to let our team feel the power of what they're doing, and how much it all means to us.

THE NO-EGO FUTURE

In a world where ego is everywhere, how can we lean into an alternative approach? Look no further than Giannis Antetokounmpo. The inspiring Disney+ movie *Rise* tells the tale of his journey from humble beginnings as an immigrant kid who hardly played basketball to becoming a Nike-sponsored, championship-winning MVP (with a lot of help from the hard work, love, and prayers of his parents). What happens when a player of this magnitude and his team with the best record in the league get swept away in the first round of the playoffs? This is where egos go to die for most players. There are months of mourning. Players leave teams. Franchises get stuck, and the blame game begins with firings not stopping "until morale improves."

What about Giannis? When asked by reporter Eric Nehm, who covers the Milwaukee Bucks for the *Athletic*, "Do you view this season as a failure?" Giannis offered a master class in ego-free living and leadership.

It seemed like a reasonable question. They were the favorite to win the title—only to get crushed in short order. Journalist Jesse Washington shared:

> Giannis Antetokounmpo said the unthinkable after his Milwaukee Bucks succumbed to the Miami Heat in an epic flameout: There's so much more to sports than winning. . . .
>
> "It's not a failure; it's steps to success," [Giannis] said. "There's always steps to it. Michael Jordan played 15 years, won six championships. The other nine years was a failure? That's what you're telling me?

"It's a wrong question; there's no failure in sports." . . .

"There's good days, bad days," he said. "Some days you're able to be successful, some days you're not." . . .

It was a much-needed reality check in a sports world that tolerates cheaters winning championships at the highest level. . . . We throw kids into competition at ever-younger ages and push them past the point of fun or injury—all because of an obsession with winning, and what we think it brings.

Antetokounmpo showed us another way to live.[10]

We can be each other's hero. Learn how to make sacrifices for each other, as a team. Let go of ego. Together.

CHAPTER 9

SHATTER THE SHARK TANK

Selfishness is . . . self-destruction in slow motion.
—Neal Maxwell

The Zoom call began. The CEO sat at a table, staring at the camera, as hundreds of employees faced their fate. He leaned in and said of the layoffs he was about to announce, "The last time I did it, I cried. This time I hope to be stronger."

Were those words supposed to be comforting? Vishal Garg had just made it painfully clear that he cared more about his own feelings than theirs.

What led to this? How could a leader be so callous? Not long before, Garg had sent out a brutal email to staff. "You are TOO DAMN SLOW," he wrote. "You are a bunch of DUMB DOLPHINS and . . . DUMB DOLPHINS get caught in nets and eaten by sharks. SO STOP IT. STOP IT. STOP IT RIGHT NOW. YOU ARE EMBARRASSING ME."[1]

Was he right? Did Garg's belief in the power of sharkiness pay off? Was it worth the bad PR tornado he unleashed on the company (ironically named "Better"), the continuing executive fallout, and the total disengagement of a workforce that is sick of such brutality in the name of short-term profits?

The success of TV's *Shark Tank*, filled with wannabe entrepreneurs begging greedy investors for cash, in exchange for the lion's share of their business, has proven one thing: entrepreneurship is alive and well. But it's also propped up the idea that success is about sitting on high and looking down at would-be successors, only to squeeze them dry. Eat or be eaten. Be the first. Be the best.

What explains this mad pursuit of sharkiness? After all, didn't *Jaws* teach us to avoid sharks at all costs? Why do people aspire to be sharks in their careers or lives?

BREAK THE SHARK TANK

Big egos are big shields for lots of empty space.
—Anonymous

Shark Tank has swept over the business world, inspiring would-be entrepreneurs with the guts to pitch big ideas. Beyond the lucky ones who get the deals and the unlucky ones who have a Shark tell them they're "a cockroach that can be crushed," what is there to learn? What if we told you that this sharky approach doesn't quite live up to the hype? Sure, it's entertainment. It's just TV. But how much of it shows up in business today?

Let's go behind the curtain, starting with this: The Sharks have invested tens of millions of dollars in hundreds of startups and have rarely seen a profit. Surprising? Given their status in the business world, wouldn't it seem that the Sharks have got it all figured out? What other surprises are there?

The Sharks aren't as friendly as they might seem. On the show, investors look like they're getting along, except when an argument flares up over a deal. But Daymond John shared that infighting among the Sharks boils over.[2] It scares the entrepreneurs. They attack each other, like real sharks in a feeding frenzy, swooping in to steal the deal. Forget relationships, the deal means money! While investment opportunities can be lucrative, is it worth it for entrepreneurs to face the real possibility that these Sharks could eventually turn on them as well?

The Sharks usually don't know what to say. Watching the show, you get the impression that the Sharks are dialed into every detail. Every time. They never skip a beat. What perfect poise. What sharp business acumen, quick math, and admirable style. Are they really this polished? No. The Sharks wear earpieces and are often told what to say.[3] They're given answers. And questions. The producers are armed with background information to feed them about the entrepreneurs.

Given how little the Sharks know about the businesses, they'll end up asking enough questions to drive contestants to tears. Great TV but a bad experience for contestants.

Shark Tank producers have a psychiatrist on site. Barbara Corcoran revealed to *Business Insider* that during the filming of the seventh season of *Shark Tank*, an entrepreneur felt so overwhelmed that he fainted, collapsing in front of the Sharks.[4] The typical pitch lasts about an hour, and they tell contestants there's a chance their pitch will never air (about 20 percent of pitches are cut). Then each contestant meets with the on-set psychiatrist who assesses their level of post-Tank trauma to ensure they aren't too emotionally scarred. This is a necessary step, as the Sharks' comments can bring enough emotional pain to haunt contestants for a lifetime.

Some entrepreneurs don't even want to be there. Watching the show, you get the impression that all contestants are dying to be on it. But according to crew member TJ Hale, some get asked.[5] This can turn into entertaining TV, seeing the back-and-forth negotiations heat up or having them walk away from Sharks' insulting offers without any remorse. For some, an appearance on the show is clearly beneficial, bringing the right kind of exposure and attention. And yet many entrepreneurs are seeking the right partner to build with together. That's hard to achieve when the *Shark Tank* is all about transactional relationships. It's a disappointing reality.

The Sharks have bought into the image of their own mythology. How many leaders have done this? Taken pleasure in squeezing people to the breaking point, expecting "blood in the water" at executive reviews? How many leaders have relied on their "executive presence," barking arrogant answers and demands at teams? How many people have suffered the trauma of a bad manager with hellish "fix it or get fired" performance reviews, leaving them scarred?

Why do people think that having a shark approach will help them get ahead? Why are shark behaviors tolerated at work? We want a different experience. It's time we shatter the Shark Tank once and for all.

THE MIRAGE OF SUCCESS

More the knowledge lesser the ego,
lesser the knowledge more the ego.
—ALBERT EINSTEIN

During World War II, indigenous people in Melanesia received packaged food, supplies, and tools brought in on airplanes. These were things they couldn't get in the jungle. But one day the planes stopped coming. The tribespeople had an idea: build their own runways. Then they'd wait for the goods to appear. If you build it, they will come, right? But when the goods didn't come, the runways were abandoned.

How often does this happen in business? Leaders, teams, and companies build up an image of something that turns out not to be real. "Fake it till you make it." Except what if people never stop faking it? And what if they never take the time to build it in the first place?

She dropped out of Stanford at age 19 to create a startup that would change the world. She had an idea for a new technology, one that could run tests on just one drop of blood, without the need for needles. Her startup rapidly hit a valuation of $9 billion, and she became universally praised, starring in *Forbes, Time,* and *Fast Company,* wearing her trademark black turtleneck that she hijacked from Steve Jobs. Those who knew her noticed that she had even altered her voice, sounding more like Mark Zuckerberg. Most people looked past the early warning signs of fraud because she showed young people everywhere how to go from would-be scientist to self-made billionaire overnight.

Fast-forward to October 2016. Elizabeth Holmes stood in front of her employees as her house of cards fell. A damning report in the *Wall Street Journal* showed the company was a sham. Its core technology, a fraud. Theranos had used competitors' equipment for its blood test and falsified the data.

How did this happen? Here she was, now 32 years old, unraveling an empire built on an idea she'd never actually executed. She may have started out with a worthwhile goal, even good intentions. But the pursuit of fame and fortune took an ugly turn. The entire venture was a facade. The deal she'd made with Walgreens to provide blood tests in thousands of locations turned into a $140 million lawsuit for breach of contract. She couldn't deliver.

Holmes was scrambling, pulling in lawyers from Boies Schiller Flexner and crisis-management consultants to fix this disaster.[6] How did it all go wrong? She had pursued her purpose, and she had worked hard to raise money. But the business was missing its core. Holmes hadn't built anything real with her team. Instead, she'd focused on building an image and a narrative.

She pushed secrecy at Theranos so far, in a misguided copy/paste of Apple culture, that she refused to let employees talk to one another about anything they were working on. Total information control. She made every decision herself, from the number of American flags framed in the hallway to everyone's pay. No one else was empowered.

Holmes told the *New Yorker* that "a chemistry is performed so that a chemical reaction occurs and generates a signal from the chemical interaction with the sample, which is translated into a result, which is then reviewed by certified laboratory personnel."[7] When the *Wall Street Journal's* John Carreyrou read this, he was shocked by the lack of depth. It sounded like a "word salad." Carreyrou called BS, investigated, and debunked the myth of Theranos technology.

Holmes had hired Cambridge graduate Ian Gibbons to solve the science behind her big idea, but she forced him to work alone. No collaboration with other departments. He struggled to make the blood test machines work. When her lies started piling up, he was asked to testify in court. Then he committed suicide. The company blamed it on health problems, ignoring the fact that she'd set him up to work in isolation on an impossible problem.

Holmes had tried to mimic a slice of Steve Jobs's leadership (innovation, secrecy, etc.) without doing the most essential work: building a core, connecting teams, and collaborating. She'd built a shell of a business, based on her persona, fueled by arrogance and delusion. She has become the poster child of synthetic leadership, showing us the "fake it, till you make it to jail" template.

We need to avoid building only the perception of success rather than the reality of it. We can avoid getting sucked into a mirage of success if we're honest with ourselves and others about who we really are, stay dedicated to the rigor of a true build, show grit during tough times, hold ourselves accountable to the promises we make, and treat people who join our cause with dignity and respect.

There is a difference between feeling insecure and projecting the appearance of success. Having awareness of both extremes can prepare us to be authentically brave with others. Let's explore this further:

Imposter syndrome. When we doubt our abilities and fear being exposed as frauds. This is primarily tied to our fears—fear of failure, rejection, criticism, or comparison to others. It can lead us to self-doubt, perfectionism, and avoidance, hindering our capacity to feel confident in our abilities. We must reframe our negative self-perceptions to embrace our true competence. Overcoming imposter syndrome involves being more compassionate with ourselves and developing a "face it till you make it" mentality.

Posture syndrome. When we brave it alone to the extreme. Independent people can get caught up in projecting an image of success, driven by an excessive need for validation and recognition. This can lead to patterns of pride and arrogance when someone believes they must portray an unwavering sense of confidence, regardless of reality. They may resort to cutting corners, fabricating achievements, disrespecting others, and even acting in fraudulent ways. Maintaining an image of success at all costs can cause people to neglect building what's important. Skipping the work could hinder their true potential and overall success in life. Those who face posture syndrome have a choice: either recognize the limitations of this approach or get lost in their own world of make-believe. To change their trajectory, they must ditch the "fake it till you make it" pursuit and consider what's core to their character.

CHANGED STEVE AND
THE FUTURE SHAPERS

All great . . . actions are accompanied with great difficulties,
and both must be . . . overcome with answerable courage.
—WILLIAM BRADFORD

When Steve Jobs was preparing his lieutenants for his death, he wisely counseled his executives "to never ask what he would do. 'Just do what's right.'" . . . He wanted Apple to "avoid the fate of Disney after the death of its founder, where 'everyone spent all their time thinking and talking about what Walt would do.'"[8]

This clarity gave Tim Cook, his successor, the freedom to be himself, and it gave other leaders permission to change the world by creating insanely great products together. But behind the scenes, inside the "spaceship" Apple Park campus in Cupertino, an unexpected tension was brewing. Other leaders who'd worked with Steve grew to believe that if they put on the black mock turtleneck and roughed people up emotionally, they'd be following in Steve's footsteps. But this was exactly the opposite of Steve's dying wishes.

Some of these leaders never personally experienced Steve's larger story arc, when his leadership perspective and tone transformed. Steve had done the deep work of personal change that Ed Catmull later shared:

> I worked for Steve longer than anybody else. I watched him throughout the changes of his life. Steve went through the classic Hero's Journey. Early on in his life, his behavior was not good. It is well documented, and well talked about. And it's kind of sexy and exciting and has a sort of a bad boy flavor to it. So, if they write movies or books, people like to focus on that part. And when I first knew Steve, he had just been kicked out of Apple. So besides going through that humiliation, he still had the characteristics at that time, which I could see. . . .
>
> I did learn that if we disagreed, that Steve could talk and think so much faster than I could. And he was so articulate, even if I knew he was wrong, that I would actually delay the thing. I'd say, "Let's talk about it later." Then I'd think for a week for my next sentence. Then I'd get back on the phone with him, and say, "About this . . ." And boom! He'd shoot it down. But there reached a point when: (1) he'd say, "I got it. You're right, go ahead"; (2) he'd convince me he was right . . . ; or (3) it was not decided, and I just did it my way, and he was fine with that. . . . So as soon as he realized he was wrong, he stopped. He was learning from those mistakes. . . . He also got married and had some kids. And he married a remarkable woman who was every bit his equal in terms of intellect and understanding. And they had a remarkable relationship. And what I found was, contrary to my original view that people probably don't learn empathy—like

you have empathy, or you don't—I was wrong. I would not describe Steve as having empathy when I first knew him. But over time, that changed. The way he treated people, the way he interacted, the way he listened, the way he cared—all changed.

He had been kicked out of his kingdom. He was going in the wilderness. Failing, creating problems. But he was learning from them. And he changed. Around the early 1990s, he changed so much that everybody that was with him stayed with him for the rest of his life. So, when it got to the point when it was getting near the end of his life, and people were doing interviewing . . . even though they were authorized by Steve, nobody was going to psychoanalyze Steve. . . . So that change in Steve was not captured in the articles or books or movies that were written about him. They were all about the early stuff, which is publicly accessible. That's not the important story. It was: Here was a person who learned from the mistakes. He got better. And then when he returned to Apple, it was that *changed* Steve that made the Apple that was so great, not the person you read about in the books or see in the movies. And it's a disservice to young people to think there's something about that behavior, which was good, when Steve would've said his behavior was not good. And what he turned into was a loyal friend.[9]

CHANGING APPLE AGAIN

When I (Chris) started working at Apple, I was amazed at the depth of culture they'd created. Here was a company that knew who it was. No mission statements on the wall. They lived and breathed their purpose: create the best products for people. Not once do I remember a conversation focused on how much money they'd make. Their purpose was to innovate as a team, with customers in mind—to enrich their lives with the best products.

Things fell short when some Apple leaders swelled with hubris. Their pride in their connection to Steve and Apple's storied history somehow led them to believe they were responsible for all of Apple's success. Those still at Apple were all part of the success story of the most valuable company in the world, not just a couple of hotshot leaders.

That's when we started to see the highly visible exits of some who claimed to be "the successors to Steve." One outspoken would-be successor told every reporter that he'd left Apple on his terms. But he'd become a demanding and brutal dictator. His best people refused to work with him. What did Steve do about it at the time? Would he tolerate this "Rough Steve" leader? He corralled that leader's entire organization into an auditorium and fired the guy in front of all of them. Unceremoniously. Turns out "Changed Steve" had no problem firing "Rough Steve," preventing a cancer from destroying the culture. It would also be the best thing for that leader, whether he knew it or not.

Maybe he could stop and reflect? Nope. He moved to a startup, bragging publicly about how much he'd led Apple. Taking advantage of Apple's secrecy-shrouded media silence to craft his own narrative, he shouted from the rooftops that his bad-boy, a-hole behaviors were OK for others if they were directed at the right goals. His startup flamed out. He's faded in influence but not from public view. He continues telling his stories, justifying "rough" leadership, sadly, never learning the joys of becoming the "changed" leader version of himself that could've accomplished so much more. But what if he had? What if he'd chosen to grow from his Apple firing by looking long and hard in the mirror like Steve had? Embrace it as "the best thing to happen to him," admit failure, and then transform into a compassionate leader? What would he have built with his team? The next NeXT, the next Pixar, or even the next Apple?

Meanwhile at Apple, another VP followed that leader's pattern of behavior, becoming so obsessed with himself that he delighted in dressing people down as they'd present to him. He'd berate his team when they'd share bad news. While sitting in a taxi in Singapore, I found myself coaching him, saying, "Why don't you just build a relationship with that VP you hate and his organization? Have you had lunch with him?" He replied, "No. Why would I? You've told me the same thing four times in this taxi ride." And I responded, "There's a reason for that."

I heard horror stories of a VP in hardware getting so angry he stabbed box cutters into the table during a meeting, just to strike fear in the hearts of everyone there. He enjoyed humiliating one person in front of 50 others and scarring them so badly, they'd never cross him again. I learned such behaviors persisted because the SVP of hardware then was known for justifying his own rage in the name of "that's what Steve would do."

But that's not what Changed Steve would've done. And certainly not what Steve would do today or get away with, at least. What bothered me most about these examples was that it all felt completely counter to everything Apple stood for. As a company designed to enrich people's lives, how could it tolerate these a-holes leading teams? Why were such abrasive and callous people being promoted in a culture that supposedly valued inclusion and compassion, with Maya Angelou videos to boot? Why were some leaders obsessed with emulating the Rough Steve who'd been fired from Apple and not the Changed Steve Ed Catmull knew, the one who'd led Apple back to greatness with empathy and humanity?

We saw many other leaders at Apple couple compassion with expertise. They cared deeply about the products, the process, *and* the people. These leaders co-created cultural movements as they became shapers of a future they were building with others.

What would become of this tension between leadership styles that were so fundamentally different?

Smartly, Steve had designed cultural checks and balances that included Apple University, headed by Joel Podolny, who was tasked by Steve with "making leaders in our own image." But which image exactly? Apple University's work centered on "managing to the Apple culture" and creating leadership frameworks, but it fell short in addressing the real gap: the Rough Steve culture that had emerged as a cancerous force that posed an existential threat to Apple.

This was a dilemma. How could Apple claim to produce the best products if the most important product (the one Steve was most proud of) wasn't the iPhone, iPad, or iPod but was, in fact, the culture? How could we amplify the Changed Steve model and build more leaders in that image? The future of Apple was at stake.

CONNECTION > CONTROL

We couldn't let the deception continue. This love affair with ego would destroy us. This powder keg of pride built over a decade, hiding behind Apple's success, had to go. The past made the executives think they had the Midas touch, that everything they'd touch would turn to iPhones and more money. Partly true but deeply flawed, this hubris-infused magical thinking could lead to the downfall of the company within one generation of iPhones. We couldn't confuse the wave of newer employees joining Apple. The future had no room for synthetic leaders.

The Rough Steves had embraced the theology of "Think Different" to the point where they'd act like they were the only ones capable of making a "dent in the universe." This self-inflated view caused newer employees to shut down rather than share, to defer rather than challenge. For a company Steve claimed "hire(s) people not to tell them what to do, but so they can tell us what to do," this was untenable. People wanted to collaborate and co-create more, not less.

Wireless capability for iPhones and other devices, for example, required deeper collaboration and convergence of voices, ideas, and skills. But some prideful executives favored bashing heads in boardrooms rather than connecting the dots. We were coming up short. Work on the future of wireless, including 5G, 6G, 7G, and whatever was next, became a road-map exercise from Hell—synthetic leaders not only perpetuated problems but became roadblocks to any crucial changes.

It would come crashing down. It started in small circles and grew. We heard escalations. The tidal wave of frustration surged as people realized they didn't want Rough Steves anymore. They wanted Future Shapers.

We worked with and designed a plan with the best leaders. We created a next-level cultural identity rooted in first principles that could inspire their future, based on what the best leaders were doing now, based on compassion and co-creation. If Apple wanted to keep changing the world, we needed to make better connections across the company and make changes to impact our culture for decades to come—not based on some bad photocopy of Steve's worst days on the job (before he was fired) but on Changed Steve's approach, which had been emulated by the best leaders themselves.

This empathic leadership approach would be an inside-out effort, one demanding a Mirror Test of leaders wanting to shape the future, transforming the company with Changed Leaders willing to make the Hero's Sacrifice, and shifting from "Thinking Different" to becoming "Different Together."

This became the cornerstone of the future of Apple. Leaders emerged as the manifestation of Different Together, designing a culture of empathy that could also be product focused. Teams were able to converge on higher-quality solutions that would otherwise have been impossible to achieve.

People came together to shape a road map for technology that included patterns of partnership. Different Together was built into Apple's inclusion and diversity DNA, and Tim Cook embraced it. Even Apple University recognized that the work was scaling and relevant to securing Apple's future.

It was a pinnacle moment for me at Apple. To see this brave work emerge within our diverse teams and the impact it had on the culture in such a grassroots way was incredible. I was offered a faculty role, which meant a lot. But I turned it down as I looked to the future with a desire to help others shape culture. This method of co-creation worked here. Why not in any other domain? Apple had become more of the brand and culture I had been promised. And I saw something unfold that I'll never forget: a culture ready to reach its true potential at the next level: Brave Together.

The future is not forged by ego. It's in changing ourselves enough to inspire the world around us. Where are you in your Hero's Journey? In your Sacrifice? Maybe your journey has just begun, or you still need to take that first step toward your adventure. Maybe you're in the messy middle trying to make sense of it all. Wherever you are, you'll find co-creative strength with a Brave Together approach.

BECOME A BETTER LEADER

If your actions inspire others to dream more, learn more,
do more, and become more, you are a leader.
—John Quincy Adams

It's time for leaders to become Future Shapers. And it begins with each of us. Start small. Make the sacrifice to be selfless. Be the change. Here's a simple framework on how to get started.

If you want to grow, build people, inspire them. You don't need to have a massive strategy or new program to do it. Start by showing up differently. Be more intentional. Show versus tell. Move, don't prove. Create a different experience with your teams. Give them permission to build, shape, and co-create together. Let yourself and them live up to Albert Einstein's charge, "Imagination is more important than knowledge."

It's hard to slow down and listen to your core—heart, mind, and spirit—and yet the key to our toughest challenges is how we inspire people. As a fragmented society, we need to become whole again.

*Leadership is not defined by the exercise of power but by the
capacity to increase the sense of power among those led.
The most essential work of the leader is to create more leaders.*
—MARY PARKER FOLLETT

Mary Parker Follet saw the future of what leadership and culture could be—in the 1800s. She became a personal consultant to President Teddy Roosevelt, and her ideas have heavily influenced the growth of future-oriented businesses like Toyota, Apple, and Pixar. She saw the potential of synthesis leadership—how we could unify by making a difference in each other's lives, by how we all come together.

In a world starving for empathy, we need to stop trying to be a shark (Figure 9.1). Dolphins are a better metaphor for the next wave of work. They live in pods and work together in teams. Dolphins help defend and protect each other. They live in relation to one another. As a leader, be a dolphin.

T1: Dependent   T2: Independent   T3: Interdependent

FIGURE 9.1 **Tiers to Navigate**

Dolphins believe in the power of selflessness and a life fueled by service. They stick with what inspires them and ignore what doesn't. Dolphins don't try to impress everyone. They don't obsess about status or social media impressions. They spend less time image-managing and more time designing an inspired life. They know authenticity outweighs smoke and mirrors any day. They inspire others to become their best. And when people don't appreciate their approach, they move on, knowing they gave it their all.

Dolphins don't obsess about winning or being right. Dolphins know better. They have goals that matter to them, but they don't let winning consume their life. They're driven by a higher purpose that's connected to creating unbreakable relationships, lifting the less fortunate, and changing the world with others.

Dolphins don't believe everything is all about them. Dolphins contribute to an ecosystem. They look outward for ways to connect and bring attention and understanding to those around them. They don't let technology distract them or stop them from strengthening relationships. Whenever they are showered with praise and attention, they share it with others: family, friends, and acquaintances.

Dolphins don't think they're above reaching out. When others ignore those in need, dolphins dive in to help. They put themselves out there constantly, giving what they can. They don't just check the box or do things to be seen. They put their heart into helping others even when it's inconvenient. When they give, they don't expect to receive in return. They aren't transactional; they're transformational.

Dolphins don't think success can make up for failure at home. They put their home life ahead of things that don't matter as much. They measure success by those who mean the most to them. This fuels them forward through any challenges they face.

Dolphins don't disregard their health. They don't let themselves get lazy, or put off sleep, exercise, or nutrition. By giving their body what it needs, they offer themselves the ultimate gift: the power to be an instrument for good in ways that keep on giving.

Dolphins don't believe they can change the world alone. They aren't into individual spotlights. They know it takes a team, a village, and a band of brothers and sisters working together as one to make change. They rely on co-creative power.

Which dolphin approach resonates most with you? How will you be more like a dolphin in work and life? Here is how to make the shift:

- **Share an inspiring vision.** Give people a deep sense of purpose, a cause to believe in that's worth pursuing, every day. Inspire them with something that gets them up in the morning, a vision that paints their dreams at night. What inspires you? Why do you show up every day? Instead of pushing an agenda, pull people in with shared purpose.

- **Give them permission to build together.** Too many companies have gotten stuck in the siloed way of doing work. Business units and experts focused on doing work separate from each other. This isn't the future. And it won't inspire people to stay and do their best work. Cut the red tape and get rid of bureaucratic nonsense.

- **Co-create the future culture with them.** People want to be part of a culture where they feel they belong, where they can build things together, where time slows down as they get in the zone, where they feel a sense of alignment doing what they're meant to do on this Earth. Co-creation can unlock people's superpowers. Create a supercharged culture together.

This is the leadership path moving forward: innovating how we work and live, paving the way for new mindsets, behaviors, and patterns shaping the workplace cultures of the future. Co-creation helps us transcend titles, politics, and social status. Our strength will emerge from inside us, leading to life-changing transformations. We will be known for who we are at our core, as we co-create with others. We will witness the results and rewards flowing naturally, seeing our lives become far richer than they are now. And we will be able to measure our progress with co-creative principles.

We can see self-inflation for what it is—a trap that has failed us. We will come to know how we can best work with others, or not, and still see a world full of potential and inspiring possibilities. We won't need synthetic leaders to tell us they are here to save the day. We will discover new superpowers in our ability to do our best work with others, to build a future that's already in our hearts and minds. And we will find ways to thrive as we begin to live this future together.

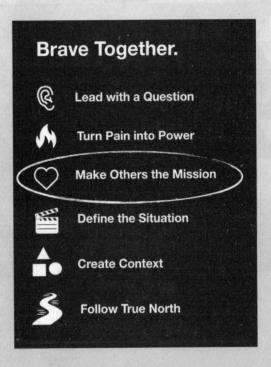

CHAPTER 10

MAKE OTHERS THE MISSION

The Compassion Principle

Give to the world the best you have,
and the best will come back to you.
—MADELINE BRIDGES

"Boom!" Debris showered the earth as another bomb detonated outside. She clung to her dad, brothers, and mom, hoping tomorrow would come, but knowing it would never be the same. Terrorists were destroying what was left of her small town of Swat, Pakistan, tearing schools apart and seeking death to all girls who sought an education.

She looked for solace in the chance that her family's suffering could mean something. More than that, she wanted to change people's lives, maybe even change the world. She needed to start where she was. Her father had named her after the legendary woman who stood against an army and won. She was about to face her own army. But her weapon wasn't the AK-47s carried by her Taliban enemies. It was her voice.

She amplified her words anonymously in a BBC blog. She wrote about the suppression of girls' education, and why everyone deserves access to learning. Through media broadcasts, she challenged the ideals of the Taliban head-on—risking her own life. She bravely proclaimed her belief in education everywhere—until a Taliban terrorist jumped on a bus she and her friends were riding, asked, "Are you Malala?," and shot her in the head.[1]

Her story could have ended there. But it didn't. After months in the hospital, and one grueling surgery after another, Malala fully recovered by the grace of God. She had a mission she still needed to carry out. So she focused her whole soul and her sincere prayers on standing up again to tell the story—not just her story, but the story of everyone deprived of an education. "Peace in every home, every street, every village, every country—this is my dream. Education for every boy and every girl in the world,"[2] she said, adding, "I don't want to be thought of as the 'girl who was shot by the Taliban' but 'the girl who fought for education.' This is the cause to which I want to devote my life."[3] She also said, "Let us pick up our books and our pens. They are our most powerful weapons. One child, one teacher, one book, and one pen can change the world."[4] She went on to win the Nobel Peace Prize and continued to inspire in powerful ways.

Malala has confronted a culture as she fights for women's education. Such courage can be part of our lives. We may not live in such brutal circumstances, but we face our own battlefields over what we believe. Our own version of those terrorizing the truth—or at least attempting to stand in the way of our best future with others.

Making Others the Mission allows us to learn from the past, live in the present, and lead others into a future of possibilities. It's grounded in an idealism that won't surrender. Most goals we carry with us have an end. When we accomplish X, Y happens, and it's over. Then we move the goalposts. This leaves us unsatisfied because whatever we achieve never feels like enough.

Stanford psychologist Jennifer Aaker studied the lives of 397 people. She found the most meaningful lives focused on moving through struggles by connecting to a larger purpose and making a positive contribution to the world. Aaker said, "People have strong inner desires that shape their lives with purpose and focus—qualities that ultimately make for a uniquely human experience."[5]

When we Make Others the Mission, like Malala, we're not afraid to look crazy in the short term because we've built a beautiful future in our minds and hearts even though our current reality may not have caught up to it yet. We boldly invite different views in pursuit of big solutions, looking to connect silos rather than build more. We shape a culture of prototyping—

exploring the joy in a relationship, a multimillion-dollar deal, or an early morning run. We live the principle-powered future.

Most people stay in a small box and don't believe they can influence much. They limit themselves. Those who Make Others the Mission reject that. They look to change things, they embrace possibilities, and they see the potential in others. The world needs people who show more compassion. Be one.

LIVING SMALL VERSUS LIVING BIG

If you want happiness for an hour, take a nap.
If you want happiness for a day, go fishing. If you want
happiness for a lifetime, help somebody.
—Chinese Proverb

Too many people focus on the wrong thing: They make themselves the mission. They build their personal brand, their lifestyle. They shout to the world, "It's my turn," ditching family, ghosting friends, and burning coworkers so they can focus on themselves.

People who pursue a selfish life act surprised when it feels empty. But what did they expect? John Gottman and Julie Schwartz have studied over 40,000 couples and can predict with 94 percent accuracy whether a marriage will last. They've discovered the one thing that makes relationships successful: How often a couple "turned toward" their partner (Brave Together) instead of "turning away" (Brave Alone) or "turning against" (Fear).[6] These couples responded to bids for connection. When their partner said something, they looked them in the eye and listened, rather than down at their phones. It all boils down to thinking more of others than yourself. Counterintuitive? Maybe. Powerful? Definitely. The future? Yes.

People who Make Others the Mission escape the void of self-obsession, which is a trap. When we're brave enough to live this way, everything changes, and life gets bigger (Figure 10.2). What if you could feel instant joy? That's the power of Making Others the Mission. As we aim to make others' lives better, we become a force of nature and our lives are filled with purpose.

FIGURE 10.1 **Live Big by Making Others the Mission**

WHY MAKE OTHERS THE MISSION?

Our world feels small when our life mission is only about ourselves. Our problems seem big. There's never enough money. Never enough success, followers, or fame. Never enough of anything because it all centers around us. By Making Others the Mission, our world gets bigger. It's about more than us. Our potential grows and our opportunities expand. There's more than enough joy, more than enough hope, more than enough impact to share with others. We are surrounded by friends, family, and faith. Here's why we should Make Others the Mission:

We create endless energy. By focusing on the endgame of education for all, Malala built endless energy into her life. She'd face the Taliban, share her voice, and fight against all odds. If you could tap into an endless source of energy and strength, would you? It's right in front of us every day: family, friends, coworkers. As we center our lives on helping others, we also feel supported.

We can take life to the next level. When others are the mission, it frees you to focus on what matters. You give up obsessing about what's next and get down to the business of serving others. Studies show that goals focused on others are far more powerful. Want to truly connect with others? Create something together.

The world is full of people who are grabbing and self-seeking.
So, the rare individual who unselfishly tries to serve others
has an enormous advantage. He has little competition.
—DALE CARNEGIE

We become more compassionate. Compassion makes us present, making our conversations the holy ground others can walk on, helping them feel safe, seen, and heard. Putting others first fuels our mood, reducing the stress hormone cortisol, and enables greater overall well-being. Compassion creates happiness all around. When we're sacrificing for others, we find real meaning without getting hung up on what's happening to us personally.

Sympathy: projecting your experience onto others through a similar situation or story

Empathy: looking to understand someone's situation but with personal motivations

Compassion: creating a deep understanding of another out of pure kindness

Pualei Lynn is a successful retail entrepreneur in Utah, but she's not interested in building a fame-focused or money-grabbing empire. She's creating a community of love and inspiration, as she reaches out to lift women in need. She helps women who've never felt respected in business or in life, including the UPS driver she met. She empowers a group of women entrepreneurs to be brave, to see beyond their limitations of self-doubt and self-sabotage.

These women are being brave together as they seek to lift up and serve other women and refugees in their community. They help them with new clothes and resources, inspiring a better mindset, so they can see themselves and their situations differently, making anything seem possible and within reach. Now they are all starting to see themselves as leaders in their own way. Making Others the Mission has changed their lives. And it has changed Pualei Lynn's as well.[7]

Selflessness is a superpower. Compassion is life-changing. Co-creation can be world-changing.

Directing the script of our life in a forward-leaning way is crucial in a world where it's too easy to get cynical. We don't have to worry about a dystopian future if we're building a beautiful one with others. This is how the best teams and leaders roll. We've seen it in the life of James Matthews, our friend from India who's worked with the world's top tech companies, FIFA, the NBA, international players, and coaches. When asked to help a top brand's team come together, rather than focus on traditional team building, he turned to creative methods and human-centered design. James, along with his team of co-creators, asked the team to write a song together. He encouraged them to get vulnerable, open, and even selfless. They created lyrics that inspired a sense of working together in brave new ways they hadn't before.

James believes in co-creation at his core. He Makes Others the Mission. His leadership approach has applied music and sports to countless other contexts. He's even done it in the slums of India, where he and his team joined an effort to help a group of children of prostitutes—who were struggling with their self-worth and life experiences—to come together and write a song. The kids were inspired to shape a beautiful melody about rising above what they face and giving others their hope.[8] How can we be brave like them? Co-creation moves us from being self-focused to becoming compassion centered, going from transactional living to transformational building and creating the best relationships and the best work life.

THE LIFE-CHANGING (AND CULTURE-CHANGING) MISSION

The company was struggling. CEO Steve Ballmer and other leaders had run the culture into the ground with winner-eat-all tactics that led to infighting, leaving employees feeling burned out and looking for the door. Enter Satya Nadella. With a net worth in the hundreds of millions, he's ranked in the top 10 on the *Forbes* list of America's Most Innovative Leaders. But do those things matter most to him? Nope. Not at all, compared to his family. He credits them for helping him become the leader he is today.

As CEO, Satya has led Microsoft to greatness by "hitting refresh" on the culture to remake it as empathic, compassionate, and powered by people. How did he become the kind of leader who embodies these principles enough to inspire others to do the same?

When Satya was 29 years old, he and his wife, Anu, were living in a rented apartment near Microsoft headquarters in Seattle, Washington, and expecting their first child. During the thirty-sixth week of Anu's pregnancy, they found themselves rushing to the emergency room. The baby was not moving. Doctors immediately started a cesarean section. "Zain was born at 11:29 p.m. on August 13, 1996, all of three pounds. He did not cry," Satya recalled.[9]

They soon learned their son Zain had cerebral palsy, a devastating diagnosis. Satya saw how his wife, Anu, took this as an opportunity to grow, not complain. She made Zain the mission. "For Anu, it was never about what this meant for her—it was always about what it meant for Zain and how we could best care for him. Rather than asking 'why us?' she instinctively felt his pain before her own."[10]

Satya was inspired by Anu's deep empathy. It changed his life and leadership. He said, "From her I have learned that when I infuse empathy into my everyday actions it is powerful, whether they be in my role as a father or as a CEO."[11]

He's become a different kind of leader. Satya wrote, "Becoming a father of a son with special needs was the turning point in my life that has shaped who I am today. It has helped me better understand the journey of people with disabilities. It has shaped my personal passion for and philosophy of connecting new ideas to empathy for others. And it is why I am deeply committed to pushing the bounds on what love and compassion combined with human ingenuity and passion to have impact can accomplish with my colleagues at Microsoft."[12]

"After Zain, things started to change for me," Satya told *Good Housekeeping*, following the publication of his memoir. "It has had a profound impact on how I think, lead and relate to people."[13]

"Anu has deeply taught me something, through all of what's happened with Zain—how to forgive myself. None of us is perfect," he continued. "Once you come to that deeper realization, you don't judge as quickly, you listen better, and you can amplify people's strengths."

Anu has also written about how her son influenced her. She wrote, "Even in his most vulnerable moments, Zain shows great resilience and strength, which inspires me."

"He has endured many painful medical interventions and will likely face more," she added. "When he brings his maximum effort to the table, I think about needing to do more for him and others."[14]

Satya has forever been changed by Zain, who passed away at the early age of 26. Satya called him "the joy of our family, whose strength and warmth both inspires and motivates me to keep pushing the boundaries of what technology can do." The experiences Satya shared with his son have shaped his approach to making Microsoft products and services more accessible to everyone, especially those with disabilities. With Windows 10, they added features such as Narrator to Hearing AI, created by Azure engineer Swetha Machanavajhala.[15]

We can Make Others the Mission like Satya and Anu have done—being present in ways people need most and changing culture with deep empathy. When we have compassion, we look to give rather than receive. It's about serving others, not ourselves. We can inspire people as we infuse more compassion into our life and leadership, strengthening relationships and breaking down silos. As we do, we'll find the path ahead of us filled with everything we need, everything that matters most.

Naval Ravikant shared a thought-provoking take on the *Joe Rogan* podcast:

> I really think socialism comes from the heart, while capitalism comes from the head because there are always cheaters in any system. So, when you're young, if you're not a socialist, you have no heart, and when you're older, if you're not a capitalist, you have no head.
>
> Nassim Taleb has a good model for thinking about this. He has said: "With my family, I'm a communist. With my close friends, I'm a socialist. At the state level of politics, I'm a Democrat. At higher levels, I'm a Republican, and at the federal levels, I'm a Libertarian."
>
> The larger the group of people you have together, the less trust there is and the more cheating takes place—the more you gear towards capitalism. The smaller the group you're in—then by all means be a socialist.[16]

Perhaps how we Make Others the Mission differs by the proximity we have to each other and the size of our groups. It's not "one size fits all." It's "one at a time," with the right focus and the best of intentions.

READY TO RESPOND

*True compassion means not only feeling another's pain
but also being moved to help relieve it.*
—Daniel Goleman

What if Making Others the Mission means going beyond our typical responsibilities? I (Ian) had an experience that made me ask this question. One day a team member came into my office and informed me that one of our competitors in San Jose, California, was struggling to keep their staff. We learned that two of their nurses were in our lobby filling out job applications.

As we spoke with them, one nurse painted the picture that the staff hadn't been paid in months, they were struggling to fully operate, and they didn't really have a leader at the time. The owner and now the acting administrator would "show up" to make an appearance once a week and make another promise they wouldn't keep, and then disappear for the rest of the week. Out of shame. Out of cowardice. The team felt totally abandoned. All the rumors they'd been hearing and the behavior of their administrator made it clear the company was pulling out of operations. And it was inevitable they would be closing their doors soon.

I could see the pain in her eyes. She was tired. The weight of her struggles made her shoulders slump. We explored her coming on board with us to give her the stability she was seeking and a team that would support her. She was interested but she pushed back saying, "I can't leave yet. A few other nurses and I are the only ones left to take care of these patients. So, I don't know when I can leave." Her response impressed me. She wasn't getting paid. And she had no director of nursing or administrator. And their owner didn't care. She and her coworkers became the true leaders in the facility. Without the titles. As we ended the meeting, we asked her to keep us posted with any help they might need.

Weeks later my admissions director received a call from their staff asking if we could provide some wound supplies. We dropped by and saw the fatigue in their skeleton crew. Many of the staff had already left. The team was grateful for the supplies we brought. We asked if they needed anything else. They had a look in their eyes that told us they needed more help.

They were reticent to show us a barren storage closet, but they did. We then grabbed a clipboard and pen and wrote down items they were lacking.

We asked about the kitchen and food. They told us they'd been bringing food from their own pantries and refrigerators at home. Our hearts sunk. We couldn't believe what we were hearing and seeing. This sad situation had affected patient care. These patients were at risk for a decline in their health because of a lack of resources. We immediate called our facility and had our team put together nursing supplies and food. Within an hour we came back with these items. This gave their dedicated staff some relief to handle operations for the next week or so. We also learned of some equipment that needed repair. So, we sent the maintenance director from our building to help.

Two weeks later I received a phone call from the Department of Public Health asking for our help. They were monitoring the proper closure of this facility and had difficulty transferring two patients to other facilities. The state informed me that other facilities in the area had declined to take them due to an issue with insurance.

My coworker and I returned to the facility. This time we encountered empty hallways and a barren facility. We found one of the remaining patients pacing back and forth in her room. She was in her early 70s and had no family. We asked if we could meet with her. She had her cell phone out and had been calling facilities on a list the staff gave her. She felt rejected. Visibly shaken, she had a tremble in her voice, fearing her uncertain future.

We sat down and introduced ourselves. When we made eye contact it was like she finally felt seen. Her rattled nerves calmed. We told her not to worry. Everything was going to work out. We had a new home for her. She looked relieved. With her things already packed, we took her back to our facility. It was lunchtime and she was greeted by our friendly staff and a bowl of soup made from scratch in our kitchen. She felt connected at our facility. Many nurses, residents, and families kept an eye out for her. They made her feel included and showed her compassion in small ways. It was beautiful to see how a tragic situation brought people together. By taking responsibility for others, we were able to find joy together.

FREEDOM = LIBERTY + RESPONSIBILITY

With great power comes great responsibility.
—Uncle Ben to Peter Parker (Spider-Man)

Freedom is liberty, but it requires responsibility. No one knew this better than Victor Frankl, a former prisoner in the Nazi concentration camps in Austria. Tortured by his captors, he witnessed the worst in human nature. He saw that when deprived of basic needs, people chose to behave in different ways. Some acted like devils. Some curled up in a corner to wait for death. And others chose to serve, giving their last piece of bread to starving strangers. Making Others the Mission kept them going. The importance of understanding their "why" made all the difference. And Victor's "why" was seeing himself teaching in a future classroom, inspiring students with survival stories from the horrible death camps. It became his will to survive.

Victor saw that he still had the ability to choose. Real freedom. After surviving the camps, he created a psychological practice inviting participants to overcome their fears by being more responsible. Victor said, "I recommend that the Statue of Liberty [on the East Coast] be supplemented by a Statue of Responsibility on the West Coast."

For several years, a small team has been working to bring this project to life, to erect a Statue of Responsibility. They've grown in numbers to make Victor's dream a reality. The prototype shows one hand reaching down from the sky to another, symbolizing the responsibility that comes with liberty. The design calls for the statue to be built 300 feet above ground level (same as the Statue of Liberty) on an island on the West Coast (www.mystatueof responsibility.com).

It's our responsibility to Make Others the Mission. How we do this and why is up to us. Serving others expands our freedom, creating possibilities.

GET PAST TRANSACTIONS AND SEEK TRANSFORMATIONS

A lot of problems in the world would be solved if we talked to each other instead of about each other.
—Nicky Gumbel

It's not wrong for us to strive for something more, to want to improve our lives. But it becomes a problem if we're consumed by the self, when everything else takes a back seat. We've been taught by all the existing systems— educational, business, political—to work hard, stick to our guns, and hold fast to our technical knowledge. Fight the other side. Point out their faults and make it clear to everyone. Brave it alone. We're told this is the key to being the best, getting ahead, and winning. What could possibly go wrong? Everything.

FIGURE 10.2 **Vertical Connections**

When we seek only Vertical Connections (Figure 10.2), we limit life, making our relationships transactional. Who can help me get ahead? If I do this for you, can you do that for me? We're told to "find your tribe and stick with it." Is this the best advice? Filling your life with people just like you sounds like groupthink. If Vertical Connections can make you self-centered, do the people around you also seem self-absorbed? What if the pursuit of Vertical Connections is holding you back?

Think about your relationships with family and friends. Are there people in your life you can be yourself around without being too self-conscious? Is it hard to keep friends or to have deep conversations with others? Do you feel supported by them? All of these insights can help you see if the people in your life are Vertical Connections. Here are the characteristics of someone seeking Vertical Connections:

- **Use of flattery.** They build up authoritative figures to gain something in the future, showering a supervisor or boss with praises, looking to appease a parent or spouse to stay in their good graces to get something later.

- **Self-promotion.** Selfish people seek the spotlight and make themselves look good to those they want to impress. They share an elaborate story about themselves at a dinner party or a brag post on social media. Getting attention is the goal.

- **Materialistic.** They use things to feel important in relationships: a new car to signal status or money or lavish gift-giving to win people over.

- **Manipulation.** Some are ready to do whatever it takes—lying, spinning the truth, blurring reality, and making others look bad so they can appear better. This makes others feel used and abused.

- **Entitlement.** They assume they deserve only the best. They won't accept it when things don't go their way. In relationships, they devalue people who, on the surface, can't do anything for them. They may be slow to respond in communications when they can't see how it benefits them.

Vertical Connections are one-sided and shallow. With energy moving only toward self-interest, we're stuck forever in Maslow's hierarchy of needs. Food, check. Safety, check. Belonging, check. Self-actualization, check, check, and check again. But Abraham Maslow realized the shortcomings of his original model later in his life. He wrote in his journal:

All sorts of insights. One big one about [self-actualization] stuff, brought on, I think, mostly by my deep uneasiness over articles . . . I realized I'd rather leave it behind me. Just too sloppy & too easily criticizable. Going thru my notes brought this unease to consciousness. It's been with me for years. Meant to write and publish a self-actualization critique, but somehow never did. Now I think I know why.[23]

Maslow grew to hate the idea he'd created: that self-actualization was the pinnacle in his pyramid of needs. He'd learned it wasn't true, that we need more as human beings. In order to feel fulfilled, we need to look outside ourselves.

Above "self-actualization" is "self-transcendence." Self-transcendence is about giving to others. It becomes the ultimate fuel in our lives and leadership. Victor Frankl said:

> The real aim of human existence cannot be found in what is called self-actualization. Human existence is essentially self-transcendence rather than self-actualization. Self-actualization is not a possible aim at all; for the simple reason that the more a [person] would strive for it, the more [they] would miss it. For only to the extent to which [people] commit [themselves] to the fulfillment of [their] life's meaning, to this extent [they] also actualize [themselves]. In other words, self-actualization cannot be attained if it is made an end in itself, but only as a side-effect of self-transcendence.[24]

How often are we stuck trading our best future away for a small win to-day? We think we're doing our best, but we're not. What if we reframed our hierarchy of needs to be healthy and whole enough to co-create the best future with others, to Make Others the Mission? It's time to let go of vain success. Instead of asking, "What more can I do to get ahead?," ask, "How can I help the people in my life get ahead?"

FIGURE 10.3 **Horizontal Connections**

Imagine a world where we reach out across boundaries, where we build relationships with those with whom we disagree, where we serve those in need, regardless of what we get in return. What if we didn't even think in terms of transactions? Zero transaction. Only transformation, only abundance.

Imagine if we rallied for those in need, had each other's backs during hard times, and built each other up? It would significantly reduce mental illness and grow relationships to a point where we help each other heal. We'd support the people in our lives, helping them navigate their biggest challenges so they no longer think they need to brave it alone.

This is all possible if we start making Horizontal Connections (Figure 10.3) to help others rise in vertical ways. You'll start to notice people you are helping are becoming empowered to help those around them transform. Here are some ideas for building Horizontal Connections in your work life:

- **Connect with your boss by seeing them differently.** See them as someone who may have the best of intentions but at times falls short—like any of us. Some of their pressure or stress may not be visible or well understood. Look for ways to serve them. Find areas of the work or their responsibilities where they might struggle and support them. This shows compassion at a deeper level. It might not make things perfect, but it will improve the relationship.

- **Connect with a coworker that you struggle with.** Relationships that are strained at work are often tied to strong personalities, passive aggression, or gossip. It may be a misunderstanding or a difference of work styles. Set clear boundaries so someone doesn't take advantage of you. Find things you have in common. Build on them. Be aware of how your behavior or communication may have complicated the relationship. Be patient. It takes time to repair relationships, but the effort is always worth it.

- **Connect with someone you wouldn't typically be friends with.** Put yourself out there in simple ways. Smile. Offer a genuine compliment. Be open to new relationships. This could be someone from a different department with a different role or someone you've seen on Zoom calls but don't know very well. Maybe even a new employee who needs support. Learn about them. It will take the pressure off focusing too much on yourself.

- **Connect with a customer or client on a deeper level.** Every job has customers, even if your role doesn't interface with them directly. Get curious about their experience with your company, brand, or a specific product. We often avoid customer issues or complaints because it can get in the way of our regular work or be emotionally draining. But it can also be emotionally filling if we approach them in the right spirit, if a true connection is made, if we serve them instead of selling.

We wonder how we can help others when we're so busy, but the answer has been staring at us all along. In those closest to us, immediately around us, who are waiting to be seen, heard, valued, loved, and served.

Combining the best in heart, mind, and spirit enables us to become the future. We're going to explore this next.

PART III

BECOME THE FUTURE

The Become the Future pattern is about transformation: manifesting the best, embodying it, and harnessing the future of influence. It's about the rise of creators who change the world by changing lives, starting with our own. We can shape our work and our lives differently as we combine heart, mind, and spirit. Our lives become a synthesis. We transform by adopting new perspectives and embracing new challenges—together.

In the coming chapters, we explore how applying timeless principles guides our actions, how creating context brings people together, and how following true north aligns us with our purpose. We'll see how a co-creative moment gave the "I have a dream" speech its lasting power and how a struggling NFL quarterback transformed his career by defining the situation. We share the story of how a ragtag team of directors saved *Star Wars* through co-creation and how a team at Burberry combined the past with future-forward artifacts that changed their culture.

The Become the Future pattern shows us how to connect, collaborate, and be brave together, enabling us to move through the messy middle of work and life with clarity. It's about going beyond goals to everlasting

themes, transforming together, and inspiring others to do the same. This

gives us a macro view, allowing us to see the potential for people, organiza-

tions, and communities to transform. The Become the Future pattern pro-

vides the building blocks for culture shaping. Co-creation powers us with

perpetual, world-changing energy. Together, we can create a story of abun-

dance, becoming transformed leaders as we shape culture with others.

CHAPTER 11

THE FUTURE OF INFLUENCE

Love is the one thing that transcends time and space.
—Dr. Brand in *Interstellar*

We've heard the mantra to work smarter, not harder. But that's not enough. The future is shared, not self-made, and the path there is to work co-creatively together. To make this shift, first, we need to understand how we've been influenced in the past.

In Part I, we saw how we've been influenced by fear, how systems were designed to control our work life, and how we've deferred to experts to tell us what to do. At worst, this Tier 1 (T1) experience has led many to experience a lack of self-worth, unclear identity, unfulfilled dreams, and a slew of mental health consequences. We're far from our full potential.

In a T1, or systemic life, we're socially constructed (Figure 11.1). A social construct is a set of ideas created through human interaction that we use to understand the world. Many people have followed similar patterns for decades, even centuries. This is a default setting we've gotten used to. We're raised in a family that follows a systemic path: get good grades to get into college, graduate college so you can land a good job, do well in your job to get promoted, and so on.

Think about it. When you start your career, the type of work you pursue may seem unique, but the systemic path is the same. Your employer establishes "what you can do" based on your degree or certifications to correlate with the role and title you receive. Your employer sets "what you are worth" based on an hourly wage or salary. Your employer tells you "how to do your

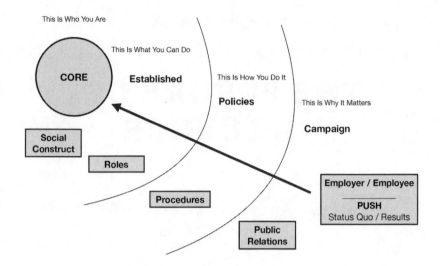

FIGURE 11.1 **Tier 1: Industrial Age**

job" based on the rules. If you raise too many questions, you run the risk of being rejected by the system, labeled as someone who can't fall in line. Systemic employees keep their heads down and figure out the manager's syllabus to stay off the radar or move up the ladder.

Traditional leaders spend their energy managing compliance and optics. They project their importance to the system: being seen in the office, dressing the part. They perceive that they are in control of others. They take credit for success and blame others for setbacks. This becomes a burden for those who grow aware of the socially constructed box they're in.

In Part II of this book, we shared the limitations of braving it alone. With a Tier 2 (T2) approach, we've relied on ego, self-reliance, being a shark, empire building, image management, and the fear of missing out (Figure 11.2). We've learned that obsessing about self-improvement and optimization gives us a shallow sense of achievement. And yet personal development is key to upgrading our work life and building a co-creative future with others.

In life, we start out by being dependent on others, but at a certain point, it turned into "single player" mode. Every man or woman for themselves. Everything looks like a competition. With a focus on self-reliance, people attempt to go out on their own. Many try to copy the entrepreneur lifestyle, amplifying "personal brand" as a rejection of a systemic life. For some

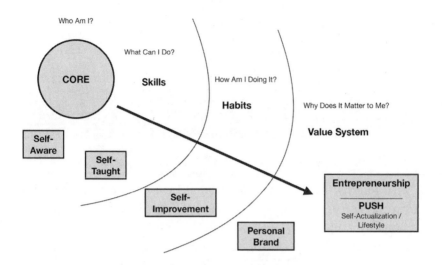

FIGURE 11.2 **Tier 2: Information Age**

entrepreneurs, it becomes a lifestyle push. "Look at me. I'm at the beach. I only worked six hours this week. I have the freedom to control my schedule and my destiny." It's easy to get puffed up when you no longer feel stuck. But with freedom comes responsibility. Those who start to see the limitations of a T2 approach realize that focusing only on oneself can't be the endgame.

DEFAULT CULTURE OR CULTURE SHAPING?

Leaders facing broken cultures they've shaped have failed themselves and their employees. And the toughest news is this: there's no quick solution for it. No overnight fix. Culture is shaped over years and decades. And if it wasn't by design, it likely isn't what the people want.

So, what's a leader to do? Look in the mirror. Get clear about how uninspiring and complacent or complicit they've become. Not that they haven't built a successful business and a high-performing team, but that they never got intentional about a culture that could sustain it all. So here we are, living in a world where people aren't getting enough empathy, appreciation, and inspiration. People in organizations are seeking more. Not just something new. They want to be part of a new work life experience.

Do you consider yourself a manager or a leader? How do your employees feel about you? How can you show up differently to inspire?

Tier 1: Manager—protects status quo (dependent on the past)

Tier 2: Leader—challenges reality (independent in the present)

Tier 3: Co-creator—shapes the ideal (interdependent into the future)

Tier 3 (T3) is the path of co-creation. It's where co-creative leaders transform culture, influencing people in simple and powerful ways and leaning into co-creation at a grassroots level to inspire others. We've seen this work. You can manifest it. Be brave together. A T3 mindset ignites this by approaching relationships as transformational and not transactional. With a T3 experience, people don't need to obsess about separating their work and personal lives anymore. There's greater fluidity between these two halves that make up a whole life. It takes deep work, but a future built in "cooperative mode" is far more rewarding when we are brave enough to do it.

Leaders who are willing to be brave with others establish a different kind of influence. A T3 approach shifts us from self to selfless. Getting intentional about culture keeps our focus where it needs to be: on people, experiences, and the greater purpose of the work.

THIS IS THE WAY: THE CO-CREATIVE CULTURE

What next steps can we take in a workplace impacted by the Great Resignation and quiet quitting? In the aftermath of a global pandemic, stacked home responsibilities, and work that seems inescapable, this is an existential moment for many. The data tells us that people aren't just leaving for more money. They're leaving toxic cultures.[1]

How do leaders address this? Not with more Ping-Pong tables and free food but by truly transforming organizational culture. In the past, culture has often been overlooked, categorized as a "soft" subject in stark contrast to the "hard" stuff of revenues, profits, and growth. Most leaders have never been intentional about culture. Some even believe they have a great culture, although their employees would disagree with that assessment. They may have said the right things, but they prioritized profits and a rapid career trajectory for themselves, while rewarding siloed "hero" behaviors. Their employees decided that they deserved better and voted with their feet.

What if the question on every leader's mind wasn't "How do I keep my people?" but rather "What do they want to feel?" "How do they want to be

THE FUTURE OF INFLUENCE

treated?" and "How can I inspire them?" What if every leader decided to shape a culture that everybody can get behind and love?

SPREADING PIXAR DUST EVERYWHERE

Look no further than Pixar. In *Creativity, Inc.*, Ed Catmull shares the power of "the Braintrust"—a collection of passionate people focused on working together with egos off the table and building blocks on the table. The Braintrust was once a small team, but Catmull says it's become "part of the DNA of the culture, and that Braintrust meetings have become the norm"—inspiring connection, collaboration, and cocreation.[2]

The Braintrust at Pixar has influenced everything from Marvel to the *Star Wars* universe. Jon Favreau was the "one Disney director who didn't just ask for advice but had gone to Pixar and experienced the Braintrust himself," Catmull shared.[3] This has led to renewed joy for *Star Wars* fans, especially those dissatisfied with movie episodes 7, 8, and 9, who love *The Mandalorian* and the undeniably cute and powerful Baby Yoda (Grogu, officially). How? Favreau built a team of directors as diverse as a band of empire-fighting bounty hunters, which included the likes of Bryce Dallas Howard, Taika Waititi, and Deborah Chow. They've selflessly created context together, rather than in silos—avoiding the mistakes of the "heads down" story-building that left J.J. Abrams and Rian Johnson forever facing online debates about the quality of their sequels. How does deep collaboration (or lack thereof) impact the larger story arc of *Star Wars*? How does this have anything to do with culture building in any domain?

The Braintrust approach is not just the hope of the future but is the re-imagining of how we engage in work and life. This involves building with pods, breaking the silence of boring meetings, and changing them from data dumps into brave conversations. This means engaging with different ideas we've never imagined, resulting in experiences, products, and services that surprise and delight us and our customers. It's the difference between a disjointed DC universe and a fully connected Marvel ecosystem—or a dispersed set of products and an intuitively connected experience. It's the difference between employees feeling detached and jaded or part of a world-changing cause, the difference between companies becoming a relic of the past or actively building the future.

SHOW UP DIFFERENTLY

Let's learn how real influence works and the abundance it creates in work and in life. Our attempts in the past to be brave may have been half-hearted. That's OK. We may have fallen back on old tactics. This is normal, even common. But we can't let fear hold us back anymore. How do we change our competitive mindset and escape the weight of a T1 shadow or the limitations of a T2 mirage? Can we overcome our desire to "be the best" and avoid the endless fight to be number one? John Nash articulated his Nobel Prize–winning theory of Governing Dynamics, which became the groundwork for how exchange happens in competition, how business games work in the market. Adam Smith's "invisible hand" of self-interest, of the greater good, was incomplete. Nash upgraded it with the notion that the collective naturally leans into *shared interest.*[4]

What if future markets won't be competitive in the same way at all? What if, to our surprise, they are far more collaborative? What if we stop asking the one-dimensional question, "Who will win?" and we start shaping the future of influence by asking, "What can we build together?"

The future can be influenced by the simple idea that personal interest and shared interest can start as a combined design amplified far beyond what we know or have ever experienced (Figure 11.3). It starts with the assumption of abundance. Everyone has what they need. We just need to unlock it. Together. We can produce far more together. The calculation is not based on the present, but on the future baked into the present: 1 + 1 = 7, or 700, or 70 million.

Co-creation unlocks infinite possibilities. How do we know? We're told the world is running out of resources when it's stocked with far more than there have ever been.[5] We're told poverty abounds, while the standard of living continues to rise higher than at any other time in human history, along with life expectancy.[6] We're told there are never enough good ideas to build the innovation the world needs, but we have hundreds of millions of people with billions of ideas just waiting to be unleashed. Fear has dimmed the light on our human experience, but co-creation is our lighthouse, helping brave ideas reach dry land where it can flourish with others.

Why hasn't this abundant future materialized fully? Because we haven't yet unleashed the full power of co-creation, the full potential of humanity.

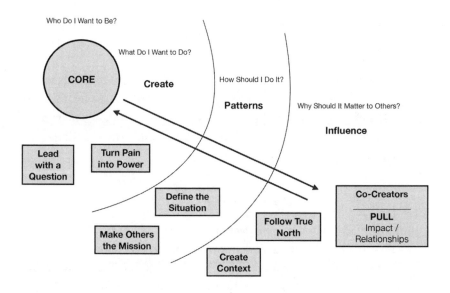

FIGURE 11.3 **Tier 3: Contextual Age**

We need a bigger vision, one that is shared, in which we turn toward and not away from each other.

These dreams can be manifested by co-creative teams in any domain. So, where do we go next? How can we influence a better, infinitely abundant future? Start by asking the quietest person in a meeting to share their private thoughts after the meeting. Sometimes your most powerful people are the ones who aren't comfortable speaking up. Don't miss great ideas because you're only listening to the loudest voices. We can start small to influence the future of our work life.

I (Chris) first learned this from my dad. When I was young, I had a lot of big ideas for inventions. I'd take them to my dad, and rather than dismiss them or laugh, he'd listen and ask, "OK, how could we actually make this?" Then we'd start sketching, and a blueprint would emerge for a multitilevel treehouse, a roller coaster, an antigravity machine (which we built with a vacuum placed upside-down, making it a kind of hovercraft—we only got a tiny bit off the ground, but it was fun). I had concepts for superhero gear, comics, book ideas, even a real electric car (well before their time) that my dad started building and dreamed of me driving to school. When we co-created together, anything seemed possible. Despite being older, grounded in the "real world," and a practical-minded engineer, my dad led with curiosity and with love.

I've since seen the best leaders do this at the best companies. They create space for brave new thinking, even if it's a bit crazy, and then they get in the trenches and build it together. This pulls people in, gives them purpose, energizes them, and fuels the future. How can we do more of this as co-creative leaders?

REAL CREDIBILITY

The future is about building connection to hearts and minds. Do others feel seen by you? How do you treat them? Recognition programs can be good, but they're not enough. Real credibility is tethered to principles, not signals propping up our own importance. Ronell Hugh has worked at storied companies like Walmart, Microsoft, Adobe, and Qualtrics, delivering the best marketing strategies with his teams. His leadership approach has given him real credibility throughout his career.

People who work with Ronell notice something different. He never gets pulled into office politics and doesn't get buried in red tape. He's open to new ways of doing things and in his words, he "doesn't drink all the company Kool-Aid." He's not afraid to challenge the status quo by asking his own leaders or coworkers when a given policy was last reviewed or updated. When the response is "This is just the way it is," he respectfully does not accept that answer. He stays more curious than rebellious, always looking to improve things.

Ronell forms deep relationships of trust with his team and asks them to challenge him. He encourages their original voices, thanking them for helping him to improve (to their shock). He continues to support team members even when they express a desire to leave for other opportunities (which also surprises them, as most leaders don't). He has inspired massive loyalty wherever he goes, along with delivering breakthrough innovations because his team members feel connected and inspired by his co-creative leadership. Here are some highlights from our conversation with Ronell:

> My first boss out of college was very authoritative, demeaning, and belittling. All the things I realized I didn't want to be, I saw

in him. That built the foundation for me to focus on people differently. All this is about people. How we treat them.

Our identities aren't the things we have, the house we live in, the cars we drive, the titles we have. Our truest identities are heaven sent, no matter where we sit or where we're from. I've always had that belief. What I believe, as a child of God. That is always going to be true. I can have the worst days or the best days, but that never changes. And I can see others that way, no matter what.

I've always been motivated to see things differently. I can't control others, but I can control how I engage with them. If I can make that positive, inclusive, where they can be open and candid, that matters. Much of what I see in the world, we tend to be passive. If you think about a buzzard circling at the carcass, that's what people do. No one wants to go down and deal with the hard conversations.

I tell people up front, "I want to be open, and working through any hard things in a meaningful way, so we can do something great." And we don't have to be passive. We can have a constructive conversation. And do incredible things together.[7]

The traditional view of credibility is that it must be earned or granted. Job titles confer credibility, held by authoritative gatekeepers, such as universities, corporate boardrooms, and other "pay to play" institutions. It's a tired old game.

The future of credibility is all about character, being principle-powered and co-creative. You become more credible with others based on how they experience you. How do you make them feel in your presence? What are you intentionally creating with others? This is the future of influence and what real credibility looks like.

Character matters. It's powerful. Take Tim Cook, for example. When the government was turning up the heat on Apple to release private data from an iPhone for a criminal investigation, Tim didn't relent. Despite pressure from the FBI, Congress, and the White House to share a "back door" into the suspect's data, Tim wouldn't give up on the principle of privacy. He knew that by giving it up to solve this one case, it would be game over. He knew if he did that, even just once, everyone's data would be in jeopardy.

Could sticking to his principles have landed him in jail? Yes. It didn't matter that he was the CEO of the most valuable company on Earth. Most people don't know this, but for those of us at Apple then, it was a scary time. We knew Tim was putting it all on the line—for his principles. His character and credibility shined through. We need more leaders of character willing to stand up for what's right, no matter the personal cost to themselves. This is real leadership, real credibility.

The future will be influenced by the power of principles—how people live, not what they say. Principles speak for themselves. The shining stars of the future will embody principles of integrity, respect, and compassion. How can we lean into this right now?

- Be willing to stand for principles, even if you stand alone.

- Notice principles in others. Shine a light on them.

- Stick to the truth. Be respectful even when you're not respected.

- Look to build others up, even if there is nothing for you to gain.

THE CO-CREATIVE MISSION

We'll only see a different future if we see it with compassionate eyes. For all the attention we give our own lives, imagine if we put the same care into creating the best relationships? Here is how we influence the future:

- **Share the vision with others.** See a future far brighter than yesterday, with no regard for personal ego and the status quo. Share the vision, manifest it with others, and reap the collective joy of bringing it all to life.

- **Show up differently.** Create a work life that enriches others' lives. Enable the best experiences as we build co-creative partnerships. When disagreements happen, find ways to continue to elevate each other. Do all you can to strengthen the team.

THE FUTURE OF INFLUENCE

- **Be credible.** Be willing to stand for principles, even if you're outnumbered. Stand in the truth, even when it's hard. Be respectful, even if it's not reciprocal. Build others up, even when there's nothing to gain.

- **Co-create the impossible.** We shape the future by doing our best work together. Never settle. Disruptive work is possible. Speak hard truths to each other, with love. Harness radical compassion.

When I (Chris) was 19, I left California and spent two years volunteering in the mountains of Peru. My friends didn't understand what I was doing. They cared about what most kids that age do: earning cash, going to college, getting a car. What I discovered in Peru surprised me. I met people who had nothing but who were happy in their relationships with family and friends. They found meaning in service.

I wrote to my dad about these experiences, and he'd share nuggets of wisdom. For 18 months, we exchanged letters. Then one day, he had a stroke and died. I lost my mentor and friend, the one I invented and built things with, the one who, when I couldn't take another step in the 100-degree heat on a 50-mile Boy Scout trek, literally carried me up a mountain—along with my backpack and his—earning himself a softball-sized blister but also my eternal respect. What would I do without him?

When I returned home from Peru, I felt a void. I sought people I could learn from, leaders, but most of all, co-creators I could build things with, things people would love. This led me to Stephen Covey and Ed Catmull, to Disney and Apple, to Ian and BraveCore, and to sharing *Brave Together* with you.

As a co-creative leader of the future, you have a mission to inspire people. This mission will be difficult. It will stretch you. This growth will lead to shared experiences you've always dreamed of having.

My dad died suddenly, so I couldn't say goodbye. Later, I was given a letter he wrote to me just before he passed. His words have inspired me ever since, and I hope they inspire you:

> Speaking of your mission—you have another one coming. A most
> difficult mission where you will be counted on to dedicate your life

to the principles you have been taught. You are like the leaven in the loaf. In the pan and rising. It will soon be time to bake your bread and bring the extraordinary flavor to the remainder of the world.

We love you and pray for you daily. Work hard and do the right things.

As Always,
Dad

What we truly believe is what we ultimately become, which is the greatest thing we can share with the world.

THE RISE OF CREATORS

To the constant beginners who sing off-key, against the beat
To those unfamiliar with convention, unmoved by rules
And reborn with every new discovery
Those open to daydreams, and night dreams, and visions, and mirages
Who can see the millions of shades of green in a field of grass
Whose days are filled with mysteries that cannot be solved with facts
You are more powerful than you think
And you are welcome here.
—Join Us. Be You. APPLE VIDEO (*Different Together*)

Singularities. They exist in black holes. In gravity, they're so intense that spacetime itself breaks down. In mathematics, a singularity is a point where a numerical object is not defined. What about in life? Singularities can happen anywhere. Where things misbehave. Where randomness takes over. They're unexpected. They disregard consistency. They're a break from order.

Peter Thiel said, "If you have a 10-year plan, you should ask: 'Why can't you do this in six months?'"[1] But we've all been handed 10 years' worth of change in six months, whether we want it or not. With all the randomness of past events, especially in recent years, it feels like the number of singularities has increased exponentially: pandemics, disasters, technology pushing us relentlessly forward. This is the paradox of our work life. We need order as a baseline to experience singularities, to see the contrast. In a time of constant upheaval, there's hope in creativity. Life is full of chaos, yet we know that chaos gives birth to art, genius, invention, and innovation.

THE CO-CREATIVE DREAM

Innovation accelerates and compounds.
—Marc Andreessen

It wasn't the singular "I." It was plural. "I," as in everyone. We are the "I" in "I have a dream." How do we know this? When 250,000 people gathered in Washington, DC, in the summer heat of August 28, 1963, with millions tuning in, change was in the air. The promise of freedom, made 100 years before, had not been fully delivered. What came next some might call a singularity event. It came at a time when tensions were high. A one-of-a-kind speech for all of humankind.

Martin Luther King Jr. was waiting to give the address of a lifetime, the culmination of years of fighting, imprisonment, death in the streets, and unfulfilled hopes for massive change. Dr. King stood up and gathered himself as the TV cameras pointed at him. Everyone was waiting on edge. He'd done plenty of speaking before. He knew what to do. But when Dr. King got to the podium, as the crowd roared, he paused. His original speech had the right themes, but in real time, it was transformed into something else. The venerable gospel singer Mahalia Jackson, whose voice had inspired a nation, stood on the steps of the Lincoln Memorial with the core group. Her songs had reached the Billboard charts, including "Move on Up a Little Higher." She was about to do just that. She shouted, "Tell them about the dream, Martin. Tell them about the dream!" And that's when he launched into "I have a dream."[2]

Dr. King's prepared speech read: "And so even though we face the difficulties of today and tomorrow, I still have a dream. It is a dream deeply rooted in the American dream . . ." But he put aside his notes to improvise his famous speech.

Jackson co-created a moment with Dr. King. It was in response to her that he shared his beautiful dream of a future where we'd all be judged "not by the color of our skin, but by the content of our character," where "all the children of God" would converge.

This moment changed history. It fired up the imagination of the nation and galvanized a people to action. That dream has yet to be fulfilled. As we look back, the story is often told as though it were just Dr. King's dream. But it was Jackson's dream, too, as it is ours as well. We're drawn to it. As a freedom-powering proposition, it offers the answer to ending all conflicts. And this shared vision was born out of co-creation.

This dream describes a brave future that continues to live in our imaginations. We hang on to the hope that it will become fully realized one day. It's up to each of us to start living this dream.

What does this have to do with singularities? If people had let the status quo or structure of the system go unchallenged, we would never have had a Civil Rights Movement. Or a Lincoln Memorial. Or a country rooted in principles of independence, life, liberty, and the pursuit of happiness. We would never have been given the infinitely powerful gift of "I have a dream." There would have been no chance for this radical yet simple idea to stir each of us to action, inspiring us to treat each other with dignity and be brave together in countless ways. This is how progress happens. True principles become the bedrock of powerful movements.

HOW TO MOVE THE MOVEMENT

It looks like work to them, but it feels like play to me.
—NAVAL RAVIKANT

As human beings, we are designed as creators. We have a *Creative Propensity*. We understand the need for structure but refuse to be limited by it. While structure may give us the comfort of predictability, we hate being boxed in by the status quo. People are rejecting the companies, leaders, and cultures that are constraining and diminishing their creative identity. And they're doing it at the most rapid pace in history.

The status quo doesn't work anymore. Everything feels like a singularity now. And leaders who shape the future are those who embrace creativity. Nolan Bushnell, visionary, inventor of the Atari, and author of the book *Shaping the Future of Education*, shared with us that leaders can't lead the future based on rules-based thinking.[3] People are seeking creative autonomy. They also need to be supported, not shamed for making mistakes. The new pursuit is progress over perfection.

Imagination creates the future, not knowledge. Creativity is informed by research and study, but it doesn't emerge from staring at Excel sheets all day. It comes from dreams, by seeing what is possible when countless voices say otherwise. Singularities can be manifested when dreams are shared.

Creativity is the last frontier . . . automation over a long enough period of time will replace every non-creative job . . . that's great news. That means that all of our basic needs are taken care of, and what remains for us is to be creative, which is really what every human wants.
—NAVAL RAVIKANT[4]

Creative propensity is our destiny. We've been put on this Earth to create and co-create. What if we built a solid foundation with the killer combination of shared dreams and innovating together? What kind of co-creative results would emerge?

We can choose to go solo and fail, or we can create as a team. We can let fear of artificial intelligence (AI) turn into an "us versus them"—the never-ending "man versus machine" battle—or we can build things together. In reality, the dystopian "robot takeover" narrative has been highly exaggerated. The robots are already here. They've been here for a while running different parts of our lives with incredible efficiency and ease. Machines have already hijacked the role of the manual worker. As AI takes over more knowledge work, creativity and co-creation will become our hidden superpower. AI is even encroaching into the arts now, with image generators winning prizes—an unthinkable prospect even a few years ago.

We've personally tested AI image generators and produced beautiful art. These visual information engines produce the final outcomes, but humans prompt the unique vision and give the AI creative direction. It takes a series of iterations to co-create effectively with AI, but it can be done.

We can embrace the fact that AI can accelerate our creations. Instead of feeling threatened, how can we use these tools to amplify our role as creators? We can build our future with the skills we have while embracing the learning curve of emerging technology. It's a beautiful combination. Technology can help us unleash the future of co-creation. These tools have been democratized. We live in a time when anyone can develop new capabilities and set up a digital business in a matter of days. It's amazing.

The future is co-creative. That's reassuring in a world facing massive change, where fear sneaks up on us and we feel lost and paralyzed by the proliferation of all that is new. But we can be brave together and lean into creativity. We can chart a different path. Angela Ahrendts, former SVP of

Apple Retail and former CEO of Burberry, said, "The acceleration and the pace of change and what AI will spawn isn't dissimilar to everything that came from the iPhone. We can't begin to fathom all the innovations that will come from this."[5]

Rapid change and radical disruption are the new norm. AI will be supplanting many roles and tasks. But this is great news for those willing to lean into creativity. Creatives are uniquely positioned to lead the future with passion, empathy, and intuition—which AI does not have. Ahrendts added, "We are going to be leaning on the creatives to look ahead and to run things. We need to amplify human attributes in an artificial world."[6]

What if we harnessed the power of intention with our Creative Propensity? What if creators didn't go their separate ways? What if we were drawn to each other's ideas and creations? Technology could help speed up these intersections and amplify our interactions.

Some people imagine the future as a gig economy filled with personal brands. While this trend may continue, a world of millions of people working in silos is not the future. We see creators emerging in the workplace, and entrepreneurs leaning into co-creative work. We see brave leaders tapping into their creativity. More and more people are moving on from being influencers to becoming creators. Influencers try to grab attention. Creators build with intention. Influencers try to impress others. Creators move others.

Creativity resides in each of us. The role of a creator is to intuit and manifest the best possible singularities. Here are four ways a leader can kick-start their *Creative Propensity*:

1. **Be playful.** Explore creating something out of nothing. Bring the best out of people.

2. **Be curious.** Lead with questions, not answers. Imagine what can emerge.

3. **Solve problems.** Get energized by addressing issues using your talents and abilities. Find ways to activate them. Focus on making a difference with others.

4. **Be a magnet.** Don't push. Pull others into your creative work, based on who you are and what you create.

ANIMATING THE FUTURE

How has an animation program that was nonexistent just a few decades ago risen to become the most Emmy Award–winning university program in the world—the feeder for Pixar, DreamWorks, Netflix, and Disney talent? The Animation Department at Brigham Young University (BYU) is a story of silo-busting, horizonal-influencing co-creation. Most animation programs set out to give students a strictly technical education, but BYU took a different approach: first, inspire them to build great teams—and then great movies. This has led to pure magic making, helping creators rise together.

At Pixar, BYU alum Meredith Moulton worked with her team on the movie *Soul*, the story of a jazz-playing Black man who taps into his passion. "The clothing in *Soul* was almost its own character," she wrote. "The style and technology developed for this film allowed it to be a lot more detailed than previous Pixar films. We were able to render cloth down to the individual weave of the fabric which added a lot of visual fidelity."[7]

To achieve this level of authenticity in the rendering of the texture of Black hair and the richness of Black skin tones, they harnessed the power of an internal "cultural braintrust" at Pixar. Black employees shared insights to shape the best visual experience. Character grooming artist Ben Porter, who benefitted from that braintrust, shared, "Those are things I never thought about and wouldn't have even known. It was exciting to get those specific insights, and it felt like a whole new world."[8]

They developed a story that takes us to the "Great Before," where unborn souls wait to come to Earth. They wanted to make the place feel real, but they also wanted it to feel ethereal. They shaped a film that asks deep questions, discusses "scary spiritual ideas," and explores the meaning of life in a commercial setting, of all places. Team member Jonathan Page said, "That was unlike anything else we were used to doing. We had to rethink most of the controls that we provided for animation and develop the system from the ground up." Page worked on the model and rigging of characters for that part of the film.[9]

"It is cool that Pixar is willing to have that dialogue with the world about what do you think the meaning of your life is?" Pixar character shader Jonathan Hoffman said. "I don't see a lot of studios doing that, so I feel privileged to have worked on something as daring as this."[10]

A co-creative dialogue with the world? Wow. By being a part of Pixar's creative culture and using the braintrust approach, Moulton found meaning in producing Pixar's first Black lead character. "As a mixed Black person, having the chance to work on Pixar's first movie that was centered around Black people was a very cool experience. I didn't see a lot of media, especially animation, featuring people that looked like me growing up, so it's especially cool for me to have the opportunity to help create more diverse animated content," Moulton said.[11]

Soul received a 95 percent on the Tomatometer and an 88 percent audience score on Rotten Tomatoes, excelling at the box office. The former BYU students who worked on it are grateful for their BYU education. "BYU fosters a great sense of collaboration, and they expose you to a lot of different disciplines within the industry, which not only helped me hone in on what I wanted to specialize in, but also has been very helpful in doing my job," Moulton wrote.[12]

The teams that come out of the BYU Animation program continue to animate one hit after another through co-creation. When we build things together that inspire us and others, we grow exponentially. Our lives become a proclamation to the world that anything is possible.

THE MISFIT MOVEMENT

What sets you apart can sometimes feel like a burden, and it's not.
And a lot of the time, it's what makes you great.
—EMMA STONE

Misfit
noun ('mɪsˌfit)
a person not suited in behavior or attitude to a particular social environment
something that does not fit or fits badly
verb (ˌmɪs'fit) **-fits, -fitting** *or* **-fitted**
(intransitive)
to fail to fit or be fitted[13]

People are the essential building blocks of the future. But we've felt categorized, treated like things, and valued only for results. There's been an awakening. The experience of working from home gave us a new view of our relationship with work: our work should fit nicely into our home life, and not the other way around. This was a massive shift in our brains and our hearts, and we'll never be the same again.

On top of that, we all feel—more than ever before—the deep need to connect, to belong, and to build meaningful things with others. Not in the name of ego, self-promotion, or career progression but in the name of joy, togetherness, and abundance.

The term "misfit" is for both one who looks at life differently and one whom life looks at differently. And yet, misfits are seen as movers and shakers, movement makers, future shapers. They get excited about being a part of things that matter. They want to use their gifts to build something bigger than themselves. They want their ideas to take on a life of their own with others. But these same people are sick and tired of being sick and tired.

A misfit could be a creative person who doesn't want to be stuck doing boring work. They ask, "Why are things done this way?" A misfit is an employee who no longer subscribes to the rewards games of their employer. A misfit is a leader who leads from the heart and treats people the way they want to be treated. They are seen by others in the company as rule breakers and anomalies.

Misfits have the proclivity to connect the dots, to see the world from different angles. Have you ever questioned why the energy you spend working for someone else feels like time wasted? Have you ever thought that you've been living inside someone else's dream? Perhaps someone else's dream equals the box people talk about. So now when you hear the phrase "think outside the box," it may take on another meaning.

Life isn't meant to be linear. When something doesn't seem right, it's because we've started to see things differently. It's as if our minds have been unplugged from the Matrix. Joseph Campbell said, "If you can see your path laid out in front of you step by step, you know it's not your path. Your own path you make with every step you take. That's why it's your path."

For some, the comfort in the known is good enough. Ignorance is bliss. For misfits like us, we prefer Campbell's notion: "Follow your bliss and the universe will open doors for you where there were only walls."

Misfits are getting wiser. We're seeing the possibilities, starting to use our creative voices, becoming brave enough to be more authentic and honest.

We're looking for brave leaders and people to build and co-create a more meaningful work life together.

Leaders: Culture is made up of people and experienced by people. Seek to understand them. Be a part of them, not above them. Notice their strengths and challenges. See how to integrate yours. Find ways to help misfits see themselves as creators. Don't just measure their performance. Recognize their potential. Measure yourself by your contributions to the culture.

THE DISRUPTIVE POWER OF MISFITS

How do we harness the power of misfits? After Pixar had succeeded with blockbusters like *Toy Story* and *A Bug's Life*, they could've stayed content by sticking with what worked—in-house directors, a proven moviemaking formula, rinse and repeat—but they didn't. They found a misfit director who'd made *Iron Giant* and other cult classics, Brad Bird, a guy who loves to disrupt things. And they challenged Brad to disrupt them.

They tasked Brad to make something great. Where did he start? By pulling together the best, proven Pixar talent? Nope. He tapped the rebels, the ones working at the edges, doing stuff other people thought was crazy. He united the misfits and the creators, like the ones tinkering away in some back office, trying to 3D animate human hair, something the industry had already deemed "impossible."

Brad formed this band of misfits, and they set about to create something insanely great, something that would meet Brad's high bar of filmmaking: "We make films that we ourselves would want to see and then hope other people would want to see it."[14] They made *The Incredibles*, a movie about a superhero family that not only delivered a wonderful story and relatable characters, with plenty of fun, but also advanced technical achievement (such as with the rendition of hair). Could this have been accomplished in a static culture, one that maintains the status quo?

> *The breakthrough innovations come when the tension*
> *is greatest and the resources are most limited. That's when*
> *people are actually a lot more open to rethinking the*
> *fundamental way they do business.*
> —CLAYTON M. CHRISTENSEN[15]

When Dell faced some of its worst days, after falling from grace as the lead PC maker, employee morale was down. The stock price was in freefall, and everything felt like a struggle. Initially, the company became strictly operations focused: cutting costs, executing faster, delivering results, squeezing all the creativity right out.

When I (Chris) got to Dell, I felt that void. People were tired. They were waiting for permission to do bigger things. Together with Gideon Hyacinth and Heather Tucker, we formed a team and set about with a different vision: we called it GenNext, a platform for connecting next-generation thinkers and innovators. We launched a think tank and ideation event we called *GameChangers*, inviting thousands of employees to join forces, across functions—from finance and marketing to product development and engineering. We offered them coaching, helped them form teams, and empowered them to innovate and do world-changing things. We told them this was their time, their chance to bring crazy ideas to life—together. They had all the permission they needed.

After several weeks of building, they came back with innovative plans they pitched to executives, shaping the future. It turns out that people who'd been at the company for 10 or 20 years had just as great ideas as those who were new. A billion-dollar app emerged from that work, along with hundreds of millions in savings in new solutions. All because we simply asked and then empowered people.

When we brought the work to founder and CEO Michael Dell, he couldn't hold back his enthusiasm, or his pocketbook. He funded the next $5 million in support. The GenNext group has grown to over 5,000 members in 32 countries, and the *GameChangers* approach lives on at Dell. The spirit of this work continues to produce powerful new ideas, shaping a different culture, one that's helping take the company to the next level in innovation.

"'We have a lot of smart people here with a lot of great ideas, and we just needed to give them a platform,' explained Vanessa Henry, a core member of Central Texas GenNext and part of the *GameChangers* competition team for four years."[16]

In one *GameChangers* season, more than 600 participants from 28 countries presented in four categories: Legacy of Good, Cognitive Technologies, IT Transformation, and an open category. Seventy Dell leaders and employees from across the globe volunteered to judge each team on presentation quality, financial impact, feasibility, innovation, and how well the solution addressed the business issue. Dell Alliance Manager Christine Sabatino said, "I love that we look from the ground up to come up with ideas and don't just rely on our executives. Dell really looks for innovation from their employees with the chance to start a grassroots project."[17]

They've even developed *GameChangers* University, a business boot camp in financial acumen, go-to-market strategies, market analysis, and presentation skills. Part of the design of *GameChangers* is to take the concepts to interested organizations, so they can have the chance to be fully executed. Stefanie Nelson, who joined one of the winning teams, shared: "I almost didn't sign up for the challenge. . . . But I took the chance and, as well as winning, I worked with four intelligent, driven, and passionate people whom I wouldn't have otherwise had the opportunity to meet."[18]

Mikhail Tolstoy said that *GameChangers* impressed upon him that "Dell is ready to spend money and, more importantly, time to work with you if you reach out."[19] All because we co-created a space for brave people to innovate. They were brave enough to ideate and incubate the future, brave enough to challenge the status quo. What can we learn from this?

1. Harness misfit energy by helping them see themselves as creators.

2. Bring people together in new ways to build brave solutions.

3. Give people permission to change things in big ways.

4. Offer real support and resources to make innovation happen.

MOVE, DON'T PROVE

We keep moving forward, opening new doors, and doing new things, because we're curious and curiosity keeps leading us down new paths.
—WALT DISNEY

Somewhere along the line, content became a volume play for creatives and brands to prove their importance: to be seen, to get more followers or customers, to generate sales. Gary Vaynerchuk said, "More content, more brand. That's how you grow." But is a stuff-producing engine useful to everybody else?

Most of what we're fed (news, posts, videos) is designed to prove it to us. Show us. Tell us. Overwhelm us with data. Yet facts and opinions have blurred into one. The noise makes it hard to think, making it harder than ever to listen to our own heart. We talk about meditation as the way to unplug, to stop what we're doing and hit a reset button away from the typical flow of life. While that practice will always be needed for our well-being, what if we practiced meditative living? Meditative living means being grounded in principles as we go from moment to moment, being present. What if we could move through life with better intention to separate inspiration from distraction in real time?

In previous chapters, we covered the ways we act to prove our authority, prove that we're right while others are wrong. When our goal is to prove, we stay static in our position. There is no growth. What if we started to see ourselves as creators and co-creators that move people through inspiring messages and challenges, building experiences that lead to action—even for ourselves. What if the future of leadership and the role of creator has more to do with moving, not proving?

HOW TO SPOT CREATORS
IN YOUR CULTURE

Connecting with creators starts with seeing them, noticing how they work, where they are, and amplifying them. How do you identify a creator?

- **Creators are brave in ways others aren't.** They take life on as a calling to challenge the status quo, not to eradicate structure but to improve it. They don't fall back on rules but seek to redefine them, only when needed. They have a bias toward dynamism, energy, and action.

- **Creators understand change takes time, and it takes a team.** They approach people and life in unique ways. They are patient with the process. Creators see one-on-one conversations as an exchange where two-way openness creates the potential to change minds. They consider these interactions the best way to build their influence. They empower others without letting ego get in the way and find ways to connect the dots.

- **Creators express their love of life.** They show that love underlies their co-creative patterns. They love people. They don't see them for who they want them to be but for who they are. They love creativity. They don't try to force the world to conform to what they want. They contribute to cultures and invite others to do the same.

> *We need leaders not in love with money*
> *but in love with justice.*
> *Not in love with publicity but in love with humanity.*
> —Dr. Martin Luther King Jr.

- **Creators pull people in.** They aren't pushing their wares at people. They're setting aside time for real conversations, heartfelt explorations of truth, and meaningful experiences that help others feel seen and heard. They're natural leaders who carve out unconventional paths. As they press forward, others get energized witnessing the progress they make, the passion they feel, and the purpose they form. Creators become a model for others to follow.

- **Creators aren't interested in competing with others.** They see every opportunity as co-creative. They hike the mountains of life with others, as a team. They find those in need and serve them. They build a selfless vision into the patterns of their lives. They embody who they wish to be now, and with patience, they intentionally seek to become their future every day. They look for creative patterns with others.

> *If you want to go fast, go alone.*
> *If you want to go far, go together.*
> —African proverb

CREATORS CAN BECOME CO-CREATORS

In the next few chapters, we will be presenting the meta principles that will help you Become the Future. We'll start with the action principle Define the Situation, do a deep dive to understand the purpose principle Create Context, and then show you how to connect dots for co-creation with the help of the alignment principle Follow True North.

Here are some things you can do now to unlock the creator inside you and embrace the idea of co-creation, leaning into becoming the future:

Own your creativity. You are an original. There is no one in history or the future of the world who is quite like you. No one with your exact talents, gifts, and powers. Bring it to life by owning it. Embrace your identity, knowing you already belong.

Be open to building together. Most artists create art for themselves and then wonder why they struggle to be successful. Building with others brings another kind of success. It's not about ego. It's about creating moments where we shape the future as one, confronting our real challenges together, transforming workplace cultures and how we approach our work life, being urgent with patience as we learn how to collaborate and co-create in powerful ways, and accepting the messiness of the moment.

Be brave enough to build original. This isn't the time to shrink. We can all do this. It starts with you and being brave. Marianne Williamson said in *A Return to Love*, "Our deepest fear is not that we are inadequate. Our deepest fear is that we are powerful beyond measure. It is our light, not our darkness that most frightens us. We ask ourselves, 'Who am I to be brilliant, gorgeous, talented, fabulous?' Actually, who are you *not* to be?"

Connect with creators. Too many leaders have failed at innovation by looking to build empires, in silos. They push others away because of fear. The future will take its shape because of co-creation. Seek heart-to-heart connection. Help creators feel seen, and value their contributions. Building with vulnerability and empathy creates unstoppable teams that can turn dreams into reality.

CHAPTER 13

DEFINE THE SITUATION

The Action Principle

Expect only the best from life and take action to get it.
—CATHERINE PULSIFER

It was a dark time. He was depressed, a laughingstock, afraid of being mocked in the city, on the verge of getting fired from the 49ers. Sitting on the bench behind the best quarterback in the NFL, Joe Montana, he'd wondered if his time would ever come. When Joe got injured, it was Steve Young's turn to lead the team. He felt the pressure. Steve was trapped in Joe's shadow. He played terribly. Would he get cut? He felt like he couldn't live up to the fans' expectations. Steve never felt respected in the locker room, and now he was losing his confidence and self-worth. He told us, "I was in a huge hole, a hole I thought others had dug for me. The expectations, the comparisons, the unfairness, the public outcry for my head. I was feeling victimized, with no control. Who wouldn't be depressed, bitter, and miserable?"

What did Steve do next? He felt like he was days away from getting fired. He got on an airplane and found himself sitting next to Stephen Covey, author of the personal growth classic *The 7 Habits of Highly Effective People*. When they started talking, Steve shared his problems—the struggle, the feeling that everyone hated him—explaining in detail how he was the victim. Steve unloaded "every bit of misery he could." After taking it all in, Covey said, "Wow, that's heavy. I feel that."[1] Then Covey asked Steve if it would be all right if he asked him a few questions. Steve nodded. It went like this:

Covey: How's the owner?

Steve: He's great. He takes care of the players. Really treats us well.

Covey: He sounds great, I'd love to meet him. How's the coach?

Steve: He's great. The best coach around.

Covey: What about Joe? Isn't he still on the team? Couldn't he mentor you?

Steve: Yeah, but *that's* the problem. Everybody's comparing me to him.

Covey's mastery of the art of listening and being a coach was on full display. Steve could feel his own attitude and thoughts shifting. He started to question his previous feelings about being the victim. Then Covey said, "I travel the world, Steve, looking for platforms that organizations have created for humans to iterate, to find out how good they can be. When I see those platforms, I amplify them. Steve, I've got to be honest with you. Of all the places I've traveled in the world, all the places I've been, and all the stories I've heard, I think that the greatest platform that I've maybe ever seen is the one that you have. So, I guess the question is: How good do you think you can get?"[2]

That question hit Steve in his core. It shifted his perspective. It changed everything. He would stop being afraid. His life became a quest, an incredible adventure. How good could he get? After he got off the plane, he couldn't sleep that night. Steve looked at his training and preparation differently. He would get up at 5 a.m. to get on the field to practice. His approach with his own team started to change. Rather than stew in fear during the pregame window, he ran across the field to thank Troy Aikman, competing star quarterback of the Dallas Cowboys. "Troy, I'm so glad you're here. Because you're the best, and I'm on a quest to see how good I can get, so I'm excited to learn from you." The Cowboy players who saw this were stunned. They stared at Steve as he headed back to his side of the field. Who does that? Steve was now looking at all his relationships with new eyes.

Fast-forward a year. Steve Young became the MVP Super Bowl quarter-back. He learned from his coach, his teammates, and even Joe Montana (his former "rival"). He took action. He got better. Steve upgraded his mindset. He changed the way he saw his situation. And he co-created success with his team.

We're going to explore how people can manifest their best life and leadership by owning the quality of their mindset and actions. Too many people react to situations, letting circumstances define them. Being co-creative helps us get out of the default situation in our lives. We can stop being scared and acting helpless. We can start living with intention by activating our principles for the future.

Do you want to change the shape of your life? Start by changing the shape of your day. Do you want to build the best culture with those you love? Define the Situation.

GETTING THE JOB FROM JOBS

Put a dent in the universe.
—STEVE JOBS

If you were looking to get hired by your dream leader, what would you do? Randy Nelson knows. He wanted to join Steve Jobs's band of rebels in what would become the rebirth of Apple, at NeXT. Randy took stock of his skills: juggling, technology, some coding, and people. He loved these most, and NeXT had it all. It was the place to be for developers, misfits, and rebels. Everyone wanted to work there. How could he possibly get a job with them?

Imagine putting together a package with your résumé in a manila envelope with "Attention: Steve Jobs" written on it. Would that be enough? No. Admins and secretaries—even with the best intentions—could easily intercept it, read it, and throw it away. What about making the package more intriguing by adding a set of red felt juggling balls? Interesting. But it could still end up in the trash. What if you took the whole package and shrink-wrapped it, like a product? For the boss who loves perfect packages. Who would dare aim to surprise and delight Steve Jobs? Randy Nelson. He'd interacted with Steve before. As part of The Flying Karamazov Brothers juggling act, he'd even performed at an Apple product launch celebration. He knew

Steve would make the connection to who he was. The beautiful, shrink-wrapped package with red felt juggling balls had a tactile look that seemed to beg for you to touch them. And his résumé in the manila envelope came with a letter making his best case for a job.[3]

The package got to Steve—and Randy got his dream job at NeXT. Later, Randy became dean of Pixar University. Then he went on to lead Apple University. Randy had an insanely great career. He made a dent in the universe, and it all started with a bold vision. He Defined the Situation by taking brave actions for his future.

BE LIKE WATER

Be like water making its way through cracks.
Do not be assertive, but adjust to the object,
and you shall find a way around or through it. If nothing
within you stays rigid, outward things will disclose
themselves. Empty your mind, be formless, shapeless, like
water. If you put water into a cup, it becomes the cup.
You put water into a bottle, and it becomes the bottle. You
put it in a teapot, it becomes the teapot. Now, water can
flow, or it can crash. Be water, my friend.
—BRUCE LEE

In a world filled with conflict, we need to become more fluid—like water—more accepting, more open. We can stick to our principles, just like water doesn't change its chemical state. We can flow with others.

How can we become more fluid in situations? We react when we're not prepared. When we're afraid, we say something we end up regretting. We can become emotional in different situations. It's natural, part of life. Suppressing emotion or pretending not to be sad or angry won't help us. Anger is an indication that a boundary has been crossed, or there's a breach of our values.

When faced with a difficult or stressful situation, it's easy to react. But it won't lead to what we want. It can make things go from bad to worse. We can slip from disappointment to sadness to anger in seconds. Anger can morph into rage. Rage can result in alienation from friends, jail time, and generational trauma in families. We've got to stop it before it starts.

To lead our best lives, we need to own our emotions. It's not about elimi-nating our emotions; it's about being responsible for them.

We're influenced by our emotions, whether we like it or not. They're shaping our work life experiences all the time, in what we do and in what we say. How we feel is how we show up with our team. Are we excited about our work? Are we facing lingering pain from the past? As we explored in the Turn Pain into Power chapter, we can reframe our painful situations by seeing things differently, seeing ourselves and others differently.

Defining the Situation is about taking things a step further by being brave with and owning our actions. Our choices matter in life. It all starts with our intentions. We choose how we respond and then we act. If we're afraid, we may react in thoughtless ways that can carry lasting consequences. When we are prepared, we open our minds and hearts to the best ways we can influence a situation by design, not by default. We can Define the Situation anywhere, facing whatever we face—financial struggles, relationship pains, or even toxic work cultures. If we don't Define the Situation in princi-pled ways, then we run the risk of situations defining us.

In the space between stimulus (what happens) and how we respond, lies our freedom to choose. Ultimately, this power to choose is what defines us as human beings. We may have limited choices, but we can always choose.
—STEPHEN COVEY

THE WORLD TURNED UPSIDE DOWN

It was late February 2020. I (Ian) was on a much-needed vacation on the island of Oahu, Hawaii, where I went to college and met my beautiful wife nearly two decades earlier. The timing for a break couldn't have been bet-ter. Little did I know that my work was about to get a whole lot crazier, that I would be tested as a leader beyond anything I'd ever experienced.

On January 21, 2020, the first known Covid-19 case in the United States was reported in the state of Washington, a person who had recently returned from Wuhan, China. There were growing indications that limited person-to-person spread was happening at the time. It was still unclear how the virus was spreading. By February 29, 2020, Public Health of Seattle and King County confirmed the first coronavirus-related death in Washington.

Dozens of patients with symptoms were reported in Kirkland, Washington, at a Life Care Center.

My wife and I flew back to San Jose, California, on March 3. As I got back into the flow of work, I watched the news closely. By March 4, the death toll in Washington state reached 10 people. I wondered how this might impact our experience in California. My mind was racing.[4]

At our facility, we helped the sick and elderly recover from health setbacks or elective surgeries. Watching what took place at the Life Care Center, I had nothing but compassion for my fellow healthcare workers. I couldn't imagine what those initial days were like, getting blindsided by the unknown, having staff, patients, and families in sheer panic, hit by sudden sickness and death.

I called for an impromptu all-staff meeting on my first day back from vacation. The team needed to be ready with our response. I was transparent. With an urgent tone, I pleaded with the facility staff to get their houses in order, to do their best to ensure they had a few weeks of food and basic supplies for their families. My reason: If they had peace of mind that their families were taken care of, we would have more than enough able staff to continue caring for patients even if things got bad.

That night when I got home, my wife and I went to a few of the major retailers in our city. An hour before midnight, we were practically the only customers in the last store. Things hadn't hit the fan yet. We walked up to the cashier with two fully loaded shopping carts. She looked at us and asked, "Is everything OK?" Little did she know that in the weeks to follow, the supplies at her store would be depleted and all the basics would be in hot demand (including toilet paper). This was the calm before the storm.

In 2019, our healthcare team had already adopted the theme Define the Situation as our mantra for the year. We used DTS as shorthand. I'll never forget how often people came into my office to describe a particular problem or challenge. Nine times out of 10 the team member would be in the middle of a sentence, and then they'd stop and realize they just needed to Define the Situation.

When we fail to act or avoid hard things, situations start defining us. Facing our problems early and often allows us to get a handle on outcomes. Over the years, our facility has received great reviews online. But on occasion, as a team, we experienced a handful of negative reviews from disgruntled family members. Whenever a review came in that seemed unfair or was emotionally charged, we'd do our best to identify the patient situation.

Often, the source of these reviews struggled to communicate effectively with us, or they just didn't have enough face time to get to know our staff. So they formed strong opinions. Other times, people had unrealistic expectations of what we could accommodate. No matter what we would do, it wasn't good enough. Either way, if we didn't identify ways to improve the relationship or failed to communicate early enough, there would be a misunderstanding.

Whenever we received an unfavorable review, we'd Define the Situation by reaching out immediately. We'd show deep empathy and aim to improve these difficult relationships. It was the right thing to do. This led to people deleting or changing their reviews.

How does this relate to the pandemic? This theme prepared our team to respond to the tornado of issues Covid-19 brought. The Bay Area of California became a hotbed for waves of outbreaks and a viral spread. By the second week of March 2020, we stopped visitations. It was hard. Families were upset. We implemented this policy before any mandates came out ordering us to do so.

Our nursing staff gave daily reports over the phone to designated family members. We had multiple tablets so patients could video chat with loved ones. We did the best we could. Families later shared how appreciative they were that we took such swift action. They felt it was part of what kept their loved ones safe. Over the course of the pandemic, the visitation protocols became more accommodating, which was good for everyone.

Once the "stay at home" order went into effect, only essential workers were allowed to report to work. The highways were empty. The feeling was unsettling. As the Covid case numbers grew exponentially in California, the hospital protocols drastically changed. I noticed large white tents staged in hospital parking lots screening people for entry. It all felt like a dystopian movie, one I wish I could've walked out of.[5]

Following New York's lead, California hospitals attempted to send Covid patients to post-acute settings like ours for recovery. This was a reaction on their part out of fear. A hospital setting had all the necessary resources, yet they didn't want to take responsibility for patient recovery. This was morally wrong and irresponsible. As a team, we took a united stand that we would not put our elderly population at risk. So we pushed back. We refused to admit Covid patients in those early months. Later in the pandemic, the healthcare community established better coordination and time frames for recovery that we participated in.

What became very apparent was that no one was prepared. A good example was the struggle to maintain personal protective equipment (PPE) supplies. The county became a hub for these donations and distributed them to healthcare providers from their emergency stockpile, but these supplies were not freely shared. The county established a gatekeeping system to control the flow of supplies. Providers had to file a formal request.

Many of the healthcare facilities in the area never received the aid they needed simply because they hadn't asked or they waited until they had an outbreak to make a request. We took the opposite approach. First, we took advantage of every private donation opportunity. We were also proactive in filling out a requisition form weekly, so we had a supply order that was ready for pickup every week. We created a working rhythm with the county and built a rapport with the shipping and receiving personnel. We sent the same two to three people from our facility to pick up these orders every time. The county personnel recognized their faces and became familiar with our facility in their system. We no longer got grilled to justify our request.

We Defined the Situation. And we created our own emergency stockpile throughout the year. Our team smiled when the county called us out of the blue one particular week to see if we still needed our routine order. They'd anticipated our call, and we must've been too busy that week. Other facilities were not getting these kinds of calls. Establishing these relationships and our consistency with seeking supplies from the county enabled us to get our hands on the highly sought-after N95 masks when many of our vendors failed to deliver what we needed in terms of PPE.

We heard countless heart-wrenching stories that spring and summer: multiple outbreaks at other facilities in the area, unspeakable deaths. We saw the impact this had on our colleagues who ran other facilities. While we had some employees test positive at times, we sent them home as soon as they had symptoms or were diagnosed even if they were asymptomatic. We did our best to reduce the risk.

Housekeeping made the valiant effort to disinfect the facility daily. It was taxing work. Our staff's dedication to the infection control screening measures was key. We took these mitigation strategies seriously. It all helped keep the facility safe. It helped Define the Situation. By the grace of God, we didn't have a single patient test positive until the end of 2020, eight months after the pandemic in the United States first started.

It was Christmas morning 2020. My family had just finished opening presents, with torn wrapping paper covering our floor. That's when I received the call. My family knew the drill. They'd been so supportive throughout. And our team responded. We showed up at the facility on Christmas day, knowing we wouldn't get that time back with our families. It took us all day and well into the night. The staff scheduled for that day needed the full team's support. We converted half of the facility into a quarantine "red zone." Half of the patients ended up testing positive. We followed the protocol. We were prepared. It was still incredibly hard. Some staff panicked; many were afraid. Our unity and resolve to do the right thing kept us going. I am proud to say we didn't need to send any patients to the hospital and there were zero patient deaths during this outbreak. Zero. Another miracle. Some patients had fevers our nurses and doctors monitored closely that only lasted a day or two, while the rest of the patients remained asymptomatic.

To this day, I am still so proud of our staff, people who were brave together and helped Define the Situation. To the department heads who may be reading this, you know who you are. Thank you for your dedication. Thank you for showing up each day, for lifting one another up during a dark time. Your light shined bright, making a difference in the lives of those who needed your help the most. It was a special time, and it was an honor to be among you. I will never forget this team and the brave things we did together.

In late January 2021, we received a surprise visit from a pair of investigators. One came from the State of California Department of Public Health in Sacramento; the other from the CDC. This was just days after our red zone was cleared, with patients integrating back into the rest of the facility. At first, we were concerned. What did we do wrong? Were they here to impose some type of citation or monetary penalty? This is what you come to expect from regulators over the years. To the contrary. We started to breathe better once we found out they were there to learn from us.

The pandemic data indicated only a handful of nursing home facilities as anomalies across the nation, outliers with few or even zero positive cases or patient deaths related to Covid-19. We were one of them. They said, "We don't understand. Santa Clara County and the San Jose region were considered a hot zone during the height of the pandemic. All of the surrounding hospitals and facilities similar to yours had multiple outbreaks and patient fatalities. What did your team do differently?"

That was a hard question to answer. It's not like we worked harder than other facilities. We cared a lot about our patients and our coworkers, but so do the vast majority of healthcare workers at most facilities. It's a caring industry. The one thing that stood out was our co-creative culture: how we worked together. We trusted one another. Our staff trusted their supervisors to such a degree that they would call to inform them of symptoms they or members of their household were experiencing without fear of reprimand. We were able to navigate each scenario that would arise. We also shared the burden and responsibilities. Our culture wasn't characterized by top-down authority. We worked together and acted as one.

The regulators couldn't understand that our staff was guided by principles. It didn't fit into their data set or matrix, but it didn't make it any less true. A principle like Define the Situation is founded on a value system. We had an excellent mission statement as a company. Our aim was to do the right thing for the patient. It resonated with the employees. So, when our team responded with DTS in mind, they had the autonomy to do the right thing. They were empowered. They didn't need permission or committee approval. They could make decisions and take actions in real time. They would always have the support of their supervisors as this was our shared goal.

So much of our work and life has room for these kinds of brave actions. Here are three keys to help you Define the Situation to become a more effective leader, no matter your role:

1. **Go from intentional thoughts to intentional living.** We judge other people by their behavior but judge ourselves by our intentions. How often have we said, "I'm sorry you feel that way. It wasn't my intention," after someone confronts us because of our behavior. We cheapen our intention when we downplay our actions. Intention has been our scapegoat. What if we upgrade our actions by living more intentionally? What if we show our intentions through better behavior, instead of trying to convince people our intentions are good by describing our thoughts?

2. **Get good at decision-making.** Delayed decisions or poor decision-making leads to inaction or unwanted consequences. Many people defer to others to make decisions for them. Critical thinking is

key when it comes to taking decisive action. Get clear about who you want to be. Then measure your decisions based on that. Does it help shape that future? A good way to frame choices is to make little decisions with your head and big decisions with your heart.

3. **Be ready to respond.** Build intention into your life. Don't let emotions rule behaviors. Follow advice like "sleep on a heated email," and let a cooler head prevail. Avoid triggering situations. Pause and take time to breathe. Sit with your thoughts. Be aware of emotions and how they affect you and shape your behaviors. Your principles will give you better direction than charged emotions. Be guided by your value system. This will inspire a true response based on what you really want—not just a self-focused outcome but one based on respect and wisdom.

> *People who fail to use their emotional intelligence*
> *skills are more likely to turn to other, less effective*
> *means of managing their mood. They are twice as likely to*
> *experience anxiety, depression, substance abuse,*
> *and even thoughts of suicide.*
> —Travis Bradberry

When you are facing conflict with someone, look for their point of view. Empathize. Have compassion. What led them to act this way? What pain are they dealing with? Trying to understand others' emotions doesn't mean we excuse their behavior. But it gives us a chance to step back, not make things worse. Being intentional with a well-crafted response brings clarity to a stressful situation.

When it comes to how you might respond to anything in the future, ask yourself, "Am I being reactive, proactive, or co-creative?"

BUILDING CO-CREATIVE MUSCLES

> *Doctors won't make you healthy. Nutritionists won't make you*
> *slim. Teachers won't make you smart. Gurus won't make*
> *you calm. Mentors won't make you rich. Trainers won't*
> *make you fit. Ultimately, you have to take responsibility.*[6]
> —Naval Ravikant

201
▲▲▲

What if we unleashed the power of co-creation in everything we do? How can we see things differently? We understand not *every* situation can be co-creative or should be. But imagine if our intentions were connected to how we respond. If our focus was co-creative. What if this helped us create the best experiences with others?

1. **Reactive = Blame.** We're reactive when we're looking externally for the culprit, witch-hunting the problem, looking for someone to blame. It's tempting to frame things as black and white, but the answer may be in the middle. We have the power to choose. Will we become bitter, or can we get better?

2. **Proactive = Responsibility.** A better future involves thinking and acting for ourselves. We can grow when we choose transformations over transactions. How can we stick to what truly matters?

3. **Co-Creative = Connecting Dots.** Co-creation is about connecting ideas to ideas, people to people, and ideas to people (Figure 13.1). We set the tone for it, knowing that co-creation can get messy and that "time and patience are our greatest warriors." The more we do it, the better we get at it. How can we bring out the best in ourselves and others?

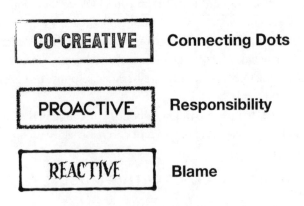

FIGURE 13.1 **The Power of Co-Creation**

How can the principle Define the Situation help leaders, teams, and cultures become co-creative? Here are some examples:

Health

Reactive: Wait until you need to go to the doctor. Take your pills. Eat different to "not die."

Proactive: Get serious about health. Choose to exercise, eat right, and get enough rest.

Co-Creative: Join forces with others to exercise together and learn new workouts, share recipes, and inspire healthy conversations. Create perpetual energy with others. How can you be an example to your family? Find ways to become a collective force for a healthy way of life.

Remote Meetings

Reactive: Stick to the agenda. Deliver the message in a one-directional discussion to ensure participants receive the necessary information, so they can carry out the plan.

Proactive: Prepare to make the meeting less dismal. Focus on topics people want to hear, encourage engagement, and keep it short.

Co-Creative: Lead with questions, build a fluid conversation, get in "the zone" together. How can you amplify the team's energy to shape things as one? Create a meeting people look forward to because they want to be there.

Planning

Reactive: Wait for things to pop up on your schedule, and deal with them as they come.

Proactive: Set time each week for planning. Wake up with a to-do list.

Co-Creative: Shape a to-be list. Share time with others. Build opportunities for co-creation, where your natural gifts, skills, and interests can intersect with those of others.

Performance Management

Reactive: Wait for the boss to ask about results or do your best to avoid the conversation.

Proactive: Deliver results. Plan for conversations. Make it happen.

Co-Creative: Build brave conversations around impact and perception. What are the collective expectations? Shape (and change) it together.

Interviews

Reactive: Ask candidates if they did homework on your organization. Why do they want to join your team? Talk about their résumé.

Proactive: Ask questions that make the conversation about the candidate. Be a good listener. Show interest.

Co-Creative: Ask questions that challenge people to reveal new things. Tap into their passion. Go deeper. Inspire each other with insights from your hearts and minds. Connect the dots on shared values. Be flexible in the moment. How can you craft a role with co-creative energy to be better aligned?

Social Media

Reactive: Get sucked into "never-ending scrolling." Watch what everyone else does, and post similar stuff. Gauge the success of your posts based on how many likes and follows you get.

Proactive: Share your authentic voice, looking to influence others. Focus on content creation, the quality of the message, and reply to comments in your feed.

Co-Creative: Go beyond the algorithms. Build better connections with your network. Find ways to co-create with them. Reach out through private messaging. Support other people. Celebrate their brave moments by responding in genuine ways.

Intellectual Growth

Reactive: Change is hard, so you become apathetic and stick to conventional wisdom. You read things at random, mostly social media reels or headline news. You challenge others who think differently than you do, trying to prove them wrong and getting into arguments online.

Proactive: You are serious about learning, consuming podcasts, books, and media that help you improve. You are intentional about the people you follow on social media and those you admire, who challenge your thinking.

Co-Creative: You shape new learning experiences for others (writing, teaching, book clubs, side hustles, etc.), and create opportunities to mentor others. How can you grow yourself as you grow others?

Goals

Reactive: Setting goals scares you. So you keep the bar low. What if you fail?

Proactive: You have a vision. Focus on a plan of attack, and go after it.

Co-Creative: Build from patterns that work. Get rid of old patterns that have become stale. Partner with others whenever possible (playing sports, starting a shared venture, building a relationship with a child, painting with your friend, etc.). What themes will you amplify to establish co-creative patterns in your life?

Self-Care

Reactive: When things get overwhelming at work, use a sick day every once in a while. Get distracted to take your mind off what you're worried about.

Proactive: Aim for a three-day weekend by asking for a day off. Plan fun things to do, and make it happen. Make self-care a part of life. Immerse yourself in nature. Skip the TV binge-watching, and get more rest.

Co-Creative: Build experiences to lose yourself in caring for others. Go after what makes you feel alive. Activate your whole soul by feeling connected to others. Develop better relationships with loved ones. Shift your life from seeking to be inspired to becoming more inspiring.

DEFINE THE SITUATION TOGETHER

Culture is the arts elevated to a set of beliefs.

—THOMAS WOLFE

We can shape culture with intention. We have more power than we know to lift, inspire, and amplify each other, to embody what we believe. We can create a magnet for others, building a place where people feel they belong, with experiences we can't get enough of as we pursue our best work and life.

What is a co-creative team? It's a team in which people work together, shaping projects, platforms, and experiences that inspire. Everyone shares, brings their best ideas, learns from each other, and moves things forward. The best cultures aren't shaped overnight by an HR program or by a *Braveheart* speech made by a charismatic leader (as good as those can be). Culture is shaped by people and built on trust.

The co-creative cultures we've experienced are established on foundational principles of integrity and honesty. Imagine a world where you love what you do, love the team you do that with, and love the experiences you create bravely together.

What culture do you want to shape?

- **Reactive: a culture of fear.** This type of culture causes people to act out of fear. Some people are stuck in the past, in dystopian thinking. Many are in pain. They stay quiet. They do the bare minimum. Leaders set the tone, but the people become tone deaf. They're reacting to current financial reports or the latest lawsuit, looking for someone to blame. A performance culture begins with the best intentions, but fear takes over. The decay of culture happens when people stop caring. It starts to rot. Fear can lead to a culture of inaction.

- **Proactive: a brave culture.** Many startups fit this mold. A new venture with fresh energy and a brave vision to do things differently. It's for an altruistic cause, but they go it alone and then reality hits. How will they make payroll in the next two months? There's a laser focus to raise more money. Venture capitalists want things to scale as they apply pressure to generate more revenue. The startup is fighting to remain independent, to be seen as a unicorn.

They've created a silo business. They think they have all the answers. They will either experience short-term success by folding back into the system they are trying to break free from, or they will crash and burn on their own. Yes, a proactive culture is about being brave and taking calculated risks. People might be attracted to join this type of adventure, but unless you're a founding member or are offered equity/stock options, your level of engagement will peak after the honeymoon stage is over.

- **Co-creative: a brave together culture.** Co-creation transforms traditional cultures. It's what gives startups the edge. It builds clients and customers into a powerful ecosystem, working as one. Together, we face what we cannot see alone. We have each other's backs. We empower each other, giving life to innovation.

  Co-creative leaders let go of control. They surrender to the ebb and flow of culture—learning from it, contributing to it, adapting to it, and setting the tone for co-creation. People know the difference by how they're treated and how they're energized. They feel different. A co-creative culture thrives on interactions.

Real power is rooted in connection to others, partnership, and the ability to inspire. You are wasting your power if you don't adjust to others' perspectives, according to research from Columbia Business School.[7] Here are ways you can be intentional when it comes to co-creative leadership and how your behavior can influence culture:

Be the calm in the storm. The world teaches, as Julius Caesar said, "I am the storm"—making more fighting, positioning, and battles necessary. The future teaches us a higher way: to lead by showing "I am the calm" and providing a way to co-create the future.

Be a deep listener. Focus on what others are feeling in conversations. Brave people stay focused on human connections. Empathy can convert acquaintances into lifelong friends—which translates into partnerships in family, business, and everywhere else in life.

Look to be inspiring even when you don't feel like it. Make things personal. Sharing real experiences can influence others to believe more, do more, be more. They will open up about the times in their lives when they've faced their Goliaths head-on and defeated them, and they will be candid about their biggest failures. When people get real with each other it creates instant bonds of trust. So be inspiring.

Be openly grateful. See the good in every situation. Thank people for their efforts and contributions. Make gratitude part of life, as it builds deeper meaning and greater happiness into everything. Everyone likes to be appreciated. Many are called leaders, but few choose to appreciate the magnitude of their stewardship.

Be creative with others in brave new ways. Do something different each day. Show up differently. Change people's daily experience by being spontaneous. They will see the value of creative expression. Focus on the outcome and the process, leading the path with faith, shared tenacity, and co-creation. Bring dreams to life with others.

Go on a quest to see how good you can get at something by being co-creative and brave with others.

CHAPTER 14

CREATE CONTEXT

The Purpose Principle

Context is to data what water is to a dolphin.
—DAN SIMMONS

People struggle to see their purpose in life—not for lack of trying. Fear leads us to believe we are lacking. We feel the need to search for something better, more fulfilling, wanting to be happier. This search can go on forever. The pursuit of more turns into a volume play. More content, more stuff, and more entertainment. It's never enough. It's hard for us to be satisfied in the moment. A superficial approach to living misses the mark. Without a clear focus, our work life feels aimless.

Purpose is a combination of the choices we make, what we're capable of, and our impact. We're going to explore why the depth of our creations matters and how striving for shared quality in all we do helps us Create Context in our lives. What kind of story do we want to weave with others? What do we want the culture of our lives to be? How can we think and be more creative with others? Our creativity with others depends on how strong we build our connections together.

Most people are addicted to consuming content or are obsessed with creating it. Not co-creators. They don't get swept up just making more stuff. They focus on the very best quality. They pour their original worldview into everything, sharing their creations with others and inspiring people for generations. There's power in leading this way. Become a magnet, not part of the noise. It's common to create or consume content. When we curate the best

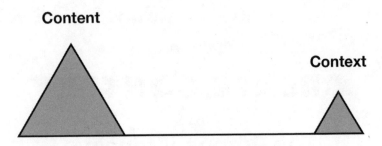

FIGURE 14.1 **Know the Difference**

parts of our work life to power others in inspiring ways, we Create Context (Figure 14.1).

We spoke with Ryan Woodward, legendary storyboard artist of *Iron Man*, *Spider-Man*, *Thor*, and *The Avengers*, and he shared:

> [As a leader] you don't have to put down the hammer. You can keep things light, and that enables everyone to destress and drop those anxiety chemicals. When that's at ease, the creative mind is more innovative. The brain releases dopamine in highly creative moments. And it opens the mind to focus on meaning over product, the "Why are you crafting this?" versus "What are you crafting?"
>
> When Sam Raimi was directing *Spider-Man 2*, he told the team, "Hey let's go to the movies and watch *Reign of Fire!*" And it was great. He created space. But when you get into production, there's no way he's going to do that. It's more intense.

There's power in the kind of co-creative leadership that creates space, like Sam did for his team. What if we did this as leaders? Story is a powerful force in our lives. We enjoy movies that move us and stories of people and teams doing amazing things. But what makes stories so insanely great? Ryan said:

> What doesn't work very well is when there is no established meaning on a project. Not just the moral of a story but the thinking process: the good versus evil, the right versus wrong. When it's not there, and you're just creating a plot-driven story, one fantastic

explosion after another. In the end, when they screen it, people say, "Meh." Then all the producers scramble, and they say, "We've got to put a moral in there! We've got to put a moral in there!"

And that's the classic *Fast and the Furious*, where you get Vin Diesel at the end of the movie saying, "It's all about . . . *family*." Are you kidding me? He didn't address family once, driving around the streets. They just threw that in there at the end to fake that they had some meaning in there.

It's 100 percent about the driving argument for the story. For example, "greed leads to self-destruction." Then you create an argument that can be sustainable with context, with all your supporting characters, your archetypes, and your relationship dynamics. You always build that thematic argument. And then when the movie is over, the conscious mind thinks about all the wonderful stuff they saw, but down deeper in the subconscious where we ingest meaning, it's stirring. And that's when you walk out of the film, and you think about it for days and you're going, "Wow! Wow! Wow!" Because it's gone deeper. And it hit on a human experience, and your conscious mind can't interpret it because, otherwise it wouldn't be a subjective meaning, it would be an objective preaching. So, crafting that right at the beginning is a real challenge, but when it's there, and everyone gets behind it, that's magic.

The best stories carry deep meaning. They help us Create Context in our own lives by showing us the power of transformation. Stories help us see the power of sacrifice and an earned life. Ryan also shared with us:

That principle of sacrifice is getting lost. It's disappearing faster and faster. And it makes me sad. Because it's so human. When I got into story, I separated myself from books, and got into the human experience. It's judging and sacrificing, and the rewards you get, making sure those are balanced. Very balanced.

You could make a movie of the most flawless person in the world. But if you miss that part, it's done. Everyone can tell an amazing story. We all live an amazing story. Think of the hardest thing you went through. That's an incredible story. The trick is not telling the story. The trick of storytelling is telling it in a way to help others feel the same way you feel. That's the trick. You could tell a story, but if you don't tell it with the right context, or the support on the argument side, people will not feel what you feel.

I've learned so much through the pursuit of story that directly relates to leadership. One of the things I say to students is that the viewer's experience is more important than the main character's experience. Way more important. We forget that. From a leader's perspective, that's about always understanding what the people on their team are going through, not what they're going through as a leader. Director Sam Raimi came into my office one time and saw my kids on a photo on my screen. Later that day he came to me and said, "Any time you need a week off to go be with your kids, it's yours." And I felt he was recognizing something that was so important, and that if those things are solid, I'll be so much better at my job. He's a big family guy too.[1]

———

To shape a more inspiring work life story, we need to explore the best books, movies, and experiences. We don't have to wait to be inspired in order to be inspiring. A purpose-driven life is not just a half-empty or half-full cup. It's a refillable cup. If you are uninspired, read. If you are flooded with thoughts and ideas, create. We Create Context by building the best stories together:

1. **Discover what others love.** Give yourself and your team the power to step back, zoom out, and breathe. Make what's important to others important to you. Lead in selfless ways by encouraging people to rest, recharge, and take the time they need with family. Make sure they stay connected to what they care about most. This will build co-creative momentum. Seeing people light up when they're fully activated connects you even more to your own purpose.

2. **Shape purpose together.** Don't push your purpose on others. Build it with them. Inspire each other by sharing personal stories about key life moments. Learn from each other. Give people social

grace, and invite brave conversations about life, not just work. Don't squeeze personal moments into work. Make your work personal.

3. **Build an inspiring character.** Show what you believe by how you lead. When people challenge you, be open to feedback. You are the main character of your own story. Tell a better story by changing the quality of your experiences. Look for ways to coach yourself and others. Get to a higher plane of living. Your story isn't about how great you are or what others can do for you. It's about how you can help make the people around you better.

4. **See the amazing stories of your life and in your team.** Build from a place of inspiration, magic, and revelation. Every joy-filled moment in your life is a teaser-trailer of what's to come. Improve the scenes and characters in your life. Grow closer with others as you continue innovating a shared story. Co-creation can help us bring out the best future together.

5. **Sacrifice time for others.** What if people you lead felt you were willing to give them exactly what they need most? What if you also felt supported by them because of the bonds you share? Give them the time. Give them your focus. Don't stare at your phone or think about the next meeting. Be fully present and show up for them. Maybe they're on the verge of an emotional breakdown after months of a brutal situation at home. How would you ever know? Your attempts to connect with others can help people in more ways than you know. A moment of your time can alleviate pain, enable healing, and power others with empathy and wisdom. Your compassion, kindness, and encouragement can help them see the best way to move forward.

ATTRACT WITH QUALITY

As we've studied how to Create Context and seen it emerge as a principle of purpose, we've asked these questions: "How do we make sense of the world around us? How do we extract meaning? How do we Create Context in a digital age flooded with so much information?" Here is the model we've

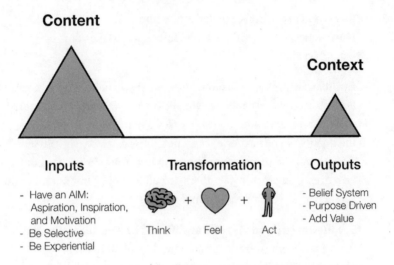

FIGURE 14.2 **How to Create Context**

developed at BraveCore to help us understand our purpose with others (Figure 14.2).

IMPROVE THE QUALITY OF YOUR INPUTS

What moves us most? How do we discover that? And how can we shape our lives with more intention?

Have an AIM

About a month after the tragic events of 9/11, Kenny Funk's father had a heart attack and died. It was an existential time for Kenny. He had achieved success leading Global Parks and Resorts Merchandise at Walt Disney World, but he felt something was missing. While driving, he passed a billboard with a target on it. He said to himself, "That's it! I don't have a target." What came next was a flash of inspiration that would redefine his leadership and life.

He developed an acrostic called AIM:

- **Aspiration.** This is the target. Goals have a finish line. Aspirations do not. They're what you want to be. Goals are what you want to do.

Ask yourself, "Who do I want to be?" and "How do I want people to experience me?"

- **Inspiration.** "When do I burn my brightest, both personally and professionally?" This is about being engaged, feeling empowered, acting with autonomy, and operating without being micromanaged. Getting clear on what inspires you helps you communicate better with coworkers, family, and friends. "If you want me to burn bright, this is how you do it."

- **Motivation.** This is what sparks the fire inside you. Ask yourself, "What drives me?" It's intrinsic: a personal interest or enjoyment tied to an activity. It could also be extrinsic. This motivation can come from factors like rewards or punishment. It may be related to Maslow's Hierarchy of Needs, where lower needs must be satisfied before higher needs can motivate.

People who never get to their ideal destination struggle to understand their identity. They have difficulty acknowledging their current reality. Just like GPS, you need to establish your starting point to get to where you're going. Establishing an AIM is no easy task. Taking the time to define this does wonders for your life.

Be Selective

Filter what you consume. Do you seek entertainment or mindless activities? Consider the content you engage with. Prioritize high-quality content that will help you grow. Be wary of sensationalism or clickbait. Most content is designed to get our attention and keep it. Curate what's best for you in terms of books, movies, podcasts, social media, and other forms of content. Take regular breaks from consuming information. Give your mind a chance to rest and process what you've absorbed.

Be Experiential

Seek out diverse perspectives and be open to hearing from people with different backgrounds, experiences, and viewpoints. This creates a more holistic awareness of issues and opportunities to adjust your belief system and approach to life. Be open to new experiences. Break out of your static routines and habits. This could lead to a deeper understanding of your purpose and position a better trajectory for your work and life.

Reflect on information you consume and think about how it applies to your life. Consider how the information helps you make better decisions, improves your relationships, and drives your goals. This makes it easier to identify patterns and themes. You can use our framework of tiers to see how you are experiencing the world or shaping experiences:

T1: Consumer—indulges in content to fill a void

T2: Content Creator—shares creations to get attention

T3: Context Creator—shapes meaningful experiences with others

TRANSFORMATION: BECOME THE FUTURE

Don't get caught up in a certain version of your past. Stop telling yourself the same tired story. It's easy to get stuck with labels, whether these are imposed by yourself or others. Discover your truest sense of self. Do the deep work to explore your future work life. Synthesize the best of your mind, heart, and spirit. Look to your future self now to know how to act in the present. Be powered by the principles of humility, love, and integrity.

Whenever you're facing a struggle, remember things aren't "falling apart" as much as they are "falling into place." Looking for a new job? Keep shaping your future. Hurting financially? Develop a new skill. Having a rough time in a relationship? Try a different approach. Create Context by becoming the bravest version of yourself.

Real and lasting influence comes through creating pull versus push. Examine the quality of your inputs. Are you stimulating your mind with knowledge and experiences that help you think critically? Are you pouring your heart into your work to add value to others? Are you powered by principles that enable you to live an inspired life? We put so much emphasis on doing things and driving achievement to become more. Creating context is about being more now to do even greater things.

Leadership of the future demands authenticity. Show the people around you that you're flexible while staying grounded in timeless principles. Create a consistent rhythm with who you really are in any domain and less of what others might expect of you.

FIGURE 14.3 **Transformational Leadership**

Transforming ourselves as leaders requires a synthesis (Figure 14.3). It takes better thoughts, being aware of our emotions, and being deliberate with our actions. It means getting intentional with others. We need a blend of logos, pathos, and now ethos to transform the future of our work life. We can't pick just one facet any longer. We need to embrace the synthesis of our lives.

Try blending your responsibilities, priorities, and relationships. Be the same person you are at work as the one you are in life. No more juggling act or code switching. We can be transformed by leaning into the best of our mind, heart, and spirit to bring it all together. Real connection is not hard. And if you do it well with others, you'll build deep relationships with people who see you for who you are.

What might that look like? Does it bring down your guard? Can you breathe better? Does it make you more open to new experiences? To lead in brave new ways while still staying comfortable with who you are?

People want to have a hands-on approach to influence the future. They need co-creation. They also need a new type of leader who can shape co-creative experiences and have brave conversations within themselves and with those closest to them.

Organizations looking to transform their cultures need to upgrade leadership. They need to employ, train, and promote co-creative leaders with a different set of skills to shape their future.

UPGRADED OUTPUTS

Creating Context means being intentional with the deep work, so it can help us transform from common leaders into co-creators. It involves building a better understanding of our belief system as we become more purpose driven and start to see the impact of the value we add to our work and how it helps others.

We need co-creative leaders who operate with a hybrid approach: brave leaders who guide the way using timeless principles and the best creatives to be bold enough to design a new way to live and work with others. The future needs this synthesis.

Co-creators see raw materials, which excites them. They see opportunities, a chance to learn from others, to be inspired and shape things together. They let principles guide their relationships and leadership capabilities, not logic or emotion alone.

Co-creative leaders are focused on character, which may surprise some. They challenge the present because they see a hopeful future. They understand that facts don't care about people's feelings, but they also know that feelings don't care about people's facts. So, there must be a middle ground rooted in converging principles: both being considerate toward others and helping establish truth. When co-creative leaders come across people who don't see the world in the same way, they don't get offended, defensive, or angry. They don't get caught up trying to convince others they are wrong. They get curious, engage, listen deeply, and invite others in. Co-creation delivers better outcomes.

GO FROM THE MECHANICS TO THE ORGANICS

Mechanics are the machinery in an organization: strategies, tactics, programs, models, software, products, services. They can deliver incremental improvement—small adjustments that can be good—but they're not the main drivers of the future. People have felt like cogs in the machine for far too long. It is our imagination and creative minds that make it possible to create a machine in the first place. Machines offer utility, some form of benefit to our lives. Humans are not machines, yet we offer so much more than utility. We can make true connections with our hearts and minds. We can imagine what's possible.

We need a higher order of inputs and quality experiences, the raw elements that can shape culture and shape us. An organic approach is open and brave. We have the autonomy to choose, act, explore, experiment, and have co-creative conversations. Our work experience feels like a lab. The core aspects of culture are organic, not forced. We break down silos naturally with storytelling and empathic thinking—connecting people, inspiring them, and bringing the best ideas to life.

Nature at its best is an ecosystem, where everything is fluid, organic, constantly working in harmony, and growing. What if we approached workplace cultures this way?

When I (Chris) was at Apple, my team and I were working to influence the entire company to shift from "Thinking Different" to living the new "Different Together" culture. And I got impatient. We'd had success with some teams but had a long way to go. I told my business partner Caroline Wang, "Why don't we just do a big rollout?"

She looked up and pointed all around us. We were sitting in the most beautiful spot in all of Apple Park: near the Reflection Pond inside the glass building, within the orchard of trees. It was secluded, quiet, the perfect place for meetings. Pure Zen. Everything around you at once: trees, water, people. Caroline said, "It's like this. It's an ecosystem. We will let it grow this way. Together. Then it will reach everyone it needs to. The leaders and teams."

I saw it. The ecosystem. All around me. I could feel it. The work we were doing would pull people in, just like the beautiful flow at Apple of design to hardware and software, engineering to operations, manufacturing to retail, until our products were in the hands of customers, enriching their lives. We had co-created the work exactly right. It would scale on its own—and it did.

CONTEXT = CONNECTING DOTS

We can Create Context by communicating our motives and intentions to others with greater clarity. We can establish better connections with our relationships by connecting the dots between different people in our lives who have different situations and different things that matter to us and them. We build a brave life together with a shared story. We start by being a great cowriter, open to shaping something inspiring with others, embracing different possibilities, willing to listen and even change our minds.

When we spoke with Guy Kawasaki—who worked with Steve Jobs when he was the chief evangelist at Apple, and now advises Canva and hosts his *Remarkable People* podcast—he told us, "You need to paint big dots in life."[2] This prepares you for luck and a variety of experiences. It's empowering. You can look back on the past and see how the dots connect, and paint big dots for the future, and be brave enough to connect them. Do what you love with others. Be prepared to pivot or double down, depending on what's required.

Leaders that focus only on optimizing and not synthesizing are destined for failure or mediocrity, at best. Getting lost in execution leaves little space for new ideas to emerge. We still need technical ability, but there's no question that leaders of the future will need crossover agility even more: the ability to see existing dots, create new ones, and connect them with others. Connecting dots doesn't mean we create things with as many people as possible. Sometimes it is just making better connections with the people we come across, building deeper empathy and establishing a better understanding.

When Elon Musk was going through a turbulent phase as the CEO of Twitter, enforcing "hardcore" work on the team, while laying off people en masse, he posted a tweet to Tim Cook, CEO of Apple. Elon was upset about Apple's approach with the App Store and their handling of advertising spend on Twitter, so he publicly attacked his adversary on Twitter, declaring a "revolution against online censorship in America," which was specifically aimed at Apple.[3]

Tim is almost monk-like in his ability to calm the storm. Time and patience are his greatest warriors. Soft-spoken and almost the exact opposite of Steve Jobs in terms of personality, Tim tends to sit back, listen, and ask questions. This may come as a surprise to those who expected Steve to groom and prepare a mini-me replacement, but it only confirms what Steve learned in his own story arc. Tim's ability to zoom out and see the bigger picture, the forest from the trees, is legendary and has led to Apple's meteoric rise to become the scaled force of producing category-winning innovations one after another. No need to break speed records; just do it organically.

Would Tim fire back at Elon to defend Apple's honor? The world was watching. Would he fight it out in the public square? Nope. Instead, he invited Elon to Apple Park and took him on a walk through innovation land. Tim considered the moment. He didn't get distracted by the fires of rage and debate. This was an opportunity to Define the Situation and Create Context. He didn't have to flex. He became fluid. Shift the dark energy from an unfair mischaracterization and online cage match into something else entirely: a mentoring moment for this talented, visionary but as still "Rough Elon." Maybe Tim could even see a bit of "Rough Steve" in him? Hoping for a bit more "Changed Elon"? Tim knew the only way was to lean in with compassion and be brave.

Tim zoomed out, and he invited Elon and his 125 million followers to do the same. What happened next? See for yourself: Elon posted a video of the beautiful Reflection Pond at Apple Park and tweeted, "Thanks @tim_cook for taking me around Apple's beautiful HQ."[4]

Then three hours later, Elon posted again, "Good conversation. Among other things, we resolved the misunderstanding about Twitter potentially being removed from the App Store. Tim was clear that Apple never considered doing so."

It was a master class in co-creative leadership and shaping the future together by Mr. Cook. It led to Musk defusing the situation himself. It came naturally, not forced. Musk changed his mind about Apple because of a story they shaped together.

CREATE CONTEXT TOGETHER

Our challenge now with co-creation is to break through our surface-level understanding of what it takes to work with others. The majority of people who work in an organization or within a department or team do not get to choose their coworkers. Teams are assigned or are made up of the people who already exist in their functions.

We all have different motivations, competencies, skill sets, and personalities, which can make it difficult to collaborate. We tend to make swift judgments about others without allowing for the proper space and time to get to know someone in depth. Co-creation doesn't need to be forced. It can become an organic experience with the right mindset, as we extend creative trust to each other.

Give Ideas Shape

We can influence how ideas flow. Most organizations push information top down. Teams are trained on what to do and how to do it. Employees experience meetings as download sessions. Most ideas at work are one-dimensional or one-directional. How can leaders help their teams connect the dots more creatively and achieve meaningful work together?

- Challenge the status quo with great questions.
- Build on the best ideas and allow things to converge.
- Follow work that energizes the people in the room.
- Have open and brave conversations.
- Avoid ego when challenges arise.
- Be patient with the messiness of co-creation.

Harness the Power of a Shared Story

How can you inspire people to feel what they need to feel? How do you lead a team in the best way? How do you achieve culture change? There's power in story, in how we design it with intention. Then we let it blend with other stories in life, becoming a much larger story. We are purpose driven with others, converging the best of our work, our team, our culture, our community, our world. What if we shaped our brave story together, with as much attention as it deserves? A shared story often leads to shared purpose (Figure 14.4).

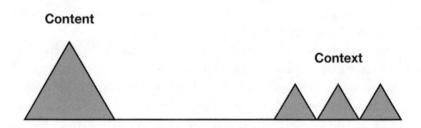

FIGURE 14.4 **Shared Purpose**

Invest in inspiring the shared voice of the team. Encourage people to share from their hearts, to be authentic. We don't all need to agree, but we should strive to have a common purpose as we find new ways to work together. Listen and observe first. Bring people closer by focusing on experiences. Act on ideas that can change the organization and the work itself.

Take things to the next level by partnering with others. Reward people for big ideas. Share the credit. Let the team flow. Share the success.

THE MAGIC POINT

When I (Chris) worked at Disney, I had the opportunity to partner directly with Imagineers and product development geniuses pulling together plans for the Marvel, Star Wars, and Avatar worlds. We wrestled with questions of how to bring the best experiences to life for people, how to create even more magic. In traditional businesses like Parks and Resorts, where innovation had slowed, we knew we could do more. Together, we applied a method we called "Magic Point." At the core, it was about bringing together the best of old and new and converging it into the best future. Following are some things we did that any leader can do.

Take Experiences to the Next Level

At the Walt Disney World Parks, guests had long become frustrated with status quo systems and old "FastPass" ticketing methods. The feedback was apparent. What wasn't clear was what exactly to do about it. We knew we had to declutter the customer experience and empower people to plan vacations better, all with a seamless experience amplifying magic for families. Around that time, there was more being done with radio frequency (RF) technology and the Internet of Things (IoT), and a heightened interest in wearables like watches. We saw the potential convergence.

What if we gave people a "Key to the Magic Kingdom"? The code-named "NextGen" platform was born and kept behind closed doors until we shaped the vision and the full execution plan. What emerged was *MyMagic+*, a wristband people could decorate with Mickey, Moana, or Darth Maul faces while using it to buy popcorn, enter their Disney hotel room, and plan Fast-Pass choices in advance. No more waiting in line for paper tickets for rides. These experiences would converge into an all-in-one solution. But the effort to move over 100,000 cast members at once to shift to this new system, with all the back-end infrastructure working together, proved a monumental task. In the end, it raised the bar for the guest experience, boosting company growth, and earning for Disney the Fast Company "Innovation by Design" Award.

Give People a Feeling They'll Never Forget

The creative teams at Disney faced the challenge of creating an Avatar-themed experience. They had the opportunity to work alongside John Landau, James Cameron, and the rest of the crew. To them, this was a special treat. These innovative legends saw things others didn't. In developing the movie *Avatar*, they had used techniques other people hadn't thought of. They were told to do it all with computer animation but refused. They wanted to merge the real and the digital worlds.

They tethered cameras to the actors' faces to capture all their facial movements, which they would then feed into digital shots—giving the audience Zoe Saldana's unforgettably piercing glares. They were very hands-on in developing the land of Avatar in Animal Kingdom, with its floating mountains and bioluminescent forest. But they weren't stuck in their own ways. They left space to co-create with the Imagineers, who shaped unforgettable experiences for guests, especially the "Flight of Passage," where you can ride a Banshee in Pandora.

Share the Power of "Yes, and . . ."

When Disney acquired Lucasfilm and all the Star Wars properties, and the product development efforts began in earnest, collaboration accelerated. This was great. Disney wanted to ensure the Star Wars brand continued to delight people and expand its reach. It helped that Lucasfilm was so collaborative. When the Disney leaders arrived to start developing products, the Lucasfilm team welcomed them with full-size figures of Boba Fett and Storm Troopers.

One of the heads of product development entered the Lucasfilm shop and saw a jacket he liked, which had a Skywalker look to it. When he asked the price, the lady running the cash register said, "It's a limited edition. There are only two of them. George [Lucas] has the other one. It's $100. Do you want it?" He bought it and has been smiling about it ever since.

Another executive leading the integration of teams set the tone for building on the power of co-creation. She shared in group meetings that instead of an "either/or" mindset for filtering ideas, she wanted everyone to start with a "yes, and" approach to collaboration. To "plus" ideas, as Walt himself would say. This built a virtuous cycle of ideation. You can do the same in any team.

As Pixar cofounder Ed Catmull shared, we need to "protect the baby" and nurture new ideas.[5] We applied this approach at Disney and achieved three- to four-times growth in our businesses. "Yes, and" is for the first phase, the expansion of ideas. This is how we can paint more dots. Later you can move to the "Yes or No" phase of contraction of ideas, to focus on what to build.

Take the Time to Get It Right

After Disney purchased Lucasfilm, we set out to launch Star Wars Land as fast as possible. Plans were set in motion. Imagineers were envisioning spaces and attractions, and it was all coming together. Meanwhile, filmmakers were fast at work producing new *Star Wars* films. But then people realized that if we launched Star Wars Land within the two- to three-year time frame back then, it could only include characters and story elements from the original episodes, and none of the new ones.

Executives could have pressured teams to go full speed ahead to deliver an amazing land, while making tons of money. But what would happen when guests wondered, "Where's everything I saw in the new movies?" They'd have no experience with the newly introduced characters or story they loved, and that is not the Disney way. This meant pushing the production schedule ahead several years to include the new characters and story elements. Although this required patience, the decision was based on the premise that guests would be much happier in a galaxy far, far away when it all came together—which is what happened.

It takes level-headed discipline and belief in the future to Create Context. The path toward co-creation and a shared purpose may be challenging, but it's worth it. If it was easy, everyone would be doing it. It's difficult to remain patient, to stay the course. It takes intense persistence. The greatest stories surface when we're brave together, but it starts with us being brave at our core. Teddy Roosevelt said:

> It is not the critic who counts; not the man who points out how the strong man stumbles or where the doer of deeds could have

done them better. The credit belongs to the man who is actually in the arena, whose face is marred by dust and sweat and
blood; who strives valiantly; who errs, who comes short again
and again, because there is no effort without error and short-
coming; but who does actually strive to do the deeds; who knows
the great enthusiasms, the great devotions; who spends himself
in a worthy cause; who at the best knows in the end the triumph
of high achievement, and who at the worst, if he fails, at least fails
while daring greatly, so that his place shall never be with those
cold and timid souls who neither know victory nor defeat.[6]

Brave Together.

 Lead with a Question

 Turn Pain into Power

 Make Others the Mission

 Define the Situation

 Create Context

 Follow True North

CHAPTER 15

FOLLOW TRUE NORTH

The Alignment Principle

Genius is eternal patience.
—Michelangelo

The world has changed. The days of toxic and transactional cultures are ending. We expect more of leaders: more humanity, more creativity, more truth—that they don't just talk about principles but live them. We are inspired by transformations and building relationships that build the future. How can we stay powered by principles when things go wrong? How do we avoid tying self-worth to achievement? How can we build alignment with our work, with others, and with our best future?

She wanted to bring electricity to kids in Africa so they could attend school and read with the light at night, rather than rely on candles they could barely afford. It turned into more when Sivan Ya'ari saw small African village "hospitals" with beds but no medicine. Sivan had studied energy at Columbia University and knew the key to changing things in the villages was to harness the power of the sun. She came back with her crew, and they installed solar panels to power lights and a fridge for the medicine. The people cheered, and Sivan felt great. But when she came back a year later, she found the kids were still not attending school and there were no replacement light bulbs or batteries. Sivan and team had been spending their efforts on the wrong solutions. They had missed the mark.

She had to think more deeply about the problem. What was driving this? Why weren't the kids going to school now if they had the light they needed to study? She walked the villages to observe more. She saw the kids were spending all their time trying to find water. Then when they'd find a mud hole, and dig out the water for their family, they'd get sick from the bacteria. People in the villages were even drinking cow blood to hydrate. Kids were cooking rats over fires to stay alive. Death from starvation was everywhere.

Sivan realized that one thing was causing the damage: the sun. She also had a powerful idea: What if she harnessed that power in a different way? What if she used it to drill hundreds of feet deep into the Earth to access fresh water for the people? This changed everything. People in the villages were now drinking clean water for the first time. They were celebrating and dancing in the streets. Soon, the people were getting healthier. They grew gardens and vegetables and were able to feed their animals. Villages were thriving, and even the kids were in school. It took time for it all to come together, but it was well worth it. This better solution changed things for millions of people in Africa. Sivan's nonprofit, Innovation: Africa, continues to change lives in a world that desperately needs it.[1]

Many people and organizations stick with their original plans and strategies, believing consistent execution will eventually deliver the desired outcome. But failure to adjust can take us off course. Being agile and building the best direction with others unlocks our ability to Follow True North.

THE MACRO VIEW

How can we zoom out and see what's core without getting bogged down by micro problems, a growing to-do list, and all the tactical approaches we've routinely applied? How do we stop giving so much attention to what doesn't serve our future? It's easy to get caught up in the little things that don't connect us to our best work life. This is the danger of micro-management and the temptation of optimization. An extreme focus can set us back or get us off track. So, how do we become our future? Start with the Macro View (Figure 15.1). Focus on the big picture: how we lead and how we treat others.

We need to shift from a to-do list to a to-be list. Whom do we need to become for our future? The Macro View helps us understand our place in the big picture of work and life, starting with co-creative patterns that help

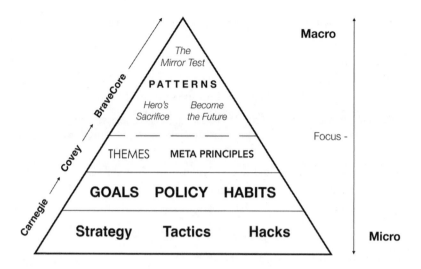

FIGURE 15.1 **The Macro View**

us connect with others. We have presented meta principles in this book that can give you direction to be brave together. A Macro View makes it possible to stay grounded at our core as we build on the unique themes of our lives. Themes carry deep meaning and have the power to inspire us long term, activating how we lead, the way we treat others, and how we approach our work with a sense of purpose.

Habits help us make changes in our lives while we work to achieve our goals. Developing habits can be like updating software for our human experience. They're meant for individuals to optimize. But new programming comes with bugs and glitches, and it takes time to smooth out the rough edges as we develop new routines. Habits tend to be achievement oriented. But taken too far, they can embolden our ego. Notice how the trends found in many bestselling books over the past few decades are all about habit forming: *The 7 Habits of Highly Effective People*, *The Power of Habit*, *Atomic Habits*, and *Tiny Habits*, just to name a few. People have become enamored with execution and a short-term focus on strategy. This obsession with the details is the tactical approach, the micro view.

Speed matters, but it is not as important as the direction we're heading. A Macro View helps us establish this. How can we sustain lasting change with consistent themes and patterns? How can we be more aligned with not only what we do but who we are, as well as with others? Invest in the Macro

View. Upgrade our relationships with goals. Create new patterns with the help of everlasting themes. No more cutting corners or searching for hacks. We need to see the sharp difference between being motivated (based on emotions) and living an inspired life (tied to principles). Embody who you want to be most—becoming your best in heart, mind, and spirit—to shape the future with others. Bring this all together with co-creation.

A Macro View can help you see the full ecosystem and your place in it. Visualize a more complete future, one that is hopeful. It's time to get your life on track. Get real about life and shift toward the ideal. Transformation is messy, but this is how we become the future.

CO-CREATIVE PATTERNS

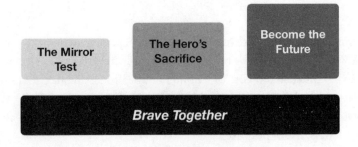

FIGURE 15.2 **The Journey of Co-Creation**

We must be brave together as we set out to experience co-creation. These co-creative patterns build on each other and connect us to a larger journey, helping us shape the future with others (Figure 15.2). How?

Patterns give us insight into our character, who we are. We connect the dots by looking backward, seeing how decisions and actions have led us here, for better or worse. We can change the direction of our patterns by being more intentional with the themes of our lives, principles that help us move forward by painting new dots. It could be a matter of articulating your first principles (as we covered in Chapters 5 and 6). Patterns are connected to principle-based themes. They help us see timeless truths. How can patterns bring out the best culture in ourselves and in others? We share the essence of co-creative patterns in each section of this book:

The Mirror Test = The Responsibility Pattern. When we see our real versus ideal self, we gain clarity. We can access new possibilities by asking better questions, acknowledging that life is filled with "and" options, instead of the familiar "either/or" dilemma. We gain better awareness. We own our role as a creator, and we strive to co-create. We take responsibility for our creations. We flow better in our relationship with ourselves and with others. If you feel stuck, look in the mirror and follow the pattern of responsibility.

Hero's Sacrifice = The Humility Pattern. We can choose to be humble instead of letting life teach us humility. We either learn to make sacrifices from a place of intention or as a result of consequences. Being humble enables us to move from the "Rough" version of ourselves to the "Changed" version of our future self, unlocking moments where ego would otherwise complicate our true potential. It can be hard to start doing things differently. It's even harder to shed bad behaviors. But sacrifice positions us for a better life. It is the price we pay for a more promising future with others. The pattern of humility helps us see others as human and makes us more approachable and therefore more likely to experience co-creation.

Become the Future = The Transformation Pattern. As we face the future in co-creative ways, we don't just believe in principles, we live them. We are them. No more need for mission statements. We embody our mission in how we wake up each day. We're transformed by living the best of our heart, mind, and spirit. When we are changed, we can inspire change in others. This becomes our brave story that inspires and helps others transform.

Why Co-Creative Patterns? The future is co-creative. People want to be more connected, heart to heart, soul to soul. They want connection to purpose, connection to what matters. Following True North is about alignment. We all want life to feel as if we're heading in the right direction with the right people. Co-creative patterns position our lives in a way that empowers us to shape the future with others.

Archie McEachern, former head of marketing for basketball footwear at Nike, said simply, "Leadership of the future is Connection."[2] Stephen Covey put it this way:

People have a hunger today for the soul side of life—a hunger created in part by our turning away from the fine arts in recent decades. I once visited a great private school that was built on a strong STEM (science, technology, engineering, math) foundation. They are moving in the fine arts as well as mathematics and science. They have come to an understanding of the need for emotional intelligence—the need to nurture other dimensions of our natures they had undervalued.

The new workers, the new worker-leaders, and the new leader-workers will seek both intellectual and emotional intelligence and focus on adding value, continuous learning, building relationships of trust, and centering on timeless principles. It's a renaissance education that leads to a renaissance in organizations.[3]

Co-creative patterns help us shatter older iterations of ourselves and our perception of others, breaking free from a "sharky" approach to business and life to be more like dolphins. The co-creative work life is playful, powered by principles, compassionate, and collaborative. We become leaders of the future by facing the reality that we're not meant to brave it alone. We can overcome fears by being brave together.

EVERLASTING THEMES

Belief is ignited by hope and supported by facts—it builds alignment and creates confidence. Belief is what sets energy in motion and creates the success that breeds more success.
—Angela Ahrendts

Why is it so hard to make the changes we want? Running five miles a day won't matter if we're eating a half-gallon of ice cream every night. If goals aren't the endgame, then what are they? Themes. Here's why.

Themes Outlast Goals

Goals are tied to achievement. They represent an accepted measurement for success. It's easy to become fixated on the gap between where you are today and where you want to be. What happens after you reach a goal? What about when you feel like you'll never reach the finish line? Themes help you focus on what is directly in front of you even when plans are disrupted. Themes challenge you to do better and be better. They help you understand why things are working and why you're winning, not just what it takes to win.

Themes give us direction and allow us to approach work life in ways we never have before—like leaning into your passions at work or being bold enough to share frustrations or ideas you've held back with your boss. Themes help us challenge ourselves to change something within us that we thought we could never change.

Themes Turn into Patterns

Goals are tied to results (lose 10 pounds, read 50 books), while themes are tied to the inspired input (build healthy exercise routines, stay in learning mode, eat Mediterranean style). Themes help us make a shift from what we need to do, to who we need to be, helping us move beyond transactions to transform our work, our relationships, and our future.

Themes help us create a solid foundation for our lives. They keep us on track. If we stick with them, we can influence our patterns. Themes keep things more fluid. We can shape new patterns, adapt, or modify our old patterns throughout our life to help us reach our goals, create new milestones, and gain momentum.

Define Your Themes

What inspires you? We've all been through a lot. We need to hope again. How do we do it? Most of us grew up in competitive environments. Youth sports. Sibling rivals. Jobs in results-obsessed cultures. We've played the game and even felt crushed by it. We compare our life to those of others and, at times, feel like we're coming up short. Themes help us transcend our constant need to win.

John Wooden, who was the winningest NCAA basketball coach, with 10 championships to his name, led with a focus on inspiring his teams to do their best, not on winning. How did he get inspired himself? Paul Putz of *Slate* shared:

The most enduring of Wooden's totems is his "Pyramid of Success," a collection of the character traits—team spirit, confidence, loyalty, and so on—needed to achieve "the peace of mind which is a direct result of self-satisfaction in knowing you did your best to become the best that you are capable of becoming." Second only to the pyramid in its exalted status is the seven-point creed handed down to Wooden by his father, Joshua. . . .

1. Be true to yourself.

2. Help others.

3. Make each day your masterpiece.

4. Drink deeply from good books, especially the Bible.

5. Make friendship a fine art.

6. Build a shelter against a rainy day.

7. Pray for guidance and count and give thanks for your blessings every day. . . .

Longtime NBA executive Pat Williams writes in *Coach Wooden: The 7 Principles That Shaped His Life and Will Change Yours*, "I believe the character and achievements of John Wooden can largely be traced to a piece of paper his father gave him on the day he graduated from the eighth grade at a little country grade school in Centerton, Indiana."[4]

Themes Make Us Brave

A career pivot. Asking for that raise. Taking the steps to launch a startup or creating a side hustle with someone else. How can you activate themes in your life and leadership? Here are some ways to start:

- **Be clear about your everlasting themes.** Consider phrases or mantras you've used in the past. How can you upgrade those messages to anchor your future?

- **Make themes personal, practical, and inspiring.** Use messages that are sticky and earthy statements that pack constant inspiration.

- **Make themes a foundation and be guided by them.** What are the themes you can set for your work life? If motivation is more like a dopamine hit, then inspiration is the light that fuels us on our journey.

Here are some examples of themes other people hold on to and hope to live by:

I speak not for myself but for . . .
those without a voice . . . those who have fought
for their rights: Their right to live in peace. . . .
Their right to be educated.
—Malala Yousafzai[5]

I like happy endings in movies.
I think life has a happy ending.
When it's all said and done, it's all something
worthwhile, and I want it to reflect that.
—Jon Favreau[6]

My mission in life is not merely to survive,
but to thrive; and to do so with some passion, some
compassion, some humor, and some style.
—Maya Angelou[7]

THE INNER SCOREBOARD

He's been called "the broadest thinker" by some of the biggest tech titans. Warren Buffett's son has called him the smartest man he knows, a ringing endorsement given the family context. Who is Charlie Munger? He's Warren Buffett's partner, considered "the man behind the curtain" at Berkshire Hathaway. Early on, Munger gave up his legal practice to focus on building financial freedom through investing. He believed in a cross-disciplinary approach to learning, taking big ideas from different disciplines to apply to new problems. This has translated into massive returns, to the tune of billions in wealth for him, Buffett, and the team. What are his everlasting themes?

Love what you do and who you do it with. Three rules for a career: (1) Don't sell anything you wouldn't buy yourself. (2) Don't work for anyone you don't respect and admire. (3) Work only with people you enjoy.

Become wise by reading great books. "In my whole life, I have known no wise people who didn't read all the time—none, zero. You'd be amazed at how much Warren reads—and at how much I read. My children laugh at me. They think I'm a book with a couple of legs sticking out."

Master the principles. "It never ceases to amaze me to see how much territory can be grasped if one merely masters and consistently uses all the obvious and easily learned principles."

Do the right thing. "There's a culture that says that anything that won't send you to prison is okay. I don't think you should come anywhere near that line. We've made extra money from doing the right thing."[8]

Bryce Dallas Howard has gone beyond being a successful actor to building a reputation as one of the most prolific filmmakers as part of *The Mandalorian* director team. She's inspired with her TED Talk, "How to Preserve Your Private Life in the Age of Social Media." What are her everlasting themes?

Learn from others. "I look up to my dad so much, . . . more than anything, as an example."

Make deeper meaning. "I love to work on material I feel has some deeper thematic or philosophical message—that is going to add to society rather than take from society. And I love to play characters where I can get lost in them."

Share inspiring women's stories. "We're faced with, right now as audience members and creative people and people with a voice, an opportunity to demand more of the stories that are being told. And to say 'It's unacceptable for women to be eye candy' . . . So these conversations are essential. But it's equally important to acknowledge that if there's a female character in a movie, she better be a three-dimensional character. She better have a personality and flaws and things she struggles with and things she overcomes and things she fails at."[9]

What do Munger and Howard have in common? They're not interested in how most people see success. They see things differently. They're in pursuit of everlasting themes and first principles. This alignment helps them Follow True North. They don't pay attention to the Outer Scoreboard, the stuff they can't control. They're focused on the Inner Scoreboard (Figure 15.3).

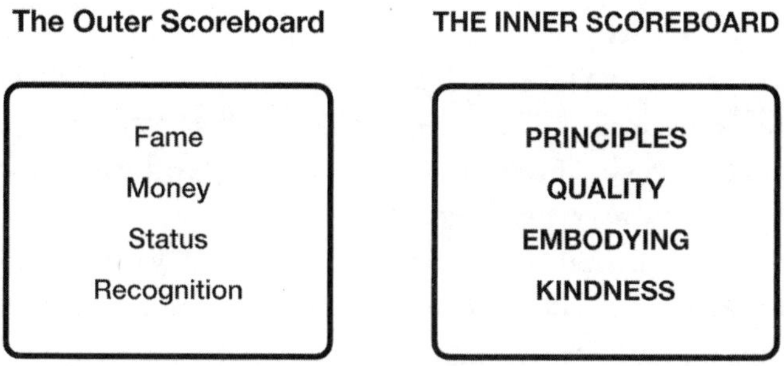

The Outer Scoreboard	THE INNER SCOREBOARD
Fame	PRINCIPLES
Money	QUALITY
Status	EMBODYING
Recognition	KINDNESS

FIGURE 15.3 **The Outer Scoreboard Versus the Inner Scoreboard**

What themes are everlasting? What about kindness? Researchers at UC Berkeley think so. Their evidence shows we're evolving to be more compassionate and collaborative in our quest to survive and thrive.[10]

They looked at more than 1,700 women who volunteered regularly to study the physical effects of giving. Fifty percent of them reported feeling "high" when they helped others, while 43 percent felt more energetic.[11] Harvard cardiologist Herbert Benson said, "Helping others is a door through which one can go to forget oneself and experience our natural hard-wired physical sensation. A runner's high happens when a runner's endorphin levels rise, the *helper's high* happens when people perform good deeds for others."[12]

When Stephen Covey and his early core team set out, they carried with them this simple, shared principle to remind them of the selfless focus of their work together: "Success to Bless, *not* to Impress."[13]

PRINCIPLE-POWERED FAMILY

Remember that hope is a powerful weapon
even when all else is lost.
—NELSON MANDELA

It was raw. It was real. It was over. I (Chris) was working a demanding full-time job at Apple, while serving Latin American families who were struggling in the community, all while staying fully involved as a father. It had long become my responsibility, on top of work, to be there for my children, always drop them off at school, help them with all their homework, and take them to all their activities, while now cooking the meals and taking care of the house. How could I sustain this? I felt zero support. Meanwhile, my marriage was falling apart. I'd grown up in a home where divorce was out of the question. How could I make all this work? It was devastating to watch it all blow up. But I did everything I could till the bitter end.

I had to walk away and let my marriage die. It was the most pain I'd experienced since the death of my dad. Betrayal by others can be brutal. I was crying for months. The pain didn't end. When I was in that valley, I did the deep work—on my patterns, my view of the world, myself, and my future. I cleared my mind, heart, and spirit. I considered the themes for the foreseeable future of my life. Questions emerged: How do I want to live? What principles are most core to me? How will I inspire my children going forward? What shared first principles will be the foundation of our family's future?

This last question led me to a place of meditation and prayer. I wondered: What are the shared first principles my children and I embody, and how can we make them stick? My oldest son was always taking things on, more responsibility, hard assignments. He was being bold, captaining teams, and challenging people, even teachers, in the name of truth. The principle that emerged for him was "Stand in the Plan." This means having the courage to face things in the name of what's core in life: the plan. This principle has inspired me and the other kids and his friends with the power to do more and be more in our lives.

The principle "Share Joy Every Day" is held by my second son, whose sense of humor is legend. He once made us all laugh so hard we couldn't stop, as our abs started cramping. He's a storyteller who shapes ideas to fit a hilarious narrative. He keeps it real. And it brings joy everywhere he goes. He makes friends easily. And he sees joy in the simple things: a sunset; our dog, Nacho; and the moments it's hard for everyone else to find. This principle has carried us.

"Be an Eternal Family." This principle came from my daughter. She's the most optimistic soul I know, brilliant, talented, and filled with light. It carried with it the tension between the Real and the Ideal. Our family was being shattered by divorce. What would this mean? The pain was breaking us, but we wouldn't let it break us apart. I would continue to be fully present in my children's lives, doing everything I could to be there for them. Building an unbreakable bond of love, with optimism for a beautiful future.

What about me? My principle is "Carry the Name of Christ." This is core to who I am. Literally, my full name ("Christopher") means "Christ bearer." The example of Jesus Christ is powerful for me. He's the ultimate example of embodying what we believe, sacrificing, teaching by example, and Following True North in the face of opposition. This has given me strength and the power to move forward when I was tempted to question everything. In doing more exercise, reading, writing, and creating, I found myself.

These principles have powered me and my family forward. We've been able to emerge from the ashes of a painful time, and move up the mountain of the future, becoming who we need to be. We're growing in our relationships with each other, co-creating art and business ideas together, while serving in the community and shaping a home filled with emotional safety, peace, and lasting joy. When we're powered by principles, we're aligned to a bright future and a life filled with growth we can experience in the most profound ways. Our True North.

CO-CREATIVE RELATIONSHIPS

Think about it. If you could tap into an endless source of energy, wouldn't you? It exists. Right in front of us every day. It's powered by human connection: in our family, among our friends, with our peers and coworkers. If we channel our selfless instincts and value what we have, we unlock unlimited potential in us and in others. Connection > Control.

We had the opportunity to advise a leader who was facing a crisis. He'd gone all in, but knew he'd missed the mark. He'd prioritized the work over everything else, leading him to say, "I don't even know who I am anymore."

Hidden behind the tough exterior was a man who knew he was succeeding at work while failing in life. He'd traded in every extra minute he could've spent with his wife and kids for more time at the office: more presentations, more profits, more results. Now he found himself feeling lost and deeply alone. Though he had a whole organization that respected him and appreciated his work, he felt empty. He realized he'd been duped. This one revelation changed everything. He wanted to transform his life. Moving forward, he became focused on the areas of his life that were lacking, that had slipped away. Slowly but steadily, he started on a path to make things right—a new alignment that led to a fulfilling life—going from static relationships to dynamic ones.

Our relationships bind us to a life bigger than ourselves. People anchor us to our purpose, empowering us to lift each other up. Success can be fleeting. People on their deathbed aren't thinking about business successes. They're thinking about loved ones. Relationships make us whole. The family is the best invention. Love makes everything come together. It's the greatest force in the universe, and it offers alignment and the best life possible.

Loving is the most critical skill and talent. After $20 million and 75 years tracking the lives and well-being of 268 Harvard undergraduate men, George Vaillant shared his now famous takeaway from the unparalleled Harvard-Grant study: "Happiness is love. Full stop."[14]

How can we build stronger relationships with others? If we're parents, with our kids? Often, parents try to live vicariously through their kids. They try to pressure them into playing a certain sport or pursuing an unwanted profession. Guy Kawasaki shared with us how when his kids got excited about a sport, he'd follow suit. He'd learn it with them. His boys got into hockey, so he did, and he loved it. His daughter got into surfing, so he did, and he loved it. The best thing of all: they spent more time together.

How we lead our kids in co-creative ways makes the difference. It can bring us together and connect our hearts in unbreakable ways, building trust. We don't need to feel social pressure about how our kids might turn out—successful or not. It's their choice and their life to live. We can still support them, build with them, and coach them—with love.

We know of one father who didn't get bogged down in negativity about raising teenagers. He saw it as pure opportunity. He also realized that one of the best inroads to influencing his daughter is through building a good relationship with her friends. As he's done this, they've asked him questions, and he's become a kind of coach for their whole group. Knowing that teenagers often look more to their friends than their parents, he's seen the power of connecting those dots by being present and interested in her friends. They all feel inspired. And after making this small effort, he's never felt closer to his daughter. It's a simple but co-creative approach that anyone can do.

CORE INTEGRITY

What if we got brave with the themes of our lives? What if we carry our best culture everywhere we go? The future is not self-made, it's shared. Everybody who's played for a successful sports team knows that. Everybody who's won together at business knows that. Too many leaders play the wrong game. They're stuck looking at the score and not at the core: shaping the culture and building the team. The best cultures hardly even talk financials. Their input is, "We're going to create the best experiences for people (products, services, etc.), and watch what happens." They do this by investing in the culture, making it a place people love, and creating massive growth.

Companies with great culture build it in the same way they build their products: with the best structural integrity. To get it right, they don't skip on quality. They treat people with dignity and respect. They Follow True North.

T1	T2	T3	Patterns
Just Follow	Lead with Answers	Lead with a Question	The Mirror Test
Seeing Loss	No Pain, No Gain	Turn Pain into Power	
Unclear Mission	Make Self the Mission	Make Others the Mission	Hero's Sacrifice
Situations Define You	Exploit the Situation	Define the Situation	
Consume	Create Content	Create Context	Become the Future
Directionless	Chase the Win	Follow True North	

FIGURE 15.4 **The T3 Operating System**

As we build principles into our lives, with a desire to lead co-creatively, we can be guided by a T3 operating system (Figure 15.4), gaining clear direction from co-creative patterns. We can lead the future with influence to move the movement of creatives. Meta principles can help us change our world from within. As you consider operating in a T3 way, you can discover your own principles and themes to help you become the future.

The key to shaping a thriving culture is to unlock creativity among your people. Show them what's possible by giving them the resources so they can build. What are the first principles, the fundamentals, that are true today, that will be true years into the future? And if you build a culture, business, and products based on those first principles, anything is possible.

Why Follow True North as a leader? Archie McEachern, former head of marketing of basketball footwear at Nike, shared a powerful experience that shows us how this works:

Another principle I learned firsthand is the power of diverse teams, inclusive teams, and ultimately empowered teams. Being open to bringing people into groups that you wouldn't have thought made sense is the right thing to do, and it's a business advantage. You're getting all these different points of view, and it's really powerful.

I wanted to create an environment where people could bring their authentic self and do their best work. I learned that working in product development at Nike with creatives. I set a tone of collaboration. The journey is everything. It's less about the result, the game, the win, the number you hit. The journey is where all the gold is. It's how you got there.

As you grow in your career, with a bigger team and more complexity, you can't do it all yourself, nor should you. The great leaders are coaches. They inspire, create clarity, celebrate execution, and package that all together through delegation, empowerment, and shaping the dynamics of that team.

When I was the head of basketball footwear at Nike in 2008, the business was not in a great place. The trends were in lifestyle. Sales at retail were down. I could feel the pressure. And before the Beijing Olympics, we created a product called "The Hyperdunk," and it ended up being an incredibly successful product, and that team went on, and that product lived on, and those principles lived on—of being lighter, more responsive, and collaborative.

When you're in a tough business, the number one thing you start with is focus. What are you trying to deliver and why? And what do you want people to feel as you deliver it? We applied incredible focus and built something super special. The product was super successful and was worn at the Olympics by the US Redeem Team. It was an amazing experience to see a group go all-in and build out a product story.[15]

Principle-powered cultures inspire us. They turn meetings into surprise-and-delight sessions, revelations where you're living in the zone of shared flow, where you lose track of time. The best teams create this kind of rhythm. Too many leaders haven't considered if they care how people feel. It doesn't seem to be a priority when results are the main focus. Maybe results could be amplified if leaders cared more about the employee experience. Involve your team in establishing themes that manifest an innovative culture.

MAKING THEMES HAPPEN

In 2006, Scott Belsky launched Behance, a platform to connect creatives and creative companies with different possibilities. Catching up with Scott, you'd have no idea how impactful his work had been, as he's one of the most unassuming people. His keen empathy for others has always been his starting point. He observes the world with a deep appreciation for different experiences. Years ago, he saw an opportunity to empower creatives who have no shortage of brilliant ideas, but rarely the patience to build them into delivered products. In that space, he found his purpose, and his pursuit paid off. After building a millions-strong community of creatives, he sold Behance to Adobe, and has since become chief product officer at Adobe. What started as an experiment connecting creators to display their portfolios and track top talent in creative industries brought the best creatives in the world together.

Scott's purpose didn't end there. He launched 99U, a think tank and annual conference devoted to execution in the creative world, based on the idea that "99 percent is perspiration." After cashing in on the sale of Behance, Scott could've bought a nice villa in Key West and retired, soaking in the sun. Instead, he's continued his pursuit of making ideas happen, inspiring others to work through the messy middle of building a great culture and company. He was an early-stage investor and advisor to some of the fastest-growing, most innovative companies, including Warby Parker, Pinterest, and Sweetgreen. He has followed his True North: "Scott Belsky has committed his professional life to help organize creative individuals, teams, and networks."[16]

Scott continues to be a leader in the creative movement, inspiring teams through hard moments to build greatness. To him, it's about building and empowering a creative team, creating alignment among creative talent, themes of the future, and shared passion. In a LinkedIn post, he shared: "A company's values should be a mix of what you aspire to be and what makes you special, they should become a part of the daily vernacular, and they should advance your mission." Here are the values that he and his team at Adobe developed:

- Create the future.

- Own the outcome.

- Raise the bar.

- Be genuine.[17]

We hear voices all around us trying to convince us of a dystopian future, but we can decide how hopeful it is. What's our story of our future? Is it one of abundance? Of lasting joy? We can shape it. Like Steve Jobs, we can "stay hungry, stay foolish" without being naive. We can stay the course even when we've been knocked down. When we feel beat down. When all seems lost. When the Fellowship of Adventurers seems to be failing. When we've lost people or things we thought we couldn't stand to lose. When the innovation we've tried isn't working and hasn't helped enough (yet).

When the pandemic hit and Airbnb lost 80 percent of their revenue in just eight weeks, CEO Brian Chesky had to make some tough decisions. He said, "When a crisis hits, you need to be decisive. However, in those situations, there's no data to base your decisions on, so you need to have courage. Courage must lean on principles. During times of crisis, you don't make business decisions, you make principle decisions."[18]

When Brian was pitching his vision of Airbnb to investors, they struggled to see it. "Investors didn't see this as a travel opportunity; they saw strangers sleeping in other people's beds."[19] By being brave together and focusing on the first principles of connecting with customers and designing an innovative service, Chesky and his cofounders created a destination brand with over one billion guests and counting.

We can reimagine our approach when we feel stuck, when struggles nearly break us. We can Follow True North. Nelson Mandela was imprisoned for 27 years for his opposition to apartheid before he was finally freed in 1990. Apartheid was abolished in 1994, the same year he became president of South Africa. Instead of avenging himself and Black South Africans against the White minority, he started the Truth and Reconciliation Commission. In choosing hope, he averted bloodshed and paved the way for a brighter future for South Africa.

What were Mandela's first principles? Sacrifice, overcoming hardship, winning freedom. Earlier in his life, he had tried militant action. Force. That didn't work. During his imprisonment, he learned something else. Forgiveness. He even became lifelong friends with his jailers. Later, he applied this love to align with others in shaping a new future of shared compassion with the whole country. He inspired them to be brave together.

CHAPTER 16

CO-CREATION
SUPERCHARGES
CULTURE

Whoever tells the best story shapes the culture.
—Erwin McManus

Everything was on the line. If this failed, the game was up. The business was done, and all their future ambitions would never see the light of day. Marvel Studios would be dead. But if it succeeded, anything was possible. Hundreds of millions of dollars were riding on it. But more than that, billions in future movies and merchandising rights, as the collective universe could unfold. But none of that mattered as much as touching people's hearts everywhere with a movie that meant something. The three sat in a room: director Jon Favreau, whose moviemaking chops were about to be tested to the extreme; Academy Award–winning actor Jeff Bridges; and another talented actor relatively fresh out of rehab with a chance at a comeback, Robert Downey Jr. They were in a trailer, where Jeff expected to get the script handed to him, just like every other movie he'd ever been in. Nope. Not this time. Instead, they sat there and started a different conversation: "What do you think you should say there?"

Discomfort is an understatement. Jeff hated it. But he saw Robert jump in and ride the wave, improvising, the same guy Jon fought Marvel to bring on. They started co-creating a massive movie that cost as much as entire companies, in real time, just as they were about to film. Sitting across from them, the Marvel executives—the "suits"—were getting visibly nervous and edgy, interjecting, "That's not something that character would say."

BRAVE TOGETHER

The suits fought for the purist comic character backdrop, while the co-creative group of director and actors channeled their raw ideas, building what they felt people wanted to feel, not just comic nerds. This had to be bigger. It had to reach everyone's hearts. Jeff said of the experience:

> This was so amazing. 200 million dollars or whatever the thing cost, you think they would have a script, but no! So here we are, coming to work, and I like to be prepared, I like to know my lines, otherwise I'm super nervous, you know. And so, we would often come to work and there'd be no script for the scene today.
>
> We would muster in my trailer with Favreau and Robert Downey and the suits, man, the guys from Marvel, and we'd all sit in there and I'd say, "Okay, Rob, you play me, and I'll play your guy." So, we'd change parts, Favreau would be calling writer friends of his and he'd be like, "Okay, so here's the scene, now you got any ideas?" Meanwhile, the crew's in there tapping their foot away, ready to go to work![1]
>
> [Robert] just surfed the big wave so beautifully. He's a master actor. He's a master improviser, as is Favreau. So, then we just jammed and had fun and great stuff bubbled out of it. And Favreau, what was so great about him was that as the director, you can imagine the pressure, but he was able to keep this thing cooking, with the suits in the room with us . . . He was just surfing the whole thing so beautifully.[2]

Iron Man became a blockbuster that crushed the box office and set up the entire Marvel Cinematic Universe as we know it, along with all the characters and stories that came with it.

Co-creation. It's pure power in moviemaking, leadership, and life. How can we do more of it? We can start by going beyond traditional answers, and choose a more fluid approach, "surfing the big wave." How can we get good at riding this wave of co-creation? How can we inspire others to join us on this wave?

We can only do it through shared principles that help us be brave together. The future isn't self-made, it's shared—and that's something worth celebrating and striving for every day. How can we be brave together? Cultures

252

that transform embrace inclusion from all perspectives. They also grow 10× or more than their competition when they master the art of co-creation.

How are you building a culture that inspires others? How are you encouraging people to do the best work of their lives? How are you giving people permission to build and be free to create together? How can you help people around you feel more connected, authentic, and valued? Be brave enough to shape culture. Throw away the old scripts.

In 1977, at Nike, Rob Strasser took the initiative to create a manifesto. Rob didn't bother to run it past cofounder and CEO Phil Knight. He just intuited the first principles. Simple, sticky, and definitive. Here are a few of them:

- Our business is change.

- Assume nothing.
  Make sure people keep their promises.
  Push yourselves push others.
  Stretch the possible.

- <u>Dangers</u>
  Bureaucracy
  Personal ambition
  Energy takers vs. energy givers
  Knowing our weaknesses
  Don't get too many things on the platter

- It won't be pretty.

- If we do the right things we'll make money damn near automatic.

A Nike historian, Scott Reames, talked with one of the key members of Nike's team at that time:

> I asked her if there was a sense back then that these "principles" were actually to be embraced or if it was just "Rob being Rob." She said, "Many of us thought there was a lot of validity to what he wrote, and over time it crept into the culture. It wasn't official policy or an edict, that really wasn't done back then, but it did become a defining moment."

Given how many people I've spoken with who kept their original copy of these principles, I'd agree that Rob not only struck a nerve, but also tapped into some key, defining tenets of who and what Nike was in the late 1970s . . . and beyond.[3]

Principles don't make us perfect, but they lead us to progress. News headlines tend to highlight egregious behaviors and scandals. They are indications that a leader or an organization (or a division of an organization) has strayed from its principles. In such cases, they must learn from their mistakes and shortcomings. Returning to timeless principles can revitalize an organization's culture and its future.

People are the culture: the collection of attitudes, beliefs, and behaviors; the values being expressed and experienced by the people, good or bad. If we can't look past performance, product-market fit, and the next quarter, we won't get there. We might see incremental gains but not the world-changing energy that's only unleashed through co-creation. Healthy cultures build on first principles, pursue a work life blend, and focus on being brave enough to transform versus fearing change. It's the difference between centering our teams or companies around a "rock star" or building a "team that rocks," between leading the future or resting on our laurels. What's in your culture manifesto? And what are your defining principles?

Let's explore the three building blocks of a Co-Creative Culture: Shared Wisdom, Deep Empathy, and Powered by Principles. This is the new road map for anyone looking to lead the future. Give people a spark and transform your culture.

THE BUILDING BLOCKS OF A CO-CREATIVE CULTURE

DNA, tree rings, fingerprints, snowflakes, lungs, veins, river networks, the Milky Way, the universe—what do these have in common? They're created out of geometric codes. What are the most basic building blocks of culture in our lives and leadership? We've talked about co-creative "Purple Zones" and shared flow in companies like Apple, Pixar, and Nike, as well as some start-ups and sports teams where cultures thrive and people can feel it. What are the core elements for building more of these experiences?

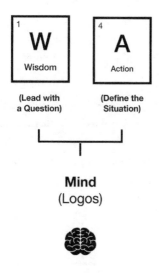

FIGURE 16.1 **Shared Wisdom**

Shared Wisdom = Wisdom (Lead with a Question) + Action (Define the Situation)

The best cultures of the future inspire people through shared wisdom. They Lead with Questions (Figure 16.1), and don't stop listening until people feel understood. It takes intention and courage to apply our collective knowledge. Taking action is how we Define the Situation. The best way to do it is to show, not tell. Shared Wisdom is experiential. The best cultures don't get stuck on balance sheets. They want results, but their obsession is teamwork and innovation. Not the other way around. They understand that people want to disrupt the status quo while building on things that already work. They love misfit thinking and ideas that challenge our work life, collective wisdom that makes us better. Here's how cultures can Share Wisdom to convert ideas into tangible builds:

- **Make horizontal connections.** We can collaborate differently each week across teams by connecting with people (cross-functional is best) to work on things that shape desired outcomes together. We must be open to new ways of working, especially with diverse teams; carving out time for meetups; sharing early;

clarifying progress and recognizing challenges; and staying fluid with different working styles, flexible to time zones and schedules. Planting anchoring questions before meetings frames the conversation.

- **Make it a choose-your-own-adventure, and let the best ideas win.** It may feel unnatural to build this way, but it invites people in. The best cultures do this well. Think different—together. We've seen teams apply these principles in simple ways that change everything. Lead with Questions to provoke a culture of curiosity, where anyone can imagine and express a better future, and partner with whoever they need to make it a reality—without fear. Show people you care about them by providing the space to create, collaborate, and shape with others. Allow the energy in the room to direct the best ideas to pursue.

- **Celebrate co-creation.** Meet people where they are and create experiences to bring out their best potential. Billion-dollar businesses have emerged from a single idea someone had for years—once they were given permission to unleash it. See people for who they are, and the gifts that they have. Recognize people for their co-creative efforts, their creative ideas, their unique talents, and their contributions to culture.

Deep Empathy = Passion (Turn Pain into Power) + Compassion (Make Others the Mission)

The best cultures of the future combine the principles of Turn Pain into Power (sharing passion) with Make Others the Mission (showing compassion) to achieve Deep Empathy (Figure 16.2). People are encouraged to join forces when a culture brings work and life together in seamless ways, when people show respect and, yes, even love. Cultures are guided by the greatest question: How do we want people to feel? They put empowerment at the center of workplace culture, not just adding it as a "nice feature." Doing this helps us go from transactional to transformational. Moving beyond the "mechanics" to experience the "organics" of culture. They see data as the side dish, not the main course. Their entrées are creativity, connection, and co-creative conversations—brave, hearty, filling, and loaded with nourishing

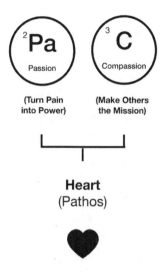

FIGURE 16.2 **Deep Empathy**

experiences that fuel the people and the culture. When we embody deep empathy, we feel more connected to each other and to our work. We're part of an environment that remains open to where things can go and less about controlling other people and outcomes. Here's how we can practice Deep Empathy:

- **Encourage people to be brave.** Don't let your culture slip into the swamp of workplace politics, personal empires, or self-inflation. Embrace the future by focusing on becoming a selfless force. Make others the mission by setting aside ego and pursuing work based on one measure: how your culture inspires the lives of others and how the "lowest-ranking" person talks about your culture to a stranger. Encourage bold empathy to help others feel seen, respected, and understood.

  I (Chris) had a leader who would ask me, "What would you do if you were in my shoes for a day?" and then he'd take my answer and start shaping the solution with me that we'd implement together. It was so empowering. What if every leader asked that question and gave power to others?

- **Start brave conversations.** Co-creation empowers people to be "cultural catalysts." Let them loose in brave conversations. Find ways to ignite their passion to build solutions. People get energized to build solutions and shape something new. Working together to solve problems by busting silos, developing cross-functional teams, enhancing collaboration not competition, exchanging best practices in regular forums, and amplifying more sharing everywhere. Under these conditions leaders are able to facilitate better meetings and better training.

- **Compassionate check-ins.** What if every week someone ensured that you felt you belonged? What if you did the same for others? Compassion builds great culture. It reaches customers and shapes how we create shared experiences. The quickest way to make better connections with others is to be more interested than trying to come across as more interesting.

- **Share inspiring meta stories.** Share passions in the form of stories. Quit saying, "we've always done it this way" and start telling stories about the brightest spots found in your culture right now. Show how people are living the principles that represent the best culture. People love to be inspired. Encourage raw, personal narratives. Move, don't prove. Stories help us reinforce a shared mission and spread it throughout the organization organically.

Powered by Principles = Purpose (Create Context) + Alignment (Follow True North)

The best cultures of the future are Powered by Principles (Figure 16.3). Pulling us out of constant division. We no longer need to pick a side. No more mind versus heart. Ethos acts as a bridge to unite us in ways that intelligence or passion alone cannot. Principles fuel our future when we start embodying values like compassion, integrity, kindness, and respect. The best work environments transcend politics and extreme ideologies and avoid the blame game with the help of timeless principles. We become purpose driven when we are inspired to be the best version of ourselves. How do we lead at the front lines of culture? How do we chart the future when there are so many unknowns? Principles become the stars that guide us.

Together as we Follow True North, we co-create the conditions for a healthy and strong culture. A random kid or dog bouncing onto the Zoom

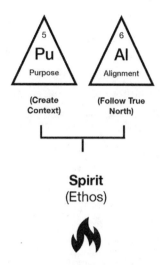

FIGURE 16.3 **Powered by Principles**

call? No problem. Asking for more pay? Let's have a brave conversation about it. Want to grow your career? Great, let's road map a plan to get there. Here's how to activate a culture that is Powered by Principles:

- **Give people permission to build.** Your people aren't as much interested in random rewards as they are in a challenge. They want to tackle impossible things, disrupt the way we work, and work better with others. They want to be trusted to expand the impact of their work in every direction. Let people loose on a big challenge and give them permission to connect with whomever they need to make it happen. Bust the barriers for them, and they'll raise the bar themselves.

- **Turn "boring work" into creative work.** If people don't feel inspired by their work, they'll eventually leave. It's that simple. People want to be part of something big and they want to feel like they belong. It may not be your job to keep their work from feeling boring, but you can create an environment where the work feels fun and is co-creative.

- **Connect dots with them.** Tell people you want them to be creative together. Let them help shape policies, systems, and processes, rather than imposing solutions established by a bureaucratic committee or management gatekeepers. Show them you care by getting in the trenches with them to see what they see and feel what they feel. There's nothing like leaders who are aligned with their team, building meaning and purpose as they shape products and solutions.

We've seen companies use these building blocks of culture to ignite new platforms of innovation, pulling different teams in that don't normally work together to build new solutions. These teams are sponsored, incubated, and powered by the top people in the company.

Burberry was founded in 1956 by Thomas Burberry, who made coats from a gabardine textile, a breathable, waterproof fabric. Fast-forward to the 2000s. The brand had become fragmented, and sales were down. They hired Angela Ahrendts, who joined forces with designer Christopher Bailey to change the future. Here's how they applied the three building blocks of culture:

Shared wisdom. They asked the right questions and listened deeply to build a vision of the future: to save the brand by blending the physical and digital worlds of retail. "We put the strategy together on a back of a napkin, and we thought how we can create the company we always dreamt of working for."[4]

Deep empathy. They brought in key leaders to connect the dots and explore the future together. The goal was to create a deeper understanding. They stayed open to learn where people were at, partnered with them, and treated them with dignity and respect, even when they disagreed. This built unbreakable trust to move the company and brand forward. Angela said, "I know it might sound weird, but empathy is one of the greatest creators of energy. It's counterintuitive because it's selfless."

Powered by principles. The team looked to reach younger markets, to become a luxury leader. They sensed the coming digital tsunami. They had to get closer to the customer. This "one brand" framing applied the principles of unity and connection, which helped create better alignment. Angela said, "When I started, we had different websites for different countries, regions shooting their own commercials, countries making their own products. We used digital to explain why they couldn't do things locally anymore. There's only one Internet—how could we have twenty websites?"[5]

They accelerated their build with the principle of humility, reaching out to top tech companies with a desire to learn how to take the brand to the next level. They harnessed the principles of storytelling and created a book, as an artifact for their future. It captured the origin of Burberry, highlighting the company's culture. And they wrote the next chapter. They tied together all the themes: "One Burberry," digital, connected to the rising generation. Their stores became digital blended experiences. Their brand became unified. And people loved it. Burberry experienced over 400 percent growth. Angela then brought her transformation chops to Apple, taking them to the next level too.

SHAPING THE FUTURE

Creativity is the last frontier . . . automation over a long enough period of time will replace every non-creative job . . . that's great news. That means all of our basic needs are taken care of, and what remains for us is to be creative, which is really what every human wants.

—NAVAL RAVIKANT

Speaking of core shapes, Plato said, "We must imagine all these to be so small that no single particle of any is seen by us on account of their smallness, but when many of them are collected together, their aggregates are seen."[6] Let's explore the true nature of these shapes in our work life.

Square: Ground Life and Leadership in First Principles

A person who has mastery over their ideas, behaviors, and emotions is represented by the square. When we have a solid foundation in life, we experience more harmony. Principles bring grounding, stability, and earthiness. They are an anchor for our lives, suffusing them with values that matter. It takes brave leadership to articulate, recognize, and live out our shared values.

We no longer need to rely on our intelligence alone. Shared wisdom enables timeless leadership.

Co-creative leadership is timeless. It encompasses these principles and a healthy amount of creative courage. Co-creators are focused on the long game. They sense the "urgency of patience." They know it takes time for people to come together. Great builds don't happen overnight. Here is what makes the leadership of co-creators different from that of synthetic leaders:

SYNTHETIC LEADERS	CO-CREATORS
Feel the need to have all the answers	Lead with questions
Get hung up on their losses	See the gains in their daily routine
Make it all about themselves	Make others the mission
Wait for approval or ask for permission	Take action
Care about image management	Curiously seek to connect ideas
Use fear tactics and desire to control things	Extend trust and show respect
Feel like frauds in front of others	Will figure things out with others
Feel threatened by others	Can get vulnerable around others
Avoid people and fail to respond	Help people feel seen and understood

Timeless leadership is leadership that endures, regardless of the specific context, situation, or people involved. It involves traits such as integrity, empathy, vision, adaptability, with a focus on leading people and not just managing tasks. Timeless leaders have a Macro View. They create positive impact, inspire others, and foster an environment of growth.

Circle: Create a Brave Space with Others

We all crave it: connection, openness, belonging. But more than that, we all crave the permission to be brave enough to share what we feel and know we are safe doing it. When we are brave with others, a circle forms. This creates a brave space where we can experience shared flow and selfless work. Where brave conversations help us see each other and the nature of our work with new eyes to achieve deep empathy. A brave space enables us to be vulnerable and respectful as we live out our creative identity. We can design this kind of space. It doesn't need to be a physical space; it could be the psychological space we extend to each other that allows us to be brave together.

In business, engineering, and technical areas, the term "skunk works" refers to a group given the freedom to break from bureaucracy and work on special projects outside their day job. Brave space is the skunk works for today, applicable to any domain. It's a blank canvas, a sandbox with toys, a big garage designed for people who want to make a difference through co-creation. Here are the core features and benefits of a brave space:

It generates ideas. A "safe space" is one in which people can experience respect and psychological safety. A "brave space" starts from a place of respect and takes brave mindsets to push the boundaries of what's possible with others. We can talk about the stuff that doesn't usually get talked about. We can face it together without fear of punishment. A brave space can become an incubator for the best ideas, creative thinking, and co-created solutions.

It encourages sharing. A brave space invites radical candor that's also respectful, where leaders and peers give honest feedback based on shared principles. It converts passive-aggressive behaviors into open minds and open hearts. In a brave space people can share big ideas horizontally, not just vertically. It breaks barriers, crossing teams, organizations, companies, and communities without boundaries.

It empowers people. Connected people feel empowered to connect dots together. It isn't an exercise in venting, even though it may seem raw. We need raw materials to build. And we need to first see how things really are, not how we imagine them to be, with the courage to make the real more ideal. In a brave space, we can lean into new insights and revelations, breaking ground, opening the floodgates, and challenging what's been done before. Not everything needs to be changed. A brave space allows us to identify what we can improve and provides opportunities to make upgrades.

We've witnessed innovation in organizations that create brave spaces. They don't wait to see if they can trust their people. They extend trust early and often. When they bring new people into their first meeting, they share a long-standing problem they've been facing and tell them, "We want to make this better. Please show us how. That's why you're here." And they mean it. This level of permission converts workplace fear into power, helping teams be brave together as they build new solutions.

It makes co-creation possible. A brave space enables better ideation of products moving through the right teams to iterate and hit the market with a splash. In a brave space, we can align ideas to ideas, people to people, and ideas to people. It allows the best projects to be crowdsourced by the culture, based on relevance and the interest of employees. These projects can be supported by senior leaders with resources to accelerate the builds.

Here are some great examples of brave spaces: the "Clapham Circle" in England, built by Hannah More and William Wilberforce, destroyed the slave trade. The "Junto" in Revolutionary-era America, led by Benjamin Franklin and polymaths from different occupations, created the first public library and other innovations. The "Camera Braintrust" at Apple is revolutionizing what a camera in a phone can do. The "Cultural Braintrust" at Pixar is shaping the future of human stories. The "Mandalorian Gallery" is bringing directors together to shape a shared vision far greater than any individual director could imagine. How can you influence the circles you're in to become brave spaces?

The size of the team doesn't matter. Just pull together people seeking to share the vision. You can start small, even with just two or three people—a mini braintrust. Co-creation isn't exclusive to leaders; anyone can engage this way as peers or colleagues or with different departments. This team can build strong co-creative muscles together and have brave conversations that spark creativity. When it takes hold, like it did at Pixar, it can grow from a small group of people to taking hold in the DNA of the organization, creating braintrusts everywhere.

Co-creative teams are the future. The answers won't be found in a committee or a new program, putting it all on HR, or hiring someone else to solve problems for you. We need to build a creative fire that spreads, a wave that grows and carries the whole organization forward, lifting people as it goes, inspiring us to do the best work of our lives.

Triangle: Make Better Connections with a Synthesis of Mind and Heart

Plato called the triangle the building block of the universe, the basic builder's tool. As the strongest shape, it's used in construction to make trusses. It's the result of connecting three dots and, when used in multiples, can form more elaborate shapes. We invite greater harmony when we're brave enough to build with others. It's the ultimate expression of connecting dots. Being powered by principles helps us lead from our head and our heart. We no longer need to pick a side. We can learn first principles from each other to shape our behavior and our experiences together. When we embody what we believe, we feel inspired.

Our work life requires a foundation of timeless leadership and brave spaces, which help us create the conditions for co-creation. How can we bring these shapes together? As we experience the Co-Creative Elements (Meta Principles) on a personal level, the building blocks of culture emerge (Figure 16.4).

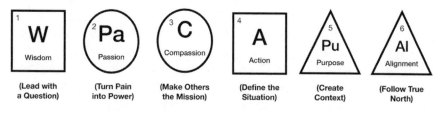

FIGURE 16.4 **Co-Creative Table of Elements**

What do we do with these Co-Creative Elements to shape our future? Personally, as a team, a family, a group of friends? Start with your personal culture, the feeling you carry everywhere you go. It takes depth of character to take brave steps toward becoming a co-creator. You need to transform yourself first, and then turn your newfound life-changing energy into world-changing momentum.

Meta Principles tied to co-creation can be experienced in linear or non-linear ways. Wisdom emerges as you Lead with Questions. You feel Passion when you Turn Pain into Power. Compassion grows by Making Others the Mission. Action is how you Define the Situation. Purpose is about Creating Context. Alignment happens when you Follow True North.

There is great power in combining the Co-Creative Elements in leadership, work cultures, and life—in hearts everywhere. Being a co-creator means being a future-shaping leader ready to inspire and be inspired by possibilities.

THE CULTURE BRAND

The future depends on how leaders and companies navigate culture transformation. Consumers can tell the difference between typical transactions and experiences that empower them. They can sense when employees are checked out and when employees exude energy tied to a greater purpose and feel connected to how their contributions make a difference. We can all get behind leaders who inspire us to do more and be more because of the way they make us feel and how we are treated. Cultures are only as good as how the lowest-ranking employees experience and describe the workplace.

A brand is no longer what we tell a customer it is—
it is what customers tell each other it is.
—SCOTT COOK, FOUNDER OF INTUIT

We tend to judge others by their behaviors, yet we judge ourselves by our intentions. It's not a great way to assess reality, much less the workplace experience. Companies can't just rely on their good intentions; they must show their people with consistent actions.

Culture shaping requires being intentional about how we, as leaders, influence people by design, not by default. Leaders must live the best principles, so their people are inspired to do the same. Leaders need to create experiences and artifacts that inspire the best in their workplace culture. Leaders alone cannot create plans and execute culture from thin air, but they can set the tone—good or bad—that influences the culture. Culture is a culmination of people's beliefs, passions, skills, and artifacts. Therefore, culture must be co-created by the people.

T1: Company Brand—building the company name over everything else. The consequence is employees and customers who feel the company is impersonal and doesn't care.

T2: Personal Brand—making a name for oneself. This can lead to detached experiences that are limiting. Even though an audience once felt connected to a person, they may grow tired of transactional sales pitches, "expertise on display," and the constant push to seem important.

T3: Culture Brand—giving people brave space to be their authentic self and to love their work. Experiences that enable a sense of belonging and even a desire to co-create together with customers.

Being a CultureShaper is all about seeing things differently and becoming a catalyst. It means living future-powering principles, enough to inspire a team. Being willing to make the sacrifices to become a selfless force. It means jumping in and bringing the full weight of creative expression, openness, and optimism to the culture.

At BraveCore we've developed a CultureShaper Assessment that measures the three building blocks of culture: Shared Wisdom, Deep Empathy, and Powered by Principles. Together, these make up the Future Culture Score (FCS), giving any leader, team, employee, and organization transparency into the current health of their culture, plus insight into their future.

We know that culture transformation is a massive endeavor in any organization, especially one with tens of thousands of people. But what if it were simpler than we thought? We learned that it only takes 7 percent of the team to adopt and build momentum for culture transformation to start taking hold.[7] This gives us hope. If we can just turn people into catalysts and start small with the most energized, brave ones, we can move the movement—together.

Here's how companies and leaders can become CultureShapers:

1. **Set the tone with co-creative leadership.** Have egos off the table, building blocks on the table. A leader of the future should possess not only emotional intelligence but also creative courage. Think of people as co-creators, not just "employees" or "managers." Know that co-creation can be painful and hard—but do it anyway. The tone you set can ensure that people feel they belong.

2. **Put culture first.** Any great company that has ever transformed has put culture first. What do customers need to feel? What do people at work need to feel? Empathy is powerful. Start by rethinking recognition. Make the experience people-centric instead of company-centric—and watch business thrive.

3. **Hire for potential to build.** Most hiring managers look for experience when filling positions, in the name of "less of a learning curve, less time to train." Some jobs require a baseline technical skill, but there's far more to consider when it comes to culture. Other hiring happens based on fit, to fill a demographic category for the sake of diversity and inclusion, or to fit a leadership preference or style. What you don't want is a room full of yes people or a culture that only appears diverse on the surface. What you do want is a room full of people willing to connect the dots and challenge mediocrity.

4. **Make culture about embodying principles.** Reimagine meetings as conversations rather than download sessions. Principles can build bridges across teams instead of more islands and silos. The best cultures are congruent with how close behaviors match values being expressed. Care about people personally. Create an environment in which joy and love may emerge. Isn't this what every single one of us wants?

5. **Look for artifacts in a culture.** Share stories, workplace lore, messages that stick. We once helped a Silicon Valley tech company identify some cultural artifacts. One of the senior software engineers got excited. He showed us a set of trees on campus, and then a gravestone. The gravestone had the name of a software engraved on it and the years 1998–2017. "That's strange," was our initial reaction. But on second thought, we realized they treasured this software they'd created together through deep collaboration. We learned that this software, even after its "death," was so great, it later came fully embedded in every laptop everywhere. Its legacy of deep collaboration lived on.

6. **Disrupt in brave ways.** The past is littered with stories of companies that couldn't make the leap into the future: Kodak,

BlackBerry, Blockbuster, Sun Microsystems. What went wrong? The future is filled with innovative cultures transforming themselves: Apple, Pixar, Microsoft, Toyota. What's gone right and when do we need to adapt to the changes around us? Are we willing to do things in different ways and to be different? What are we willing to sacrifice to get there?

7. **Skip outsourcing and be resourceful.** The thought of finding someone else who has all the answers or could be the solution is attractive. Too many consulting practices and programs make us feel like we're getting the help we need but fall flat. Sure, there are outside partnerships that can help us grow, but the real magic happens when you let your own people loose. Put that red tape in the recycle bin. Pose the challenge to your teams, give them tools, and let them fly. Then get out of the way!

8. **Launch co-creative builds.** Encourage cross-teaming. Create new ways to approach the work, with cross-functional collaboration and co-creative muscle built into the organization. Nurture horizontal connections, not just vertical. Make these pathways clear to people. Bring new team patterns to life. Realize transformation with small steps. Shape actual solutions together. Form teams to tackle solutions.

9. **Keep an open mind.** Constantly ask the question, "What if?" But don't just solicit feedback with employees and customers, involve them. Explore ways to co-create. Hal Gregersen, executive director of the Leadership Center at MIT, said, "Questions have a curious power to unlock new insights and positive behavior change in every part of our lives. They can get people unstuck and open new directions for progress, no matter what they are struggling with."[8]

10. **Become future-powered.** What do we need to amplify? Fast-forward 10 years from now. Who are we? What have we done for others? If our current culture could embody the best parts of our future now, then what is it? A great way to answer this is to focus on who we want the leaders and people "to be" versus what we want them "to do." This is how principles can amplify our future culture.

11. **Practice the 85 percent rule.** Hugh Jackman, legendary actor of *Wolverine* and *Les Misérables* fame, shared that the best Olympic coaches ask runners to "give 85 percent," not "100 percent." Why? This seems to go against all the self-help advice ever. Carl Lewis applied this rule. As a runner, he'd start out dead last, but then slowly speed up to his striding pace. As all the other runners would clench, overexert, and tighten up, Carl would just breeze past them, earning him an unprecedented nine Olympic gold medals, Jeff Haden of *Inc.* said:

> The premise works in nearly any pursuit. Take Hugh Jackman; [he] said: "If I were the coach and Hugh Jackman was on my team, I wouldn't put more pressure on him, push him more. I wouldn't yell at him, scream."
>
> Jackman feels his best moments have come from doing the research, doing the work, doing the preparation, and then leaving room for impulse and spontaneity. "I actually think you need to risk being bad," and "just let it be." . . .
>
> First, put in the effort ahead of time. Know your stuff. Know how you'll respond to questions. Know how you'll react to objections. . . . And then relax. Let your preparation and practice . . . take over, and operate at 85 percent. At 85 percent, you'll be able to read the room. At 85 percent, you'll be able to adapt to whatever happens. At 85 percent, you'll be able to smile, and engage, and establish genuine rapport. At 85 percent, you'll appear more confident and self-assured—because you actually will be. Which means your performance will actually improve. Even though you won't be trying as hard.[9]

MAKING THE FUTURE HAPPEN

Walt Disney had set out to create happiness for people, but he didn't do it alone. It would've taken him a lifetime just to animate a single movie himself. Walt braved it with his team of innovators. He wanted to share magical moments with his daughters—and with everyone else. He envisioned a magical place where they could live the stories they loved from his movies. When Disney studios faced an existential crisis with competitors MGM winning awards and Warner Bros. winning the box office, Walt and team wondered if maybe the theme park idea could save the business. They imagined "Mickey Mouse Park," with an old-fashioned square, a fire station, and shops for guests to enjoy. But the city of Burbank rejected it. Shareholders shut it down. What would Walt and team do?

On April 6, 1953, Walt cashed in his life insurance he'd been paying into for 30 years and sold his house in Palm Springs to pursue this project. He launched a skunk works team he called WED (Walter Elias Disney) and bought a 145-acre property in Anaheim, California. Then they let their imaginations run wild. Disneyland opened in 1955, and millions showed up. It became an iconic dream place for all, with a "hub and spoke" design and Main Street leading to the castle. Disney may have started with a mouse, but Disneyland started with a dad and his daughters. Walt's dream has inspired generations.

Walt and his team kept dreaming. They found some orange groves in Florida to build a bigger "Disney World." But Walt had even larger ambitions: an actual community, a place where people and cultures innovate the future together, a real Tomorrowland. It was called EPCOT: Experimental Prototype Community of Tomorrow. Then Walt died of lung cancer, and the world mourned. As they were completing Walt Disney World, the remaining leaders rushed to finish what they could, but EPCOT became a theme park instead of an innovation community. Would the dream ever be realized? Decades later, as Disney's core animation business was waning in the hands of money-obsessed executives, people wondered: Would Disney even survive at all?

Fast-forward many years. People sat quietly waiting in Cupertino City Hall on a Tuesday night. Steve Jobs stepped to the podium, his body frail. The pancreatic cancer had long taken over. He looked like an old Jedi, ready to fade away and become one with the Force. He glanced around with a weak smile. He wasn't here for theatrics. No big magic. He was going to tell them about the future he envisioned. Plainly.

He leaned into the microphone and walked them through the story. "Apple is growing like a weed" right there in Cupertino. They needed a bigger campus, but not just that. They wanted to build a landmark to the soul of innovation, a place that would make people's hearts sing. Something other-worldly, something that would inspire us all to innovate even more.

He referenced the new "spaceship" campus that would have 6,000 trees, including apricot orchards, sitting on the land of his mentors, the founders of Hewlett-Packard. The campus would look more like a nature preserve than the ugly asphalt that had preceded it. The massive form-fitting glass around the circular building would be forged like nothing else in the world. It was meant for crazy dreamers, designed for the human spirit to converge with technology in the most intimate way, intended for teams of misfits to continue changing the world one surprising and delightful product at a time. Apple Park was the future, even though he wouldn't live to see it with his own eyes.

It would build on the legacy of Apple's old campus, Infinite Loop—named after a computer program that repeats itself without end. Apple Park would adhere to the same circular theme. The perfect circle. A brave space. They wouldn't need any power supply from the city. They'd make their own. Cleaner, better—that's the Apple way.

Mayor Gilbert Wong thanked Steve and wondered out loud how else Apple might give back to the community. He showed Steve his iPad 2 and praised the product. Then he asked about getting an Apple Store in Cupertino. Steve hesitated, "The problem with putting an Apple store in Cupertino is that there just isn't enough traffic. So, I'm afraid it might not be successful. If we thought it might be successful, we'd love to."

Wong said, "We'll help you make it successful."

Another co-created moment? They went on to build the Apple Store in the Visitor's Center right across from Apple Park. And it's had plenty of foot traffic ever since.

Steve Jobs and his team weren't just creating a building; they were making the ultimate Apple product: a bold expression of the culture of Apple itself. This was a culture where Steve had reimagined design as the heartbeat and rebuilt the company with one skunk works project after another. And they were carrying forward the same spirit of Walt's work. Steve and Ed Catmull had built Pixar by telling stories people love through 3D technology, restoring Disney animation to greatness. They had even helped inspire the successful acquisitions of Marvel and Lucasfilm.

Steve had nothing left to prove. Pixar was leading Disney into the future, Apple was on track to become the most valuable company on Earth, and Apple Park would be the fulfillment of it all. This place would be a hub for people to share the best ideas, blending with Walt's dream of a community inspiring a culture of ongoing innovation and leading Tim Cook to talk in terms of Apple's future not being "10 or 100 years, but 1,000 years."

The design of Apple Park was shaped by Steve's son, who told his dad to change its shape to a circle, literally changing the shape of the future.

What if we changed the shape of our future?

OUR 1,000-YEAR PURPOSE

Courage is the most important of all the virtues,
because without courage you can't practice any
other virtue consistently.
—MAYA ANGELOU

I (Chris) was in the thick of my personal struggles. The pain was overwhelming, and the fear was crippling. I didn't know where to go. I decided to power through. Be brave on my own. "I'll get past it," I thought.

It wasn't working. I just felt more alone. My phone rang. It was Ian. He could sense my struggle and said, "You need to go out into nature. Go put your hand on a tree." He shared with me the benefits of grounding with nature and challenged me to actually do it.

Seriously? I didn't need a tree! I needed to get through what I was feeling: buried, stuck, paralyzed under the weight of the world. But what if he was right? What if nature was exactly what I needed? After all, I was the guy telling the world to be brave together. Was I ready to do that during my hardest moments? I set out and walked the same trail I had 100 times before, but instead of blasting my favorite music or chatting with friends or family on the way up, I hiked in silence. No distractions. Just listening. I noticed birds chirping. Were they singing? Light danced over the fields and between the trees. It felt different. Maybe I was part of all of this.

I got to the top of the hill like so many times before. I was in the same spot with the same tree next to me, but I saw it differently. Half of the tree's branches were on the ground, chopped into pieces. What had happened? Was it firewood? Did someone cut down part of this tree to improve the view?

I stepped up, softly placing my hand on its hard bark. I felt something. This tree had suffered greatly. Tears streamed down my face. I could feel all my pain and all my struggles. I was this tree, too. We had both suffered. We had both struggled. Then I walked to the other side of the tree, placing my hand on it again. And I felt a shift. Like a voice was coming through the tree to me, a higher power. "Look up. Look what I get to see."

I looked up and saw an incredible view of the valley below. Beautiful! It had always been there. Then I saw that the branches on the ground had mold. The cuts hadn't hurt the tree; they had saved it. The suffering was part of the healing. I knew this was true for all of us.

In that moment, I felt one with nature, part of a larger ecosystem. I felt more connected to the core of who I am. The future was bright again. I even felt closer to Ian, my co-creative partner and coauthor of this book.

How brave could we all be? What if we were brave enough to help each other heal? To co-create our best moments together? The world tells us to "follow your heart." It's not enough. We must be brave enough to allow time-less principles to fill our hearts and inspire our minds, activating a better future through co-creation in our lives. What if we we're brave enough to build cultures people love?

———

Here's to the brave ones. The ones who see with love. Facing their fears. The ones who build bridges. Who move beyond silos. They don't let ego hold them back.

Here's to the creatives. The ones who paint big dots. And take the risks. Who challenge what's been. To those who've felt like misfits. They create momentum. Creative Propensity. Shared flow that changes everything.

Here's to the leaders of the future. Who give others hope. Those who embrace singularities. Who give more than they take. They seek to transform. Guided by timeless principles, empathy, and wisdom.

Here's to the Co-Creators. Sharing the builds. Connecting the dots. The champions of culture. Shaping the future. They are Brave Together.

ACKNOWLEDGMENTS

We're grateful for our sons Austin (Chris) and Von (Ian) for bringing us together and starting it all . . . even though we don't owe you guys all the royalties you think we do ☺.

I (Chris) am thankful for my daughter, Faith, for inspiring me to be the best dad I can be; to my son Daniel for standing in the plan; my sister, Marianne, for inspiring the best; my mom, Devi, for always being there; my brother, Ed, for the brotherly coaching; and my father, Tom, for being a co-creative dad and valiant follower of Jesus Christ. To Joseph Lewis for boldly living principles, Dale Warren for sharing the power of transformation, Loren Dickson for his advice, and Mercedes Giron-Cerna for helping me make time and wisdom my greatest warriors.

I (Ian) am thankful for Alisa, my life partner, for being a co-creative mother and such a supportive wife. I love you dearly! To my daughters: Addison, keep living life to the fullest; I am inspired by your courage; and London, you have been given the gift to make friends easily because you're a good friend. To my parents, Bret and Marsha Clawson, thank you for giving me opportunities to be curious, to learn, and to grow throughout my childhood and for helping me get through college. I will never forget your support. To my three beautiful sisters, Shandra, Chelcie, and Brooke, I love that we are still close as siblings. You are such great mothers. I consider your husbands to be my brothers. I hope our families will remain lifelong friends.

We express gratitude to our co-creative editor, Casey Ebro, and McGraw Hill for helping to make this book everything we've dreamed it could be. To Mark Fortier and his incredible team for helping us share it with the world. To our amazing agent, Jill Marsal, for patiently shepherding our work of a lifetime.

We are grateful to Ed Catmull for inspiring us with his braintrust leadership approach, for being a Jedi-level culture-shaper, and for helping us believe that co-creation can work in "any domain." To Stephen Covey for showing us the way with timeless principles. To Angela Ahrendts for challenging us to "share what we love, and what breaks our hearts." To Steve

Young for giving us a glimpse into how to shape a life filled with love and meaning, despite all odds. To James Matthews for being an early believer and connector of deep co-creative relationships. To Rob Callan for setting the stage for brave conversations on the *Lead with a Question* podcast. To Dave Arcade for bending our minds with his killer art. To Joel Peterson for infusing enthusiasm into our endeavors at an early stage. And to Ryan Woodward for inspiring us with the classic Marvel character-building lens and seeing the "epic" nature of possibilities.

We would like to acknowledge all our friends from Apple: Randy Nelson for his insights, Jaydeep Ranade for his example, Mattia Pascolini and Matthew Costello for their selfless leadership, Graham Townsend and Lynn Youngs for being a force of braintrusting innovation, Priya Balasubramaniam and Jen Edwards for embodying the future, Stacey Smith for challenging the culture, Lucky Luckay and Donna Cerny for leading with curiosity, Caroline Wang for inspiring co-creation, Tim Cook for his steady and thoughtful leadership—thinking different enough to work different together—and all the industrial designers manifesting the best future. To all our friends at VMware: Lauren Schlangen Kalafsky for being an all-in co-creative partner, Michaela McCollin for never being satisfied with the status quo, Betsy Sutter for staying open to a revolution, and Victor Rojas for being a master teacher. To all our friends at Disney: Mahjabeen Rafiuddin and Jeanette Dennis for their perennial changemaking, Emily Empel and Louise Murray for painting a big future, Jon Landau for bringing the impossible to life, Kenny Funk for building space for brave conversations, and all those "disruptive" Imagineers like Ryan Wineinger. To our friends at Dell: Gideon Hyacinth for starting something amazing, Heather Tucker and MaryBeth Mongillo for pushing us to be more, Allen Bowers and Lisa Graham for joining the movement, Erin Nelson for her enthusiasm, and Michael Dell for being open to reinvention. And to the International Mentoring Network Organization team, particularly Jetmir Hysi for building breakthroughs. To friends at Generations Healthcare: Tom Olds for seeing potential in a guy after crossing paths in Huntington Beach, California, and giving him an opportunity to learn and grow as a leader, to serve others, and to shape cultures with healthcare teams and selfless heroes.

NOTES

Introduction

1. Apple Event, Sep 7, 2022, https://www.youtube.com/watch?v=ux6zXguiqxM.
2. Jason Aten, "Tim Cook Says This Is the Single Most Important Skill That Separates Successful People from Everyone Else," *Inc.*, October 22, 2022, https://www.inc.com/jason-aten/tim-cook-says-this-is-single-most-important-skill-that-separates-successful-employees-from-everyone-else.html.

Chapter 1

1. Wildcat Venture Partners, "Why 80% of All Startups Fail, and What You Can Do to Succeed," Medium, Jan 11, 2019, https://medium.com/wildcat-venture-partners/why-80-of-all-startups-fail-and-what-you-can-do-to-succeed-6a1ca11e3b79.
2. "Mohammad Anwar: How Love as a Business Strategy Saved Softway from Bankruptcy," *Leadership from the Core*, podcast, episode 183, https://www.marcelschwantes.com/mohammad-anwar-love-as-a-business-strategy-ep-183/.

Chapter 2

1. Emma Hinchliffe, "35-Year-Old Canva Founder Melanie Perkins Got Rejected by VCs. Now Her $26 Billion Design Startup Is Ready to Take on Microsoft and Google," *Fortune*, Oct 4, 2022, https://fortune.com/longform/melanie-perkins-canva-founder-ceo-interview/amp/.
2. Max Chafkin, "How Kiteboarding Became the New Golf," *Men's Journal*, Dec 4, 2017, https://www.mensjournal.com/sports/how-kiteboarding-became-the-new-golf-20160210.
3. Trey Williams, "Google Is Toughening Its Performance Reviews to Identify 10,000 Low Performers. Employees Fear Layoffs Are Next," *Fortune*, Nov 23, 2022, https://fortune.com/2022/11/23/google-toughening-performance-reviews-employees-fear-layoffs/.
4. Minda Zetlin, "Malcolm Gladwell Says Remote Work Is Bad for Employees—and a Lot of People Are Mad at Him," *Inc.*, Aug 11, 2022, https://www.inc.com/minda-zetlin/malcolm-gladwell-criticizes-remote-work-engagement-podcast.html.
5. Lean Collins, "Job Unhappiness Is at a Staggering All-Time High, According to Gallup," Workforce Wire, CNBC, Aug 12, 2022, https://www.cnbc.com/2022/08/12/job-unhappiness-is-at-a-staggering-all-time-high-according-to-gallup.html.

Chapter 3

1. Chris Jones, "How Can a Return to Principles like Love Heal Our Communities?," *Lead with a Question*, podcast, Oct 4, 2022, https://open.spotify.com/show/1vZBQf9O8iMo6HWWgG1UdE.

2. "The Blue Zones: Lifestyle Habits of the World's Longest-Living Populations," Fullscript, Sep 15, 2022, https://fullscript.com/blog/blue-zones.

3. Tim Hughes and Mario Vafeas, "Happiness and Co-Creation of Value: Playing the Blues," Jul 19, 2021, *Marketing Theory* 21, no. 4, https://journals.sagepub.com/doi/full/10.1177/14705931211032255.

4. Rebecca Komp, Simone Kauffeld, and Patrizia Ianir-Dahm, "The Concept of Health-Promoting Collaboration—a Starting Point to Reduce Presenteeism?," *Frontiers in Psychology*, Jan 13, 2022, https://www.frontiersin.org/articles/10.3389/fpsyg.2021.782597/full.

5. Trisha Greenhalgh, Claire Jackson, Sara Shaw, and Tina Janamian, "Achieving Research Impact Through Co-Creation in Community-Based Health Services: Literature Review and Case Study," *Milbank Quarterly*, Jun 2016, https://www.ncbi.nlm.nih.gov/pmc/articles/PMC4911728/.

6. Erin Blakemore, "'Top Gun' Is Back. But Is the Elite Navy Fighter Pilot School Really like the Movies?," *Smithsonian* magazine, May 26, 2022, https://www.smithsonianmag.com/smithsonian-institution/top-gun-is-back-but-is-the-elite-navy-fighter-pilot-school-really-like-the-movies-180980149/.

7. Patrick J. Kiger, "You've Seen 'Top Gun.' But What's the Real TOPGUN Program Like?," Howstuffworks, Jul 20, 2022, https://science.howstuffworks.com/TOPGUN-news.htm.

8. Katie Lange, "TOPGUN's Humble Beginnings in a Parking Lot Revealed," Aerotech News, Feb 7, 2022, https://www.aerotechnews.com/blog/2022/02/07/topguns-humble-beginnings-in-a-parking-lot-revealed/.

9. Lange, "TOPGUN's humble beginnings in a parking lot revealed."

10. Andre De Waal, Michael Weaver, Tammy Day, and Beatrice van der Heijden, "Silo-Busting: Overcoming the Greatest Threat to Organizational Performance," *Journal of Sustainability*, Nov 7, 2019, https://www.mdpi.com/2071-1050/11/23/6860/htm.

Chapter 4

1. "Leonardo da Vinci's Elegant Design for a Perpetual Motion Machine," Open Culture, Aug 14, 2019, https://www.openculture.com/2019/08/leonardo-da-vincis-elegant-design-for-a-perpetual-motion-machine.html.

2. Scott S. Smith, "Nikola Tesla Revolutionized World with Grid, Wireless," Investor's Business Daily, Dec 7, 2015, https://www.investors.com/news/management/leaders-and-success/nikola-tesla-created-much-modern-technology/.

3. Mind Tasting, "The Mind of Nikola Tesla and the Power of Visualization," Medium, Feb 3, 2019, https://mindtasting.medium.com/the-mind-of-nikola-tesla-4305e3d5ee1e.

4. Nathan Coppedge, "History of Perpetual Motion Machines," ResearchGate, Mar 2020, https://www.researchgate.net/publication/340364116_History_of_Perpetual_Motion_Machines.

5. Christopher McFadden, "The Mysterious Disappearance of Nikola Tesla's Files After His Death," Interesting Engineering, Feb 22, 2019, https://interestingengineering.com/culture/the-mysterious-disappearance-of-nikola-teslas-files-after-his-death.

6. Peter Economy, "Steve Jobs on the Remarkable Power of Asking for Help," Inc.com, June 11, 2015, https://www.inc.com/peter-economy/steve-jobs-on-the-remarkable-power-of-asking-for-what-you-want.html.

7. Economy, "Steve Jobs on the Remarkable Power of Asking for Help."
8. Ed Catmull, interview and conversation with the authors, Apr 18, 2019.

Chapter 5

1. Brandon Kyle Goodman, Twitter post, Jan 17, 2021, https://twitter.com/brandonkgood /status/1350837356073414657?lang=en.
2. Tom Huddleston Jr., "Billionaire Investor Charlie Munger: 'The World Is Not Driven by Greed, It's Driven by Envy,'" CNBC, Dec 11, 2022, https://www.cnbc.com/2022/12/10 /billionaire-charlie-munger-world-is-driven-by-envy-not-greed.html.
3. Chip Heath and Dan Heath, "Made to Stick SUCCESs Model," 2008, https://heathbrothers .com/download/mts-made-to-stick-model.pdf.

Chapter 6

1. Dan Farber, "Tim Cook Maintains Steve Jobs' Beatles Business Model," CNET, Jun 12, 2013, https://www.cnet.com/tech/tech-industry/tim-cook-maintains-steve-jobs-beatles -business-model/.
2. "Join us. Be you.," Apple, https://www.apple.com/careers/us/.
3. Zach Baron, "Tim Cook on Shaping the Future of Apple," GQ, Apr 3, 2023, https://www .gq.com/story/tim-cook-global-creativity-awards-cover-2023.

Chapter 7

1. Barry Brownstein, "Why Positive Thinking Doesn't Work," Intellectual Takeout, Feb 21, 2019, https://intellectualtakeout.org/2019/02/why-positive-thinking-doesnt-work/.
2. Arjun Julka, "10x Scoring Champion Michael Jordan Once Admitted How Donning the Role of a 'Sponge' Was His Greatest Skill," The Sports Rush, Apr 12, 2022, https://thesportsrush .com/nba-news-10x-scoring-champion-michael-jordan-once-admitted-how-donning -the-role-of-a-sponge-was-his-greatest-skill/.
3. Mel Robbins, Facebook post, Dec 5, 2018, https://www.facebook.com/melrobbins/photos /passion-is-not-a-person-a-place-or-a-thing-its-a-state-of-mind-its-how-you-feel-/1949 229695172905/.
4. Mel Robbins, Facebook post, Jan 4, 2021, https://www.facebook.com/melrobbins/posts /theres-an-enormous-difference-between-passion-and-purposeyour-passion-is-for -you/3641947065901151/.
5. Edmund Flagg, Edmond Dantès (Chicago: Donohoe Henneberry & Co, 1909), 106.
6. Dave Arcade, "How Can People Co-Create Even When It's Messy and Hard?," Lead with a Question, podcast, Jun 24, 2022.
7. Eric Barker, "6 Secrets You Can Learn from the Happiest People on Earth," Time magazine, Mar 7, 2014, https://time.com/14296/6-secrets-you-can-learn-from-the-happiest-people -on-earth/.

Chapter 8

1. John Hollinger, "The Grizzlies Keep Winning Without Ja Morant. What's Going On?," Athletic, May 13, 2022, https://theathletic.com/3309223/2022/05/13/the-grizzlies-keep-winning -without-ja-morant-whats-going-on/.

2. Jason Reed, "Are the Los Angeles Lakers Actually Better Without LeBron James?," *Lake Show Life*, Nov 23, 2022, https://lakeshowlife.com/2022/11/19/los-angeles-lakers-better-lebron-james/.

3. Martin Rogers, "Why Do NBA Teams Keep Winning Without Their Superstars?," *USA Today*, Feb 26, 2019, https://www.usatoday.com/story/sports/2019/02/25/why-do-nba-teams-keep-wining-without-their-superstars/2982256002/.

4. Michael Jordan, "On Who's the Greatest Team of All Time," YouTube, Jul 16, 2022, https://www.youtube.com/watch?v=5h8fFhh8aUM.

5. Erving Goffman, *The Presentation of Self in Everyday Life* (New York: Doubleday, 1959).

6. Suzy Menkes, "Retail Is Broken. Apple's Angela Ahrendts Has a Plan," *Vogue Business*, Jan 29, 2019, https://www.voguebusiness.com/companies/angela-ahrendts-apple-retail-strategy.

7. Anuj Talwalkar, "'That's a Really Powerful Combination': Steve Kerr Reveals How Stephen Curry Differs on the Floor Than off the Court," Essentially Sports, Feb 1, 2022, https://www.essentiallysports.com/nba-basketball-news-thats-a-really-powerful-combination-steve-kerr-reveals-how-stephen-curry-differs-on-the-floor-than-off-the-court/.

8. Scott Cacciola, "Traffic Cones and High-Fives: A Glimpse Behind the Warriors' Curtain," *New York Times*, Oct 11, 2017, https://www.nytimes.com/2017/10/11/sports/basketball/golden-state-warriors-practice-secrets-kerr.html.

9. Cacciola, "Traffic Cones and High-Fives."

10. Jesse Washington, "Giannis Antetokounmpo's 'Failure' Was a W for the Game," Andscape, Apr 28, 2023, https://andscape.com/features/giannis-antetokounmpos-rejection-of-failure-was-a-w-for-the-game/.

Chapter 9

1. Jack Kelly, "Better.com's CEO Called Workers 'Dumb Dolphins'—Three Executives Quit," *Forbes*, Dec 8, 2021, https://www.forbes.com/sites/jackkelly/2021/12/08/bettercoms-ceo-called-workers-dumb-dolphins-three-executives-quit/?sh=38e451681e35.

2. Philip Etemesi, "Shark Tank: 10 Fakest Things About the Show, According to Cast and Crew," Screenrant, Sep 7, 2022, https://screenrant.com/shark-tank-fakest-things-cast-crew/.

3. Janaya Wecker, "All the Rules Entrepreneurs Who Go on 'Shark Tank' Have to Follow," Feb 9, 2023, *Good Housekeeping*, https://www.goodhousekeeping.com/life/entertainment/g42266474/shark-tank-entrepreneur-rules/.

4. Richard Feloni, "Why All 'Shark Tank' Entrepreneurs See a Psychiatrist After Their Pitch," *Business Insider*, Nov 5, 2015, https://www.businessinsider.com/shark-tank-entrepreneurs-see-psychiatrist-2015-11.

5. Etemesi, "Shark Tank: 10 Fakest Things About the Show."

6. Lucas Manfredi, "Elizabeth Holmes Pushed for Theranos-Walgreens Deal Despite Test Reliability Concerns, Former Scientist Claims," Fox Business, Sep 22, 2021, https://www.foxbusiness.com/lifestyle/elizabeth-holmes-theranos-fraud-trial-walgreens-partnership.

7. Nick Bilton, "Exclusive: How Elizabeth Holmes's House of Cards Came Tumbling Down," *Vanity Fair*, Oct 2016, https://www.vanityfair.com/news/2016/09/elizabeth-holmes-theranos-exclusive.

8. Joe Svetlik, "Jobs Told Cook: Don't Ask 'What Would Steve Do?,'" CNET, Oct 26, 2011, https://www.cnet.com/tech/tech-industry/jobs-told-cook-dont-ask-what-would-steve -do/.

9. Ed Catmull, "Steve Jobs: The Books & Movies Got It All Wrong," YouTube, Mar 2022, https://www.youtube.com/watch?v=jyw28WrGt-c.

Chapter 10

1. Mishal Husain, "Malala: The Girl Who Was Shot for Going to School," BBC, Oct 7, 2013, https://www.bbc.com/news/magazine-24379018.

2. Malala Yousafzai, *I Am Malala* (New York: Back Bay Books, 2015), 313.

3. Yousafzai, *I Am Malala*.

4. Malala Yousafzai, Speech to the United Nations, Jul 12, 2013, https://www.theguardian .com/commentisfree/2013/jul/12/malala-yousafzai-united-nations-education-speech -text.

5. Bea Karnes, "Stanford Research: The Meaningful Life Is a Road Worth Traveling," Patch, Jan 11, 2014, https://patch.com/california/paloalto/stanford-research-the-meaningful -life-is-a-road-worth-traveling.

6. Dr. John Gottman and Dr. Julie Schwartz, "Here's the No. 1 Thing That Makes Relation-ships Successful, Say Psychologists Who Studied 40,000 Couples," CNBC, Nov 11, 2022, https://www.cnbc.com/2022/11/11/the-no-relationship-hack-according-to-psychologists -who-have-been-married-for-35-years.html.

7. Pualei Lynn, "What If We Didn't Have to Achieve Our Way into Feeling Worthy?," *Lead with a Question*, podcast, Aug 9, 2022, Spotify, https://open.spotify.com/episode /3BckCewDz7FATJ5Ji7qNIZ.

8. James Matthews, "How Can You Attract Your Best Future, Right Now?," *Lead with a Ques-tion*, podcast, Jul 15, 2022, Spotify, https://open.spotify.com/episode/050F7YmXDclURy VbeMSnSB.

9. "Zain's Birth Was a Turning Point in Satya Nadella's Life; Tech Boss Says His Son Taught Him Empathy, Influenced Microsoft's Vision of 'Accessibility,'" *Economic Times*, Mar 3, 2022, https://economictimes.indiatimes.com/magazines/panache/zains-birth-was-a-turning -point-in-satya-nadellas-life-tech-boss-says-his-son-taught-him-empathy-influenced -microsofts-vision-of-accessibility/articleshow/89918905.cms.

10. "Zain's Birth Was a Turning Point."

11. Jane Their, "Microsoft CEO Satya Nadella's Son Died at Age 26. Here's What He Taught the Leader About Empathy," *Fortune*, Mar 2, 2022, https://sports.yahoo.com/microsoft-ceo -satya-nadella-son-155307499.html.

12. Brett Molina, "Zain Nadella, Son of Microsoft CEO Satya Nadella, Has Died," *USA Today*, Mar 1, 2022, https://www.usatoday.com/story/tech/2022/03/01/zain-nadella-son-microsoft -ceo-dies/6978789001/.

13. Maria Pasquini, "Microsoft CEO Satya Nadella's Son Zain Has Died, Company Says," *People*, Mar 1, 2022, https://people.com/human-interest/microsoft-ceo-satya-nadella-son -zain-dies/.

14. Pasquini, "Microsoft CEO Satya Nadella's Son Zain Has Died."

15. Satya Nadella, "Satya Nadella: "The Moment That Forever Changed Our Lives," IndiaCurrents, Oct 23, 2017, https://indiacurrents.com/satya-nadella-microsoft-ceo-the-moment-that-forever-changed-our-lives/.

16. Naval Ravikant, "Naval Rakivant—The Joe Rogan Experience," Podcast Notes, Jun 5, 2019, https://podcastnotes.org/joe-rogan-experience/naval-joe-rogan/.

17. History.com, "Harriet Tubman," Mar 29, 2023. https://www.history.com/topics/black-history/harriet-tubman.

18. "Why an Ex-CIA Operative Decided to Adopt 2 Children He Saved," LDSLiving, June 23, 2016, https://www.ldsliving.com/why-an-ex-cia-operative-decided-to-adopt-2-children-he-saved/s/82455.

19. Jamie Armstrong, "Rescuing Children from Sex Slavery: One Latter-day Saint's Inspired Mission," LDSLiving, Oct 18, 2018, https://www.ldsliving.com/rescuing-children-from-sex-slavery-one-latter-day-saints-inspired-mission/s/78169.

20. Armstrong, "Rescuing Children."

21. Armstrong, "Rescuing Children."

22. Armstrong, "Rescuing Children."

23. Heather Harper, "Maslow's Hierarchy of Needs . . . and His Big Revision," The Career Project, Jan 9, 2021, https://www.thecareerproject.org/blog/maslows-hierarchy-of-needs/.

24. Heather Harper, "Maslow's Hierarchy of Needs . . . and His Big Revision."

Chapter 11

1. Donald Sull, Charles Sull, and Ben Zweig, "Toxic Culture Is Driving the Great Resignation," *MIT Sloan Management Review*, Jan 11, 2022, https://sloanreview.mit.edu/article/toxic-culture-is-driving-the-great-resignation/.

2. Ed Catmull, Interview and conversation with the authors, Apr 18, 2019.

3. Ed Catmull, Interview and conversation with the authors, Apr 18, 2019.

4. John Cassidy, "The Triumph (and Failure) of Nash's Game Theory," *New Yorker*, Mar 27, 2015, https://www.newyorker.com/news/john-cassidy/the-triumph-and-failure-of-john-nashs-game-theory.

5. Matt Ridley, "The World's Resources Aren't Running Out," *Wall Street Journal*, Apr 25, 2014, https://www.wsj.com/articles/the-worlds-resources-arent-running-out-1398469459.

6. Max Roser, "Proof That Life Is Getting Better for Humanity, in 5 Charts," Vox, Dec 23, 2016, https://www.vox.com/the-big-idea/2016/12/23/14062168/history-global-conditions-charts-life-span-poverty.

7. Ronell Hugh, "How Can Great Questions Challenge the Status Quo in Positive Ways?," Jun 24, 2022, in *Lead with a Question*, podcast, https://podcasts.apple.com/us/podcast/lead-with-a-question/id1631887896?i=1000567882431.

Chapter 12

1. Kathleen Elkins, "Here's What Billionaire Peter Thiel Wishes He'd Known in His 20s," CNBC, Feb 10, 2017, https://www.cnbc.com/2017/02/10/heres-what-billionaire-peter-thiel-wishes-hed-known-in-his-20s.html.

NOTES

2. History.com, "Mahalia Jackson Prompts Martin Luther King Jr. to Improvise 'I Have a Dream' Speech," History Channel, https://www.history.com/this-day-in-history/mahalia -jackson-the-queen-of-gospel-puts-her-stamp-on-the-march-on-washington.

3. Nolan Bushnell, "How Can We Create the School of the Future?," *Lead with a Question*, podcast, Feb 3, 2023, https://open.spotify.com/episode/1yup4J7uW106Q6WnJwLM54.

4. Marvin Liao, quoting Naval Ravikant, "The Future of Work: Are You Above or Below the Algorithm?," blog, https://www.marvinliao.com/blog/the-future-of-work-are-you-above -or-below-the-algorithm.

5. Moira Forbers, "Leading in the Age of AI: Angela Ahrendts on How Creativity Will Set Future Business Leaders Apart," *Forbes*, Apr 28, 2023, https://www.forbes.com/sites /moiraforbes/2023/04/28/leading-in-the-age-of-ai-angela-ahrendts-on-how-creativity -will-set-future-business-leaders-apart/?sh=4215239b7c2f.

6. Forbers, "Leading in the Age of AI."

7. Trent Toone, "Former BYU Animation Students Now with Pixar Discuss the Inno-vations Behind Disney's 'Soul,'" *Deseret News*, Jan 24, 2021, https://www.deseret.com /faith/2021/1/24/22214081/former-byu-animation-students-at-pixar-discuss-the -innovations-behind-disneys-soul-black-culture.

8. Toone, "Former BYU Animation Students Discuss Disney's 'Soul.'"

9. Toone, "Former BYU Animation Students Discuss Disney's 'Soul.'"

10. Toone, "Former BYU Animation Students Discuss Disney's 'Soul.'"

11. Toone, "Former BYU Animation Students Discuss Disney's 'Soul.'"

12. Toone, "Former BYU Animation Students Discuss Disney's 'Soul.'"

13. Collins Dictionary, s.v. "misfit," https://www.collinsdictionary.com/us/dictionary/english /misfit.

14. James Gurney, "Brad Bird Quotes About Animation," Gurney Journey, Nov 2, 2016, http:// gurneyjourney.blogspot.com/2016/11/brad-bird-quotes-about-animation.html.

15. Katherine V. Smith, "Inclusion = Innovation," Boston College Center for Corporate Citizenship, Mar 1, 2021, https://ccc.bc.edu/content/ccc/blog-home/2021/03/inclusion-innovation.html.

16. Meredith Harrison, "Changing the Game at Dell," Dell.com, Nov 17, 2015, https://www .dell.com/en-us/blog/changing-the-game-at-dell/.

17. Harrison, "Changing the Game at Dell."

18. Harrison, "Changing the Game at Dell."

19. Jenn Koiter, "Changing the Game with Innovation," Dell.com, July 18, 2017, https://www .dell.com/en-us/blog/changing-game-with-innovation/.

Chapter 13

1. Steve Young, "How Can We Become More Selfless Leaders?," *Lead with a Question*, podcast, May 5, 2023, https://podcasts.apple.com/us/podcast/lead-with-a-question /id1631887896?i=1000611847147.

2. Steve Young, Interview and conversation with the authors, Nov 3, 2022.

3. Randy Nelson, "How Can You Create a Culture of Curiosity?," *Lead with a Question*, podcast, Aug 19, 2022, https://podcasts.apple.com/us/podcast/lead-with-a-question /id1631887896?i=1000575990178.

4. Casey McNerthney, "Coronavirus in Washington State: A Timeline of the Outbreak Through March 2020," KIRO 7, Apr 3, 2020, https://www.kiro7.com/news/local/coronavirus -washington-state-timeline-outbreak/IM65JK66N5BYTIAPZ3FUZSKMUE/?outputType =amp.

5. San Francisco Chronicle Staff, "The Bay Area's Battle Against Coronavirus," San Francisco Chronicle Timeline, Jun 19, 2020, https://projects.sfchronicle.com/2020/coronavirus -timeline/.

6. Naval, Twitter, Aug 9, 2018, https://twitter.com/naval/status/1027776399329898496?lang =en.

7. Columbia Business School, "Power Isn't Enough: Study Reveals the Missing Link for Ef- fective Leadership," Sep 17, 2014, https://business.columbia.edu/press-releases/cbs-press -release/power-isnt-enough-study-reveals-missing-link-effective-leadership.

Chapter 14

1. Ryan Woodward, "How Can Character Development in Storytelling Improve Our Leader- ship?," *Lead with a Question*, podcast, Jul 30, 2022, https://podcasts.apple.com/us/podcast /lead-with-a-question/id1631887896?i=1000573227095

2. Guy Kawasaki, Chris Deaver, and Ian Clawson, "What's the Best Career Strategy?," *Lead with a Question*, podcast, Jan 5, 2023, https://podcasts.apple.com/us/podcast/lead-with-a -question/id1631887896?i=1000601371294

3. Kate Conger and Tripp Mickle, New York Times Service, "Elon Musk Takes on Apple's Power, Setting up Clash," Nov 29, 2022, Boston.com, https://www.boston.com/news/technology /2022/11/29/elon-musk-takes-on-apples-power-setting-up-a-clash/.

4. Brett Molina, "Elon Musk Says He Met with Apple's Tim Cook, Issue with Twitter 'Re- solved,'" *USA Today*, Dec 1, 2022, https://www.usatoday.com/story/tech/2022/12/01/elon -musk-tim-cook-apple-twitter/10809126002/.

5. Andy Boynton, "Pixar Chief: Protect Your 'Ugly Babies,'" *Forbes*, Mar 17, 2014, https:// www.forbes.com/sites/andyboynton/2014/03/17/pixar-chief-protect-your-ugly-babies -your-unsightly-ideas/?sh=7219288e74e1.

6. Theodore Roosevelt, Address at the Sorbonne in Paris, France: "Citizenship in a Republic," Apr 23, 1910, https://www.presidency.ucsb.edu/documents/address-the-sorbonne-paris -france-citizenship-republic.

Chapter 15

1. Tzufit Herling, "The Entrepreneur That Brought Electricity and Water to Africa," *Forbes Israel*, Sep 7, 2017, https://forbes.co.il/e/and-then-there-was-light-the-female-entrepreneur -that-brought-electricity-and-water-to-villages-in-seven-african-countries/.

2. Archie McEachern, "How Can Deep Connection and Trust Lead to a Culture of Innova- tion?," *Lead with a Question*, podcast, Sep 2022, https://open.spotify.com/episode/78xfVH zUMgOSPCLB8J1Nfo?autoplay=true.

3. Stephen Covey, *Primary Greatness* (New York: Simon & Schuster, 2015), 66–67.

4. Paul Putz, "John Wooden's Homespun Creed Was Not So Homespun," Slate, May 17, 2017, https://slate.com/culture/2017/05/john-woodens-seven-point-creed-came-from-a -1931-magazine-article.html.

5. Malala Yousafzai, Speech at United Nations, Jul 12, 2013, https://malala.org/newsroom/malala-un-speech.

6. Jesse David Fox, "Talking to Jon Favreau About *Chef*, Returning to Indies, and Maintaining a Vision Inside Blockbusters," *Vulture*, May 9, 2014, https://www.vulture.com/2014/04/jon-favreau-on-chef-going-indie-getting-older.html.

7. Maya Angelou, "Maya Angelou in Her Own Words," May 28, 2014, https://www.bbc.com/news/world-us-canada-27610770.

8. Kathy Elkins, "Warren Buffett's Partner Charlie Munger Says There Are '3 rules for a Career,'" CNBC, Aug 17, 2017, https://www.cnbc.com/2017/08/16/warren-buffetts-partner-charlie-munger-has-3-rules-for-a-career.html.

9. Yahoo Style Contributors, "Bryce Dallas Howard Thanks the Karadashians for Teaching Her to Accept Her Curves," Yahoo! News, Oct 19, 2015, https://www.yahoo.com/news/bryce-dallas-howard-thanks-the-kardashians-for-210835040.html.

10. Yasmin Anwar, "Social Scientists Build Case for 'Survival of the Kindest,'" Berkely News, Dec 8, 2009, https://news.berkeley.edu/2009/12/08/survival_of_kindest/.

11. Jenny Santi, "The Science Behind the Power of Giving," *Expert Voices*, Nov 30, 2015, https://www.livescience.com/52936-need-to-give-boosted-by-brain-science-and-evolution.html.

12. Santi, "The Science Behind the Power of Giving."

13. Stephen M. R. Covey and Pete Mockaitis, "Stephen M. R. Covey Reveals How Great Leaders Inspire Teams," *How to Be Awesome at Your Job*, podcast, Apr 28, 2022, https://awesomeatyourjob.com/763-stephen-m-r-covey-reveals-how-great-leaders-inspire-teams/.

14. Liz Mineo, "Good Genes Are Nice, but Joy Is Better," *Harvard Gazette*, Apr 11, 2017, https://news.harvard.edu/gazette/story/2017/04/over-nearly-80-years-harvard-study-has-been-showing-how-to-live-a-healthy-and-happy-life/.

15. Archie McEachern, "How Can Deep Connection and Trust Lead to a Culture of Innovation?," *Lead with a Question*, podcast, Sep 2022, https://open.spotify.com/episode/78xfVHzUMgOSPCLB8J1Nfo?autoplay=true.

16. Scott Belsky, "Creating in the Era of Creative Confidence," Medium, Dec 22, 2022, https://scottbelsky.medium.com/creating-in-the-era-of-creative-confidence-b4e251d725f; "TEDxPugetSound—Scott Belsky—Making Ideas Happen," text description of YouTube video, https://www.youtube.com/watch?v=lsQtptwMCFI.

17. Scott Belsky, LinkedIn post, Feb 7, 2023, https://www.linkedin.com/posts/scottbelsky_a-companys-values-should-be-a-mix-of-what-activity-7024253649988001793-BK9t?utm_source=share&utm_medium=member_desktop.

18. Brian Chesky, Stanford University Graduate School post on LinkedIn, Mar 3, 2023, https://www.linkedin.com/posts/stanford-graduate-school-of-business_when-a-crisis-hits-you-need-to-be-decisive-ugcPost-7037199938560135168-Dep5/.

19. Chesky, Stanford University Graduate School post on LinkedIn, Mar 3, 2023.

Chapter 16

1. "Jeff Bridges on Filming 'Iron Man' Without a Script (2014)," The Howard Stern Show, Nov 6, 2022, YouTube video, https://www.youtube.com/watch?v=Mud3eouMMBw.

2. Thomas Pritchard, "Jeff Bridges Spills on Surviving the No-Script Chaos of MCU's Ice-Breaker," Startefacts, Dec 5, 2022, https://startefacts.com/news/jeff-bridges-spills-on-surviving-the-no-script-chaos-of-mcu-s-ice-breaker_a116.

3. Scott Reames, LinkedIn post, Jan 26, 2023, https://www.linkedin.com/posts/scott-r-1b59527_despite-what-you-may-have-read-recently-on-activity-7024628353617854464-s12C?utm_source=share&utm_medium=member_desktop.

4. Almog Goldstein, "How Angela Ahrendts Transformed 150-Year-Old Burberry into the Most Innovative Fashion Company," LinkedIn, Nov 27, 2020, https://www.linkedin.com/pulse/how-angela-ahrendts-transformed-150-year-old-burberry-almog-goldstein/.

5. Goldstein, "How Angela Ahrendts Transformed Burberry."

6. Plato, "Timaeus (55d-56c)," 1181.

7. Laura London, Stephanie Madner, and Dominic Skerritt, "How Many People Are Really Needed in a Transformation?," McKinsey & Company, Sep 23, 2021, https://www.mckinsey.com/capabilities/transformation/our-insights/how-many-people-are-really-needed-in-a-transformation.

8. Leah Kral, "Three Must-Read Books to Get People Out of Their Comfort Zones and Spark Innovation," Discourse, Jan 30, 2023, https://www.discoursemagazine.com/ideas/2023/01/30/three-must-read-books-to-get-people-out-of-their-comfort-zones-and-spark-innovation/#:~:text=Gregersen%20writes%2C%20.

9. Jeff Haden, "Exceptional Performers Like Hugh Jackman and Usain Bolt Follow the 85 Percent Rule. So Should You," Inc., https://www.inc.com/jeff-haden/optimal-performers-like-hugh-jackman-usain-bolt-follow-85-percent-rule-so-should-you.html.

INDEX

ABOUT THE AUTHORS

Chris Deaver is cofounder of BraveCore, a leadership consultancy that helps leaders shape cultures people love. He's influenced Fortune 500s from the inside, including Apple and Disney, taking leaders to the next level and inspiring teams shaping iProducts and Star Wars experiences. He has coached leaders, including Tim Cook and Michael Dell. Chris is cohost of the popular podcast *Lead with a Question* and has cofounded startups, including a mentoring network with Stephen R. Covey. He is passionate about building Marvel-like worlds that give us greater hope for the future. He earned his MBA at the Marriott School at Brigham Young University and received his BA in Art with the first animation class at BYU that has now become the top Emmy Award–winning program in the country. Chris loves co-creating stuff with his kids, exploring the outdoors, and listening to U2.

——

Ian Clawson is cofounder of BraveCore, cohost of the *Lead with a Question* podcast, and a regular contributor to *Fast Company*. He is an advisor to startups and accelerator programs and has contributed to organizational growth through leadership coaching. Over the past decade, Clawson has led culture change initiatives in the healthcare industry. He is also cofounder of and story architect at StoryCircle, a development studio focused on co-creative storytelling that brings together artists and writers who have a passion for worldbuilding. He earned a BA in International Cultural Studies at Brigham Young University–Hawaii, where he developed a high interest in world philosophy and communication theory.

CONNECT WITH BRAVECORE

BraveCore helps leaders shape cultures people love, powering people to become co-creators. We've taken companies to the next level, including Fortune 500s like Apple and Disney, startups, and individuals. We offer culture coaching and Brave Sessions to inspire growth. Learn more at www.brave core.co and get connected with the community here:

The *Lead with a Question* podcast offers space for leaders to be more creative, and creatives to be better leaders. We see broken cultures everywhere. We need a deeper focus on humanity and the courage to let go of power and ego. Experience the movement here:

Spotify:

Apple: